THE WAY OF SIDDHARTHA

A Life of the Buddha

David J. Kalupahana
Indrani Kalupahana

ERSITY
SS OF
RICA

BIP88

LANHAM • NEW YORK • LONDON

Copyright © 1987 by

University Press of America,® Inc.

4720 Boston Way
Lanham, MD 20706

3 Henrietta Street
London WC2E 8LU England

Printed in the United States of America

British Cataloging in Publication Information Available

Copyright © 1982 by
David J. and Indrani Kalupahana

Library of Congress Cataloging in Publication Data

Kalupahana, David J., 1933-
   The way of Siddhartha.

   Reprint. Originally published: Boulder : Shambhala
Publications, 1982.
   Bibliography: p.
   1. Gautama Buddha.   2. Buddhists—India—Biography.
I. Kalupahana, Indrani.   II. Title.
BQ882.K34   1987   294.3'63 [B]   86-28223
ISBN 0-8191-6066-0 (pbk. :   alk. paper)

All University Press of America books are produced on acid-free
paper which exceeds the minimum standards set by the National
Historical Publication and Records Commission.

To all the beloved children in the world,
including ours:

NANDANA KAMALASILA,
DIMATI CANDRIKA, AND
MILINDA SANTIDEVA.

Preface

Information regarding the life of the Buddha, available in the earliest portions of Buddhist literature known as "discourses" (*sutta*), found both in their Pali and Chinese versions, can be grouped into two. The first consists of scanty references to the life of Siddhartha before his enlightenment, and the second includes the numerous dialogues he had with his disciples and other personalities of his time. Long after these discourses were collected and when the disciples felt the need for a connected account of his early life, especially for the edification of the pious devotee, this information was utilized to reconstruct his life history. But as time passed radical changes were taking place with regard to the very conception of the Buddha. He was being gradually elevated to the level of a superhuman being, a subject that was hotly debated among the Buddhists by the time of King Asoka (see *Kathavatthu*, London, 1894, pp. 221 ff.). Although the Sthaviravadins or the Elders of the Buddhist Order themselves rejected the view that Buddha was a transcendent (*lokuttara*) being, yet like the Mahayanists, they could not resist the temptation to present a story edifying to the unenlightened. The result was that whatever meager information available in the early discourses regarding incidents such as the renunciation, striving, the attainment of enlightenment, the first preaching and the founding of the order of monks and nuns was given a rather supernatural coloring when the story came to be finalized. This elevation of not only the Buddha but even Siddhartha to the level of a transcendent being was carried out in the account of his life prefixed to the *Jataka* stories, and it is not much different from those that are found in texts with Mahayana leanings such as *Mahavastu* and *Lalitavistara*.

Most of these stories ended either with Buddha's attainment of enlightenment or with the founding of the order of monks and nuns.

For some inexplicable reasons, no complete account of his life story was attempted until recent times (see Nanamoli's *The Life of the Buddha,* Kandy, 1972), even though much information regarding his later life was available in discourses such as the *Mahaparinibbana-suttanta.*

The present story, therefore, attempts to achieve two things: (1) to eliminate the mythology that came to be associated with Siddhartha's early life as a result of his being elevated to the level of a transcendent being and to present him as a historical person, and (2) to provide a connnected account of his later life on the basis of the information available in the discourses. For several reasons, the second proved to be the more difficult task. First, the discourses delivered by the Buddha that came to be included in the *Nikayas* and *Agamas* are so numerous that all of them could not be accommodated in a story like the present one. Secondly, there is no way to decide the sequence in which they were delivered. Therefore, the material for the story was selected with several purposes in view. First, to portray as many leading personalities as possible who were associated with the Buddha. Secondly, to give a reasonable idea of the geographical area covered by the Buddha's visits. Lastly, to present the teachings of the Buddha in a concise and coherent form.

In presenting this story, we have been influenced primarily by two recent works on the subject. The first is Martin Wickremasinghe's *Bavataranaya,* written in Sinhala and published in Sri Lanka. The work was an imaginative creation by one of Sri Lanka's leading novelists of the century. One of the major contributions of that work is the elimination of the mythology that had grown around Siddhartha's life history. Unfortunately, the work contained several inaccuracies relating to the sociological background as well as some glaring misinterpretations of the enlightenment and teachings of Buddha. Like many other traditional stories, it ended with Buddha's enlightenment and the conversion of some of the early disciples.

The second is a work of rare scholarship by Bhikkhu Nanamoli: *the Life of the Buddha.* Here the life of the Buddha is presented beginning with birth and the early years until the great demise and the convening of the First Council. It consists of translations of selections from the entire Pali Canon. These selections have been carefully sorted out and identified, especially with regard to their authors, as for example, reports by Ananda or Upali who were Buddha's immediate disciples, or explanations provided by traditional commentators, like Buddhaghosa. We have drawn much inspiration from these two works and have been greatly influenced by them in presenting our story. However, the interpretation of Buddha's philosophy as presented here is entirely ours.

We are thankful to Professor Graham Parkes of the Department of Philosophy at the University of Hawaii and to Ms. Chitra Stuiver of the Hawaii State Library for reading through the original draft and making many useful suggestions for improvement. Our thanks are also due to Mr. Larry Mermelstein, Associate Editor, Shambhala Publications, Inc. for his interest in this work. Ms. Floris Sakamoto has once again extended her ungrudging help in preparing the final manuscript for the press, for which we are very grateful to her.

David J. Kalupahana
Indrani Kalupahana

Honolulu, Hawaii
September 10, 1981

Note on the Proper Names Used in the Story

Buddhists in India adopted Sanskrit as a literary medium long after the original discourses were collected and classified into the four (and sometimes five) *Nikayas* or *Agamas*. These early discourses were available in some form of Prakrit, Pali being one of them. With the use of Sanskrit, the proper names were rendered into Sanskrit, and even to this day there is not much unanimity regarding the correctness of these Sanskritizations. Since the Pali version of the discourses is the only one available in a complete collection in any Indian language and since the material for the present story has been taken from the Pali version, it was felt that the more sonorous Pali forms should be utilized than their more cumbersome and sometimes uncertain renderings into Sanskrit. The following exceptions have been made: (1) The name Siddhartha has been retained, instead of its Pali form, Siddhattha, primarily because the English-speaking public have come to be familiar with it as a result of the popular novel, *Siddhartha* by Herman Hesse. (2) The names occurring in the non-Buddhist texts, such as the Upanishads, have been presented in the form in which they occur.

The usage of diacritics in transliterating Pali and Sanskrit words has been omitted, and the palatal and retroflex *s* has been rendered *sh* to better approximate the correct pronunciation.

People appearing in the story

Abhaya, a prince, believed to be a son of King Bimbisara, and a disciple of the Jaina leader, Nigantha Nataputta.

Ajatasattu, son of King Bimbisara of Magadha, who usurped the throne and conspired with Devadatta to kill the Buddha.

Ajita Kesakambali, one of the six heretical teachers mentioned in the Buddhist texts. He was an ascetic who used to wear a cloak made of human hair, hence his name Kesakambali ("wearing a hair blanket"). He could be considered the first and foremost materialist thinker of India.

Alara Kalama, a contemplative (yogin) who instructed Siddhartha on the techniques of meditation before the latter attained enlightenment. Kalama probably belonged to the so-called Upanishadic tradition.

Ambapali, a famous courtesan of Vesali. She was noted for her beauty. Her character is here portrayed on the basis of her confessions, which are recorded in *Therigatha* (vv. 252–270).

Ananda, A Sakyan who became a disciple of the Buddha and also was his constant companion. Tradition has it that he attained enlightenment only after the passing away of the Buddha.

Anathapindika, a famous merchant from Savatthi, whose real name was Sudatta. Because of his munificence towards the poor and the destitute, he came to be popularly called "Feeder of the Poor" (Anathapindika). He became a disciple of the Buddha and the leading benefactor of his disciples.

Angulimala, so-called because he wore a "necklace of fingers," and tradition says that he did so in order to fulfill a vow he had made. He is believed to have killed many people in order to obtain fingers for his necklace.

Anuruddha, one of the Sakyan princes who became a disciple of the Buddha along with Ananda. He was present when the Buddha passed away at Kusinara.

Asita Kaladevala, a brahman priest adept in the Vedas and the related disciplines. He was the spiritual adviser of Suddhodana, father of Siddhartha. Tradition has it that it was he who suggested the name Siddhartha after reading the signs on the body of Suddhodana's newly born baby. As Suddhodana's spiritual guide it was natural for him to serve as Siddhartha's instructor.

Assaji, one of the five ascetics in whose company Siddhartha practiced self-mortification. He later became one of the first five disciples of the Buddha.

Bhaddiya, one of the five ascetics with whom Siddhartha practiced self-mortification and who also became one of the first five disciples.

Bhaddiya, a Sakyan prince who joined the Buddha as a disciple along with Ananda and others.

Bhagu, another of the Sakyan princes who joined the Buddha as a disciple along with Ananda.

Bharadvaja, a brahman who is often referred to in the discourses. He is here represented as Siddhartha's teacher in political philosophy.

Bimba, the mother of Yasodhara, wife of Siddhartha.

Channa, Suddhodana's stableboy who accompanied Siddhartha when the latter left Kapilavatthu to adopt a homeless life.

Cunda, a goldsmith's son from Pava from whom Buddha had a meal, believed to be of hog's meat (*sukaramaddava*). Buddha is said to have taken ill after partaking of this meal.

Devadatta, a cousin and playmate of Siddhartha. He joined the Buddha as a disciple along with Ananda, but unfortunately came under the evil influence of King Bimbisara's son, Ajatasattu. Tradition depicts him as the most evil-minded person among the Buddha's disciples, probably a later exaggeration.

Dighanakha, a wandering ascetic (*paribbajaka*). The two famous disciples of the Buddha, Sariputta and Moggallana, are said to have attained enlightenment after listening to a conversation between Dighanakha and the Buddha.

Dighatapassi or **Tapassi,** a disciple of the Jaina leader, Nigantha Nataputta.

Gaggamantani, the family name of Angulimala.

Gavampati, literally meaning "Lord of Cattle," a fictitious character.

Gotami or **(Maha) Pajapati Gotami,** Suddhodana's sister-in-law whom he married after the death of his queen, Maya, Siddhartha's mother. Gotami was responsible for Siddhartha's upbringing.

Janussoni, a brahman philosopher, who often confronted the Buddha with metaphysical questions.

Jeta, a prince from Savatthi whose property was bought by Anatha-pindika to construct a monastery for the Buddha and his disciples.

Jivaka, a famous physician, also believed to have been the Buddha's personal physician.

Kaccayana, a noted disciple of the Buddha who was the interlocutor in a discourse, named after him as *Kaccayanagotta-sutta,* in which the Buddha presented his famous theory of "dependent arising" as a middle position between the two extremes of absolute existence and absolute nonexistence. This discourse is quoted by almost all of the later Buddhist schools of thought, in spite of their great divergencies.

Kaludayi, a son of one of Suddhodana's ministers. He was sent to Rajagaha by Suddhodana with an invitation for the Buddha to visit Kapilavatthu. He was the first Sakyan to become a disciple of the Buddha and attain enlightenment.

Kalamas, the residents of a small town called Kesaputta. Buddha's discourse to the Kalamas has been hailed as the first "Charter of Free Inquiry."

Kapila, recognized as the first systematizer of Sankhya philosophy, is here represented as a childhood friend of Siddhartha in order to explain the influence of Sankhya, if any, on the Buddha's own thinking. The nonappearance of Kapila on the scene after the Buddha's attainment of enlightenment may be taken as indicative of the differences in their philosophies.

Kassapa, of Uruvela, was an ascetic who had developed psychic powers and who enjoyed enormous popularity among the people in that region. His character is here portrayed on the basis of his reminiscences recorded in *Theragatha* (vv. 375–380).

Kimbila, one of the Sakyan princes who joined the order along with Ananda.

Kolita, the name by which Moggallana, one of the famous disciples of Buddha, was known before his conversion. Previously he was a disciple of the famous skeptic of the Indian tradition, Sanjaya Bellatthiputta.

Kondanna, one of the five ascetics with whom Siddhartha practiced self-mortification, and who was the first to attain enlightenment after listening to the Buddha's first discourse, the *Dhamma-cakkappavattana-sutta,* delivered at Isipatana in Baranasi.

Mahanama, one of the five ascetics with whom Siddhartha practiced self-mortification and who also became one of the Buddha's first five disciples.

Mahanama, Yasodhara's father, who constantly met with the Buddha when the latter visited Kapilavatthu.

Mahavira, another name for the leader of the Jaina religion, better known in the Buddhist texts as Nigantha Nataputta.

Makkhali Gosala, one of the six heretical teachers mentioned in the Buddhist texts, who propounded an extremely deterministic view of life.

Mallika, queen of King Pasenadi of Kosala.

Maya, Siddhartha's mother, who is believed to have died a few days after he was born.

Moggallana, one of the leading disciples of the Buddha who, before his conversion, was a disciple of the skeptic Sanjaya Bellatthiputta and was known as Kolita.

Mutta, a female disciple of the Buddha.

Nalaka, here represented as a person from whom Siddhartha learned about the contemplative tradition before his renunciation.

Nanda, Siddhartha's stepbrother.

Nanduttara, a female disciple of the Buddha.

Naradatta, here portrayed as a materialist with whom Siddhartha came to be associated during his adolescence and from whom he learnt to be critical about the Brahmanical traditon.

Narayana, the mythical sage who is considered to be the author of the famous *Purusha-sukta* of the *Rgveda* in which the divine ordination of the fourfold caste system is first enunciated.

Nigantha Nataputta, the historical founder of the Jaina religion, who is also known as Mahavira.

Pakudha Kaccayana, one of the six heretical teachers mentioned in the Buddhist texts, who is also a materialist.

Pasenadi, king of Kosala.

Prajapati Paramestin, the mythical sage considered to be the author of the *Nasadiya-sukta* of the *Rgveda*.

Pukkusa, a follower of Alara Kalama.

Purana Kassapa, one of the six heretical teachers with materialist leanings.

Rahula, son of Siddhartha. Rahu, according to ancient Indian mythology, is a demon whose head was cut off by Vishnu when he attempted to drink the nectar obtained at the churning of the ocean. However, he became immortal, retaining his head only, and periodically took revenge from his betrayers, the sun and the moon, by swallowing them at the time of eclipse. Solar and lunar eclipses generally cause confusion not only in human beings but also in animals. The confusion created in the mind of Siddhartha with the birth of his son, especially at a time when he was contemplating the suffering associated with life and was getting more interested in a life of asceticism may have induced him to name his baby Rahula.

Rohini, a Sakyan woman, depicted here as a constant companion of Yasodhara.

Saccaka, a disciple of Nigantha Nataputta.

Sakyans, the citizens of the city-kingdom of Kapilavatthu.

Sanjaya Bellatthiputta, one of the six heretical teachers considered to be the foremost of skeptics in India.

Sariputta, one of the leading disciples of the Buddha. Before his conversion by Assaji, he was a disciple of Sanjaya Bellatthiputta, and was known as Upatissa.

Sela, a female disciple of the Buddha.

Soma, a female disciple of the Buddha.

Sona, a female disciple of the Buddha.

Subha, a female disciple of the Buddha whose encounter with a sensuous man trying to seduce her is poignantly described in *Therigatha* (vv. 366–399).

Subhadda, the last person to become a disciple of the Buddha before the latter's demise.

Sudatta, another name for Anathapindika.

Suddhodana, Siddhartha's father and king of the Sakyans.

Uddaka Ramaputta, one of the contemplatives under whom Siddhartha received instruction regarding the techniques of meditation before his enlightenment.

Uddalaka Aruni, one of the leading sages of the Upanishadic tradition whose ideas are embodied in the *Chandogya Upanishad.*

Upajjhayaka, a fictitious brahman, who is here portrayed as an upholder of the moral values inculcated in such texts as the *Bhagavadgita.*

Upaka, a wandering ascetic.

Upali, a barber from Kapilavatthu, who joined the band of disciples of the Buddha in the company of Ananda.

Upali, a lay disciple and benefactor of Nigantha Nataputta.

Upatissa, another name for Sariputta.

Uppalavanna, a female disciple of the Buddha.

Vajiri, the daughter of King Pasenadi and Queen Mallika.

Vappa, one of the five ascetics with whom Siddhartha practised self-mortification and who became one of the Buddha's first five disciples.

Vassakara, Ajatasattu's minister of state.

Vessamitta, a fictitious character who is here represented as Siddhartha's instructor in martial arts.

Vimala, a female disciple of the Buddha.

Visakha, the famous female lay devotee of the Buddha who, like Anathapindika, spent most of her wealth on the welfare of the Buddha and his disciples.

Yajnavalkya, the well-known Upanishadic sage who figures prominently in the *Brhadaranyaka Upanishad.*

Yasodhara, Siddhartha's wife.

ONE

IT WAS THE SOWING SEASON in the land of the Sakyans, a small independent kingdom at the southern foothills of the majestic Himalayas. Kapilavatthu, the capital city of the Sakyan kingdom, was unusually busy at this time, for the king and his retinue were going forth that day to take part in the ceremonial beginning of the sowing activities. This was one of the few occasions when the ruler and the ruled mingled freely to invoke the blessings of nature for a bountiful harvest.

Living in the hostile regions of the Himalayas, the Sakyans turned out to be a rough and rugged people. Yet they were peaceful and very religious and extremely conscious of their identity as a nation. At this time they were ruled by Suddhodana, held in high esteem by the Sakyans as an honest and just ruler. They were aware of the expansionist intentions of their more powerful neighbors, the Kosalans and Magadhans, and were therefore ready to rally around their king in case of an invasion. Suddhodana was thus the symbol of unity for the Sakyans.

The country was primarily agricultural and generally self-sufficient. Rice and wheat constituted the staple diet of the people and were produced in abundance. Every family, if it belonged to the agricultural class, owned a plot of arable land, though not very large in extent. Labor was shared, each family helping the other in the work of plowing, sowing and harvesting of the land.

There were no property rights but mere conventions that everyone in the community respected. Customs, or a general concensus as to what was right and proper, were strictly observed. Disputes were settled by the village chief, who was ultimately responsible to the king. Cattle rearing, carpentry, wood work, pig farming, masonry, weaving and many other arts and crafts provided the villagers with a variety of vocations thus producing a reasonably healthy economic atmosphere. Most of the wealthy business people, who enjoyed a more luxurious life compared to that of the villagers, lived in the city. A whole class of entertainers—musicians, singers and dancing girls—catered mainly to the more wealthy classes in society. Community social events and religious festivals were popular and frequent.

Although the kshatriya or the ruling class was the more dominant in society and was extremely conscious and proud of its status, the brahmans or priests with their highly elaborate rituals dominated the religious life of the people. Ascetics inhabiting the surrounding forests occasionally went to the villages in order to collect whatever meager requisites they could not find in their forest habitation. But they were few and their way of life was not very attractive to the Sakyans.

Elaborate arrangements were made for the very important ceremony connected with the first sowing of grain. People worked day and night to prepare the ceremonial ground, to decorate the roads leading to it, to build the altars needed for the rituals and to construct the pavilions for the chiefs. It was customary for the king to play a leading role at this ceremony. Suddhodana, accompanied by his son, Siddhartha and other members of the royal household, arrived at the place where the ceremony was held.

Siddhartha lost his mother, Maya, immediately after his birth. Pajapati Gotami, Maya's younger sister, who was now Suddhodana's consort, was responsible for nursing Siddhartha in his childhood. Siddhartha was about ten years old when he came to know that his real mother died on the occasion of his birth. He began to have confused feelings. He grew up in Gotami's lap, feeling and enjoying her warmth and affection. All this time he was under the impression that such warmth and affection could be associated only with the mother. Now he was beginning to realize that it could be a common possession

2

of anyone who plays the role of mother. It is not possible to know whether it was this realization that made Siddhartha come closer and closer to his childhood playmates, Kapila, a few years older than he; and Devadatta, his cousin who was younger. When Siddhartha joined his father at the ceremonies connected with the sowing of grain, he was with Kapila and Devadatta.

The highly ritualistic ceremony did not appeal to either Siddhartha or Kapila nor to little Devadatta. The children were fascinated by the elaborate decorations along the path leading to the small area of the field where the first grains were to be spread. They were also attracted by the four altars built at the four corners of the field dedicated to the guardian deities of the four directions. Yet the offerings of various oblations and the singing of Vedic hymns by the brahman priests watched by the elders with religious awe did not make much sense to Siddhartha. The brahman priests officiated at the ceremony with Suddhodana leading the congregation of people. Siddhartha, trained to act like the son of the king, did his best to live up to the dignity and sacredness of the occasion.

OFTEN DURING THE CEREMONY, Siddhartha's mind would stray away as a result of his inability to understand the meaning and significance of all that was taking place. He had seen how for several days people worked day and night in preparation for this festival. He did not fail to observe the inconvenience to which the people, including his father, subjected themselves in order to make preparations for this occasion. They seem to be moved by some sort of religious feeling. The absence of such religious feeling was sufficient reason for Siddhartha to be driven out of the heat of the midday sun to seek the pleasant shade of a nearby rose apple tree. Under the cool shade of this tree, Siddhartha felt comfortable. It was an incredible relief. In his ignorance of what these people were engaged in, Siddhartha asked himself: "Why should these people go through all these inconveniences? What are they going to reap as consequences?" One ferocious frown from his father was sufficient to bring him away from the lovely shade he was enjoying back to the agonizing heat of the sun-god.

Ceremonies were concluded by early afternoon. Everyone assembled enjoyed the milkrice prepared in abundance for the occasion. The children who until now had been indifferent to what was going on, began to enjoy the milkrice. After the conclusion of the ceremony, while returning home, Siddhartha, who felt somewhat guilty for offending his father by his un-enthusiastic participation in the ceremony, questioned him:

"Sir, I did not understand any of those hymns sung by the priests. What were they singing and what language could that be?"

"Son, it is the sacred language of the Vedas. Those Vedic hymns are deep in meaning and were revealed to the sages of yore by Brahma. They were preserved for us by a long line of priests. Only those born into the brahman clan are entitled to recite them at these ceremonies, for they are the only people who can generate the magical and protective power of these sacred hymns."

Siddhartha was silent, not because he accepted his father's explanation, but because he feared the wrath he might earn by further questioning.

Suddhodana was disturbed by Siddhartha's silence. He felt that his explanation did not appeal to the inquisitive mind of his young son. The predictions of his friend, Asita Kaladevala, on the day Siddhartha was born came back to his mind. It made him uneasy. Asita, who had mastered the traditional learning, including astrology and the interpretation of the auspicious marks on the human body, upon hearing that Suddhodana was blessed with a son, visited him in his palace. After being greeted by Suddhodana, Kaladevala asked:

"O King! I understand that a son was born to you and Queen Maya."

"Yes, indeed. We have a son. He is an unusually handsome boy."

"It is proper that he be initiated according to the rites of the brahmans who are spiritual guides of the mighty kshatriyas. May I see the baby?" asked Kaladevala.

"It would be an honor," replied Suddhodana. He went into

4

Maya's chamber, picked up the little baby wrapped in silken cloth and showed him to his friend and spiritual guide, Kaladevala. Kaladevala stood looking at the child for a moment. Observing the child's physical characteristics, he divined that he had great potential.

"This child will develop unusual intellectual capacities," warned Kaladevala. "He may not have much respect for authority and tradition, and will be very revolutionary in his attitude."

"What can I do to prevent him from becoming a revolutionary?" asked Suddhodana, greatly agitated.

"I do not know how to prevent him from becoming one," replied Kaladevala. He was himself agitated by the possibility that the future king of the Sakyans would be intolerant of Brahmanism. If Siddhartha had no respect for authority and tradition, the brahmans would not enjoy the same privileges that they enjoyed under Suddhodana. He felt that instead of the kshatriyas paying respects to the brahmans, the brahmans may have to bow down to the kshatriyas. Feeling powerless to safeguard his own tradition and also being unable to help his friend, Suddhodana, Kaladevala rejected the idea of initiating the child according to the brahman rites and left the palace wiping tears from his eyes.

Suddhodana recollected this incident and decided to remain silent, even though he felt that Siddhartha was not satisfied with his explanation of the value of the Vedic hymns. He realized that further explanation may force Siddhartha into greater and greater confusion.

TWO

THE LARGER CITIES and townships in Central India, such as Rajagaha, Baranasi and Savatthi, were centers of learning, where the brahmans and kshatriyas were struggling for superiority and where the brahmans and ascetics were engaged in all kinds of debates on philosophical and religious issues. Takkasila, the capital of Gandhara in the northwest, prospered as the meeting point of Indian and foreign cultures—especially the Greek. It was in Takkasila that the famous Upanishadic philosopher and sage, Uddalaka Aruni, had his education. Uddalaka may have inherited the basic temper of his philosophy, which was a systematic reconstruction of a world view based upon human experience, from his contact with the Gandharan culture. Although Uddalaka's teachings spread over to the central parts of India after he came to be associated with the educational institutes at Baranasi, the more mystically oriented thought of Yajnavalkya, his junior contemporary, was dominant in this region.

Kapila was fifteen years old when his father decided to send him to far away Takkasila for his formal education. The elder Kapila thought that the more liberal atmosphere in Takkasila would provide his son with better opportunities for learning than in Central India where the Brahmanical tradition played a rather dominant role. Moreover, being a Sakyan, he not only disliked the ideological supremacy of the larger kingdoms of the south, but also resented their political aspirations.

Kapila's reactions were rather mixed. He was excited about the opportunity to travel, but was not very pleased at the

6

prospect of having to leave his parents as well as his childhood companions, Siddhartha and Devadatta, for a lengthy period of time. Kapila thought that his next meeting with his friends was not going to be a very pleasant one, if he were to break the news of his impending trip to Takkasila. While playing a game of dice, Siddhartha noticed that Kapila was rather inattentive to what was going on, and could not resist inquiring:

"Hey, Kapila! What is bothering you? You are not with us in this game today."

Kapila did not have the courage to break the news to his friends.

"Are you not feeling well?" asked Devadatta.

"No. I am alright."

"Is there anything that you do not want to tell us?" inquired Siddhartha. Finally, Kapila picked up his courage and said:

"My father has decided to send me to Takkasila. I am excited about the prospect of traveling, but I am uncertain of the problems I may have to face in a distant country. I had very few friends here and I am not sure whether I will be able to make any when I get there."

Siddhartha was more encouraging than Kapila thought he would be.

"It has been the practice of the parents here to send their young ones for education in Takkasila, Baranasi or Rajagaha if they can afford it. I have heard that there are more teachers there than here. I am looking forward to my father sending me to one of these places. We surely are going to miss you right now. Maybe, we can all come back to Kapilavatthu when we have completed our education," suggested Siddhartha.

Siddhartha's more mature response did not appeal to Devadatta, who suggested:

"Why don't we ask our parents to let us continue to study under Asita Kaladevala? He likes us, and we like him. Then we won't have to leave our parents. Nor would we be separated from each other."

"Devadatta, how long do you think we will be able to continue playing like this?" questioned Siddhartha, looking at Devadatta. Devadatta looked away, and remained silent.

When, in the evening, his family assembled for meals, Siddhartha thought of breaking the news about his friend Kapila, hardly realizing that it was no news to Suddhodana who was already informed by the elder Kapila regarding his decision.

"Father, Kapila told me that he will be going to Takkasila. I think it is a good idea, though we will surely miss him."

Siddhartha assumed that his father would say: "Yes, your turn will come very soon." Instead he merely said:

"Kapila's father told me the other day that he will be sending Kapila to Takkasila. I wonder why he decided to send him that far away, when he could have sent Kapila to Baranasi or Rajagaha. It will be a very tedious journey for Kapila. I know you are going to miss a close companion."

Gotami, wanting to console Siddhartha, joined the conversation.

"Siddhartha, you should not be too upset over Kapila's leaving Kapilavatthu. When he returns from Takkasila he will be able to help you with your responsibilities. Who knows? He could be your chief adviser when you become the king of the Sakyans."

Siddhartha felt uncomfortable at these remarks. He was not certain whether his parents wanted him to follow Kapila's footsteps and go out to Rajagaha or Takkasila to complete his education. Suddhodana, in the meantime, was looking for some way of changing the topic of conversation. It was only a few days ago that he met with his friend and spiritual adviser, Kaladevala, and discussed the prospect of Siddhartha's moving out to another city for his education. On that occasion, Kaladevala was very explicit in his views about Siddhartha.

"O King," said Kaladevala, "your son, as I predicted when he was born, is a very inquisitive person. He will not accept anything on the basis of authority or tradition. Takkasila provides too liberal an atmosphere for a person of your son's temperament. Rajagaha and Baranasi seem to be pervaded by the same spirit of freedom, especially because of the large number of ascetics and wanderers roaming around this area. If you want your son to be the ruler of the Sakyan clan, keep him here in Kapilavatthu and train him for the kind of duties he will have to perform when he succeeds you."

"You are right, Sir," said Suddhodana. "It is not a good thing to expose Siddhartha to all the different views expressed by the sophists. He has a specific function in this society and he needs to perform that function well."

Looking out through the window into the moonlit night Suddhodana saw two persons approaching the palace. It was the opportunity he was looking for to end the conversation.

"We have guests," said Suddhodana, getting up from his seat. He walked up to the door, opened it and welcomed the visitors. First to enter the house was Vessamitta, followed by Bharadvaja. Vessamitta was the best known instructor in martial arts in the Sakyan territory, while Bharadvaja was highly regarded as an expert in the science of royal polity. They were close associates of Suddhodana, who often enlisted their services in the administration of the Sakyan kingdom. Their visit was not casual or accidental—it was prearranged. Suddhodana, upon hearing that Kapila, his son's closest friend, was to be sent to Takkasila, decided to make arrangements for his own son's education, without having to send him outside Kapilavatthu. Asita Kaladevala was already instructing Siddhartha in the regular curriculum such as language and literature, which in the more advanced stages would include the study of the Vedas, their philosophy and religion. It was now time for Siddhartha to begin training as a warrior and a politician.

Siddhartha, unaware of his father's planning for his training as the future ruler of the Sakyan kingdom, retired with his mother to the family room where he spent the rest of the evening discussing the possible adventures of Kapila in his travels to the northwest. At the end, he raised the inevitable question:

"Mother, where do you think my father is going to send me for my education and when?"

Gotami was careful not to break the unpleasant news to Siddhartha.

"Dear, your father is the king of the Sakyans. Upon his retirement, the responsibility of administering this country

9

will fall upon you. Kapila has no such responsibilities. Therefore, he can do whatever he wants. But in your case, it is necessary to have training appropriate for a ruler. I think your father knows what is best for you."

Siddhartha was disappointed. His future responsibilities seemed to stand in the way of his going out into the open country. His hopes were shattered. Nanda, his three-year-old stepbrother, ran up to him, climbed onto his lap and wanted to play. Siddhartha was deeply attached to his little brother. His dandling and laughing on this occasion helped Siddhartha to forget his disappointment.

THREE

WITH KAPILA'S DEPARTURE, Siddhartha became more and more involved in his educational activities. He accepted with resignation his father's decision to keep him in Kapilavatthu. He spent more of his time with Asita Kaladevala and Vessamitta than with Bharadvaja. Under the careful and meticulous guidance of Asita, he gradually gained proficiency in the Vedas, together with their ancillary studies such as grammar, semantics and poetics. He enjoyed the company of Vessamitta who was closer to his own age than Bharadvaja. He learned martial arts such as sword fighting and archery. One of the things he enjoyed most was horse riding, for it provided him with an easy means of exploring the remote areas of the Sakyan territory.

The study of the Vedic tradition was of historical importance for Siddhartha. It was necessary for him to understand what the ancient traditions were, though he did not possess the temperament to accept everything in them. But his attitude towards the science of polity, which he learned from Bharadvaja, was different. Many of the smaller nations, such as the Sakyans, were suspicious of the expansionist intentions of their more powerful southern neighbors. Siddhartha was gradually becoming aware of these suspicions. He would often get into arguments with Bharadvaja.

"What can we do if the king of Magadha wages war against us?" he once asked Bharadvaja.

"It would be foolish for us to stand against him if he decides to do so. We are like small fish in the ocean and could be devoured by the larger ones without our being able to put up a struggle. This is nature, and we cannot go against it," responded Bharadvaja.

Siddhartha could not reconcile himself to this position. His inquiring mind turned on to the question of justice. He insisted:

"How can nature be so unfavorable to some and favorable to others? I cannot see any justice in this."

"This is the way the world is made. Brahma, the creator, was aware of injustice. He knew that there could not be justice, if there was no injustice. Brahma's intentions are not bad. He is inherently good. But he had to assume that there may be some among his creation who would not conform to his wishes. He anticipated that there would be evil ones who would disturb the natural equilibrium that he set up."

As a result of his study of the Brahmanical tradition, Siddhartha knew that Bharadvaja was struggling to reconcile the notion of a creator with the belief in karma. But he was not satisfied.

"Does this mean that we, the Sakyans, are the evil ones and that the Magadhans, who are more powerful are the good ones?"

Bharadvaja interrupted. "No, no. I did not mean that. Brahma did not create the world yesterday and place all us Sakyans here in the rugged and mountainous land because we are evil and leave the Magadhans in the more fertile and prosperous parts of the earth because they are good. We have to take into

11

consideration the long historical development of human society. We have to ask ourselves the question, 'Why are we born in this part of the country, and not in Magadha or Kosala?' Each one of us is responsible for his own present life. Karma is an inexorable law that determines what we are and what we will be. So at some stage in our evolution we have contributed to our present situation, and we are now at the mercy of those who have fared better. Let us take our own society. We have kshatriyas who are rulers and are more powerful than others. We have the brahmans who are well respected by all of us. The merchants, farmers, artisans and those others who work harder than the kshatriyas and brahmans do not possess the same status that the latter enjoy in this society. Finally, there is a large population that leads a life of servitude. How can we account for these differences?"

Siddhartha was silent for a moment. He needed time to reflect on his own standing as the son of the king of the Sakyans. He reflected on the temperaments and attitudes of those who served in his household. They were different. Why? Before he could say anything, Bharadvaja began explaining the traditional view of society that he was alluding to earlier.

"Siddhartha, have you heard of the great sage Narayana?"

"Yes," replied Siddhartha, "I have heard of him from Asita. In fact, we read his famous hymn the *Purusha-sukta.*"

"But, have you reflected on the significance of this hymn?"

"I am not sure I understand clearly what Narayana is trying to say," replied Siddhartha.

Bharadvaja thought that this was a good opportunity to explain to Siddhartha the philosophical tradition that Bharadvaja himself had accepted. He began by distinguishing two aspects of Narayana's *Purusha-sukta.*

"As you may have noticed, this hymn has two sides—the philosophical and the social. But they are not unconnected. Narayana's ideas about the nature of society are based upon his world view. His world view, on the other hand, is based on experience. For example, we know that every event has a cause. Now, the effect that is produced by the cause cannot be completely different from the cause; it must be substantially related to the cause. This is why Narayana considered the cosmic person as the principle of all that has been and of all that is to be."

Siddhartha interrupted, "But this is mere speculation!"

"No," said Bharadvaja, "it is not mere speculation. It is reflection based upon experience of cause and effect. Sages like Narayana who possessed unlimited powers of reflection and retrocognition were able to see for themselves what the original state of the universe was. Such unlimited powers of reflection they attained as a result of revelation."

"I am not sure how one can relate this cosmic person to the universe as it is," remarked Siddhartha.

"There is both identity and difference," responded Bharadvaja. "As every particular thing is the cosmic person, the sum total of all particular things is also the cosmic person. Yet, in appearance they are different. Inasmuch as the cosmic person has transformed into the universe, the universe does not resemble the original person. Now see, we can take a lump of gold, divide it into several pieces and make different ornaments with the different pieces. We do not want to say that the gold is different. It is the form that the different pieces of gold assume that is different. Similarly, we say the cosmic person is the universe, and yet it is not the universe."

"Does this mean that according to Narayana the world as it has come to be now, together with its social and political institutions, is in essence the cosmic person?" queried Siddhartha.

"Of course," asserted Bharadvaja. "That is why Narayana maintained that the brahman was the cosmic person's mouth, the kshatriya the arms, the vaishya the thighs and that the shudra was born from his feet. Since the brahmans represented the cosmic person's mouth, they have inherited the function of reciting the Vedas, which no one else should attempt to do. The kshatriyas represented the arms and, therefore, they have the responsibility of wielding the sword or kshatra, to fight battles and to rule the country. The vaishyas who represent the thighs have to be involved in the production and distribution of various commodities that the society needs. Since the shudras are born from the cosmic person's feet, they are born to serve the other three castes. These four classes in society are in essence the cosmic person, for, as you know, nothing comes out of nothing."

"If that is the case, either the cosmic person is evil, or, if there is a creator of that cosmic person, that creator is evil. Otherwise there could not be shudras in this world," maintained Siddhartha.

"We do not have to attribute evil either to the cosmic person or its creator. The shudra as he has come to be is not identical with the original shudra-part of the cosmic person. He has come to be in the present state as a result of a long period of transformation."

Siddhartha could not discover a conception of justice in this kind of theory, and thought it would be futile to go back to his original question regarding what needed to be done in case the king of Magadha waged war against the neighboring kingdoms.

At this time, a young man named Naradatta returned to Kapilavatthu having spent some time in Rajagaha and Baranasi where he had gone for his education. In fact, he did not stay there as long as his parents expected him to stay. Gradually Siddhartha was able to make friends with him, and Naradatta was able to fill a vacuum in Siddhartha's life that was created by Kapila's departure. Siddhartha found Naradatta to be a friendly person in spite of his dogmatism. His dogmatism was of a different sort. It was different from the dogmatism of the brahmans whom he almost hated. He was critical of the dogmatism of the brahmans, but yet carried a strain of hardheadedness that Siddhartha could not understand. Apart from that, there was a common bond between them: both of them were lovers of horse riding.

One day Siddhartha and Naradatta went out riding their horses and decided to travel a little further than usual in order to visit some of the villages in the outskirts of Kapilavatthu. While riding together thus, Siddhartha reluctantly asked Naradatta:

"How long did you stay in the south?"

"Three years."

"Did you not like it there?" asked Siddhartha, trying to learn more about his experiences.

"I like traveling around and getting to know people,"

14

responded Naradatta, "but I am not sure whether I liked the educational atmosphere in the south. I understand it is much better in the northwest, in Takkasila."

Siddhartha was eager to know more about it.

"In what way is it different from Takkasila?" questioned Siddhartha.

"Oh, well! The south is not yet free from the yoke of Brahmanism. Yajnavalkya's mysticism has caught the fascination of the people. He is a shrewd debater and many a wanderer has been humbled by him."

"Surely, there is some reason for the popularity of his teachings. What does he teach?" inquired Siddhartha.

"He is a syncretic thinker who attempts to reconstruct a philosophy by putting together the essential ideas of many of the sages of the past. He believes in the existence of a self in every individual. The existence of this individual self, he thinks, is self-evident and it is always felt and known. One is absolutely certain of one's self. It is eternal, immutable, permanent and pure in nature."

Siddhartha interrupted Naradatta. "If it is pure in nature, what is the purpose of leading a religious life?"

"Yes," continued Naradatta, "I would ask the same question. Yajnavalkya's reply is that although this self is pure, it is in bondage because of our ignorance. Through our ignorance, the self comes to be associated with individuality, that is, with the senses, the mind, the intellect, feeling and will. The real self is above all these."

"What happens to this self when it is freed from individuality?" inquired Siddhartha.

"Yajnavalkya maintains that when this individual self is freed from its individuality, it becomes one with the universal self, or Brahman, which is the absolutely real. I myself have difficulty in understanding the relation between the individual self and the universal self. Yajnavalkya seems to think that the individual self is both reality and unreality. It is reality because it is part of the universal self, but it is unreality since it is individualized by us through our ignorance."

"I assume this is not the whole story," remarked Siddhartha. "This is his explanation of the individual self, and he thinks it both is and is not—it is both real and unreal. How does he explain the universal self or the absolutely real?"

"Siddhartha, you are very sharp," responded Naradatta. "Yajnavalkya assumes that this ultimately real self is indefinable and is not identifiable with anything that we see with our eyes, hear with our ears, smell with our nose, taste with our tongue, feel with our body or even conceptualize in our mind. It is beyond all forms of discrimination and distinction. Whenever somebody wants to identify the universal self with something, Yajnavalkya would say, 'It is not this, it is not this.' "

"Does Yajnavalkya want to say, 'It is not this, it is not this, but it is?' "

"I think so, Siddhartha," continued Naradatta. "Surely, he would not want to say that the ultimately real self is not or does not exist."

"If this ultimately real self is not known to us through our senses, including the mind, how do we get to know it?" was Siddhartha's next question.

"We do not get to know it in the same way in which, say, we get to know that this is a horse. For in such a case, we have a duality of subject and object. The ultimately real self is nondual. Yet, Yajnavalkya does not say that it is what the *yogin* experiences as the highest bliss, though I assume that he would not have any objection to anyone's saying so."

Siddhartha and Naradatta had been riding for a long time and Naradatta was beginning to feel tired. He was merely explaining to Siddhartha ideas he had collected during his stay in the south, ideas which did not appeal to him, and was, therefore, not emotionally involved in the discussion. But for Siddhartha, who had not had the opportunity of going outside the Sakyan territory, it was a great learning experience. He knew that Naradatta did not approve of these ideas and that this was the reason for his early return to Kapilavatthu. Therefore, with the hope of guiding the discussion in a direction in which Naradatta could express his own ideas and criticisms, and thereby getting him more involved in the conversation, rather than being a mere expositor, Siddhartha said:

"I am not sure how Yajnavalkya can explain moral life in the light of such a view of man. What is the purpose of my doing good to others, if their individualities are not real? Even if I were to hurt another, I would not be doing anything wrong, for that other person is not a reality."

"I agree with you, Siddhartha. I myself have difficulty in explaining the good life by assuming that our individualities are not real, but that the real is a permanent and eternal self without distinctions. It is such difficulties that led ascetics like Ajita Kesakambali and Pakudha Kaccayana to scorn the notions of good and bad and propound a materialistic doctrine. But Yajnavalkya has a way of explaining it, though such an explanation would not be appealing to many an inquirer."

"How does he explain it?" inquired Siddhartha.

"Yajnavalkya believes that a man loves his wife, not because he loves his wife, but because he loves the Self. A father loves a son, not because he loves a son, but because he loves the Self. A man loves wealth, not because he loves wealth, but because he loves the Self. A good man loves all beings, not because he loves all beings, but because he loves the Self, and so on."

"Does he say so because he thinks the different individual selves are, in the ultimate analysis, one with the universal self?"

"I suppose so," was Naradatta's reply.

Their conversation was interrupted when a group of little children, who had been playing in a nearby field that had been just harvested, came running towards them. Siddhartha and Naradatta dismounted from their horses. To Siddhartha, who had not gone beyond the city limits of Kapilavatthu, the difference between these children and those whom he was familiar with in Kapilavatthu was significant. They were dirty and ill-clad, though they certainly were not ill-fed. On the contrary, they looked healthy. Yet they did not appear to be tender at all, compared to the children of their age who lived in more prosperous parts of the territory.

Siddhartha and Naradatta decided to rest a little and took refuge under a tree, letting their horses free to graze for a while. They sat on a log, which was part of a tree that had fallen or had been cut down by the villagers for firewood. The children sat on the ground, and Naradatta got into a conversation with them, the older ones being more talkative and the smaller ones displaying shyness. The oldest was about ten years old and his hands and feet indicated that he was involved in some kind of rough work. Naradatta pointed his finger at him, and asked:

"You over there, what is your name?"

"Gavampati," replied the boy.

"How did you get a name like that?" asked Naradatta.

"I don't know," was the boy's response. But Naradatta immediately realized that this probably was the son of a dairy farmer.

"So, you are the lord of cattle?" questioned Naradatta smiling. The boys laughed. They probably did not know what was meant by "gavampati." For them it was just a name.

"Do your parents own many cattle?" questioned Naradatta.

"Yes," said Gavampati, "we have about fifteen. We make curd and ghee with the milk we get from them and sell them to the merchant in the village."

"Do you help your father with his work?"

"Yes, I take care of the cattle when they are let out to graze. Sometimes I go out and cut grass to feed them in the night."

"Don't you go to the village priest to learn to read and write?" asked Naradatta.

"No," said the boy. "We visit the priest only when my parents want to offer sacrifices to the gods. We take a lot of ghee and other kinds of food when we go to see him."

"Does the priest give you anything in return for all the ghee and food that you offer him?" asked Siddhartha, wanting to join the conversation.

"No. My father says that when we offer sacrifices, the gods protect our cattle and help us to get more and more milk from them."

Naradatta looked at Siddhartha. Siddhartha realized what was going on in Naradatta's mind. His look indicated his annoyance at the brahman priest who was exploiting the poor villagers. Siddhartha wanted to go into the village, meet some of the older folk and get to know more of their beliefs, their life-styles. But it was getting too late for them not to return home.

"I think it is time for us to go back," said Siddhartha, getting up and walking towards his horse. "I would like to come some other day. We should start in the morning so that we can get here early and spend more time. My father will be unhappy if I get home too late."

"Alright," said Naradatta, even though he did not worry about getting home late.

They rode in silence, enjoying the peace and quiet of the late afternoon, listening to the melodious singing of the birds flying hither and thither, looking for their nests to rest in during the night. The sun was going down, spraying the sky with a beautiful combination of colors soon to disappear in the darkness of the night, as if providing proof of the enduring truth that even the good and the beautiful are subject to change and impermanence.

It was a restless night for Siddhartha. What he had learned from Asita and Bharadvaja regarding the Brahmanical views about theology and karma, and what he heard today from Naradatta about Yajnavalkya's ideas concerning the self, conflicted with what he learned of the life of the little children whom he met in the afternoon. To him it appeared that their lives were determined by the environment in which they came to be born. "Are they to be held responsible for what they are? Why did they ever come to be born in such a situation? Why am I enjoying all the comforts in life, when those little children have to work all day long to help their parents to eke out a meager existence?" Such were the disturbing thoughts that crossed his mind. He was tired physically and mentally. Sleep came to his rescue.

FOUR

SIDDHARTHA WAS BEGINNING to develop a close friendship with Naradatta. The fact that Naradatta did not complete his education in Baranasi and Rajagaha intrigued him. He remembered Naradatta saying that the south was heavily under the influence of Brahmanism. Was that the reason why he returned to Kapilavatthu? Weren't there other teachers who could accept him as a disciple? Was Siddhartha going to experience the same kind of frustration if his father decided to send him to the south? These questions and reflections helped Siddhartha to gradually overcome his disappointment at not being able to leave Kapilavatthu. But his desire to know more about human life continued to grow like a creeper undeterred by obstacles. He was on the verge of completing his education under Asita, Vessamitta and Bharadvaja. Suddhodana was eagerly looking forward to Siddhartha's participation in the administration of the kingdom.

Every now and then, Suddhodana would ask Siddhartha to join him in his tours of the various provinces in the Sakyan kingdom. Suddhodana had several residences in the provinces that he would occupy during these tours. These residences were also meant to be occupied by the royal family during different seasons. Siddhartha enjoyed accompanying his father on these tours, not because he was interested in learning about the administration of the kingdom, but because they provided him with an opportunity of learning more about people, their life-styles and aspirations.

Occasionally Siddhartha would invite his friend Naradatta

and cousin Devadatta to go on these tours. Whenever he found the opportunity, he would go out with Naradatta and Devadatta into the forests bordering the villages to watch the deer and antelopes, the waterfowl and other rare birds inhabiting these forests. Naradatta and Devadatta were interested in hunting and would carry bows and arrows with them when they went out into the forest. Though Siddhartha did not enjoy hunting, he would not stand in the way of his friends' amusing themselves.

On one occasion, a waterfowl shot by Naradatta fell down close to Siddhartha who immediately ran up to the bird, pulled out the arrow from his body and was trying to nurse him. Naradatta approached him laughing.

"O, Siddhartha, the compassionate one! You seem to be a believer in Yajnavalkya's philosophy. Do you think that the bird has a soul, and therefore it is wrong to hurt him?"

"I do not know whether it has a soul or not. But don't you see that this poor creature is in pain? You seem to have no regrets for the suffering of others," rejoined Siddhartha, looking at his friend with disappointment.

"I am not sure whether the bird is experiencing any pain," retorted Naradatta. "All I see is that it is flapping its wings and is trying to fly again, which is a natural tendency in a bird. Do you think I have done something wrong in shooting the bird?"

"Yes, I do," said Siddhartha in disappointment.

"In that case, all those poor people who have no other means of livelihood than hunting are committing wrong deeds all the time, and if we are to believe the so-called moral philosophers, all of them would end up in hell."

"I am not speaking about people who are compelled to adopt professions like hunting for lack of any other opportunity. I am only speaking about people like you who are doing it merely for amusement."

Naradatta was not willing to make such a distinction between his action and that of a regular hunter. He argued:

"Do you mean to say that an action is wrong when it is done by one sort of person and right when it is done by another? This is the double standard of morality that some people advocate. Siddhartha, don't you think that our actions are the same? What the hunter and I have both done is to send an arrow through a lump of physical elements. Aren't good and bad, right and wrong, meaningless discriminations made on the basis of individual dispositions, having nothing to do with reality?"

Siddhartha knew that Naradatta was very critical of traditional views of morality. But until now he did not realize that his friend was an avowed materialist. He remembered Naradatta's sympathetic reference to Ajita Kesakambali and Pakudha Kaccayana on the day they rode together to the village on the outskirts of Kapilavatthu. He was able to piece things together.

In the meantime, Devadatta returned with a pretty little bird whom he had knocked down with a slingshot. He was excited about cleaning up the bird's flesh, drying the skin and stuffing it up with cotton so that he could decorate his room with it.

After taking care of his official duties, Suddhodana returned to Kapilavatthu with his entourage. When they got home late in the evening, Siddhartha's stepmother informed him that his old friend, Kapila, had returned to Kapilavatthu after completing his studies at Takkasila. In fact, Kapila had visited the palace several times looking for Siddhartha. Siddhartha was excited about the news and was impatient to meet him. He had to wait till the following day, and for him it was one of the longest nights he had lived through. Early in the morning, Siddhartha got ready and was off to see his childhood friend, and on his way picked up Devadatta. The reunion of the three childhood friends turned out to be an occasion of unbounded joy.

"Now that Kapila has returned after becoming proficient in all the branches of human knowledge, it would not be appropriate for us to address him as 'friend.' Instead, we should call him 'Sir,' shouldn't we, Devadatta?" questioned Siddhartha, looking at his cousin.

"Your majesty, now that I have completed all my training, I am at your service," retorted Kapila.

All three of them laughed.

"Did you enjoy your stay in Takkasila?" questioned Devadatta.

"Yes. It was a great learning experience. I met many teachers and enjoyed studying under them. They are very systematic and rational. The science of supreme reality or *brahma-vidya* was nothing for them, unless it was possible to give a logical account of it. They were skeptical about those who wanted to remain silent about questions relating to reality. Studying under them, you had to think of some possible explanation, and that kind of exercise was considered to be good for the soul."

"What have you been doing all this time?" asked Kapila, after a moment's silence.

"We have been studying the Vedas from Asita Kaladevala, the science of politics from Bharadvaja, and the martial arts from Vessamitta. Except what we picked up from Vessamitta, everything that we learned here was really the science of the brahmans rather than the science of supreme reality," replied Siddhartha, rather despondently.

"I am sure that would still prove to be profitable one day," remarked Kapila. "They say, no knowledge is useless, so long as one does not get overly attached to it."

"By the way, there is a person named Naradatta who has returned from Baranasi. He left Baranasi even before he completed his studies. Maybe you would like some of his ideas," said Siddhartha.

"When I am rested and have completed visiting all my relatives, I would like to meet him," said Kapila.

The three friends spent the whole day together recounting their experiences before they bade good-bye to each other.

By now Siddhartha had passed his adolescence and had grown up to be a tall and handsome young man. Suddhodana and Pajapati Gotami were becoming more and more concerned about his future role as chief of the Sakyan people. They were perturbed by the fact that the heir to the throne was more interested in questions relating to justice and moral values than matters pertaining to the administration of the kingdom. Nor was he showing any interest in following the obligations of household life by choosing a suitable kshatriya maiden to be his wife. However Gotami had noticed that Siddhartha was attracted to Yasodhara, daughter of Mahanama and Bimba. Yasodhara was a beautiful young woman, bright, intelligent and outspoken. She was also well educated, having made full use of the opportunities given her by birth. At religious ceremonies and social occasions where young men and women had the opportunity of meeting each other, Yasodhara would be a very noticeable figure.

One evening when Suddhodana and Gotami were out on the balcony of their palace, they saw Siddhartha running around and hiding behind the bushes in the garden below. A moment later his little brother, Nanda, appeared and he was looking for Siddhartha. Siddhartha was trying to entertain and amuse his younger brother. He enjoyed playing with his little brother in spite of their difference in age.

"Look," said Suddhodana, drawing Gotami's attention to the two sons playing in the garden. "Siddhartha has not yet outgrown his childhood. When he is at home, he plays with Nanda. Other times he is out with his friends. He does not seem to have any interest in learning the duties and responsibilities of a chieftain. I think it is time to get him settled. When he gets married he will have to be more responsible in his behavior."

"Siddhartha is not an irresponsible man," responded Gotami. "He is very keen to learn more about people, their hopes and aspirations. When he plays with Nanda, he is observant of Nanda's behavior, his spontaneous responses to situations. Sometimes Siddhartha argues with me when I try to control Nanda's behavior. Siddhartha thinks a child should grow up without inhibitions. Anyway, I agree that it is time for Siddhartha to think of marriage."

Suddhodana looked far into the horizon and pondered for a moment. "I would be at fault if I did not make arrangements for Siddhartha to choose a suitable young woman," said Suddhodana.

"Have you spoken to Siddhartha about marriage?" asked Gotami.

"No," responded Suddhodana. "We should first look for someone suitable and then arrange for them to meet."

Gotami thought this was the moment to let Suddhodana know what she had observed on a number of occasions.

"It may be true that Siddhartha has not yet thought of marriage. But I have noticed him being decidedly partial towards Yasodhara. Maybe he has some interest in her."

Suddhodana was not enthusiastic about this news. He knew Yasodhara's parents well. They were too liberal in their outlook. Yasodhara did not have to conform to the restrictions that a young girl in that society had to follow. Suddhodana was haunted by the predictions of Asita. He felt that Yasodhara with her liberal upbringing would only precipitate what he was trying to prevent.

"Do you think Siddhartha is very interested in Yasodhara?" inquired Suddhodana. Gotami agreed to find out.

Siddhartha had been a precocious child and had grown up to be a thoughtful and considerate young man. His royal upbringing did not prevent him from experiencing the most natural feelings of any other young man of his age, and his attraction to Yasodhara was one of these. Yet Siddhartha had a tendency to restrain himself from undue indulgences and still more from the exercise of his princely charms and powers. Furthermore, Yasodhara herself was more enlightened than any other female of his acquaintance, thus contributing to Siddhartha's attraction towards her.

It did not take long for Gotami to confront Siddhartha with the question regarding his marriage and his interest in Yasodhara. She had just returned from a sports festival at which young men of the kshatriya clan participated. Notable absentees at this festival were Siddhartha and Kapila. Being interested in having a close conversation with Yasodhara, Gotami decided to occupy a seat next to her in the pavilion specially constructed for the occasion. Naradatta and Devadatta were taking part in the various competitions. To Gotami's surprise, Yasodhara herself raised the question:

"Where is Siddhartha? Is he not attending the festival?"

"I am surprised Siddhartha is not here," replied Gotami. "He left home early in the morning with Kapila and I assumed they were coming here to participate in the games."

"Well, Siddhartha met his friend after so many years and

they may have enough things to discuss. He certainly would have provided good competition to Naradatta who is now dominating the games," remarked Yasodhara, who joined her companions cheering the participants in the competition.

Gotami realized that just as Siddhartha was attracted to Yasodhara, Yasodhara herself was showing some interest in Siddhartha. She was unhappy that Siddhartha did not show up at the festival. Deep inside her Gotami felt that she liked Yasodhara. But she knew that Yasodhara was not Suddhodana's choice for Siddhartha.

Siddhartha was at home when Suddhodana, Gotami and Nanda returned from the festival. They enjoyed the evening meal together, and Suddhodana retired to his bed chamber without asking where Siddhartha had been during the day. Nanda's maid was there to take him to bed. Siddhartha and Gotami were left alone.

"I met Yasodhara today," said Gotami.

"Where did you meet her?"

"At the sports festival. She was inquiring about you," replied Gotami, looking sharply at Siddhartha for his reactions.

"I was interested in participating in the competitions. But Kapila suggested that we visit a village. How did the competition go?"

"Devadatta came first in archery. Naradatta defeated everyone in horse racing. Yasodhara was sorry that you were not present. She felt that you would certainly have beaten Naradatta."

"How did you get to know that?" asked Siddhartha, trying to hide his embarrassment.

"Well, that's what she told me."

Siddhartha was curious. His restraint in his relationship toward young women of his age was being gradually overcome by his attraction towards Yasodhara. He wanted to know more about her feelings.

"Why did she think I could defeat Naradatta?"

"She probably has a lot of confidence in your abilities. She thinks highly of you. What do you think of her?"

"Why do you ask that question?"

"Isn't it important?" asked Gotami.

Siddhartha realized the importance of Gotami's question. It was time for him to decide whether he should get married or not.

"Yes, it is important. But there is a question that is more important than that," said Siddhartha.

"What is that?" questioned Gotami.

"Shouldn't I first decide whether I want to get married or not? If I decide to get married, shouldn't I have the freedom to choose the person I want to marry? Also, is it not important that I get to know the woman I want to marry?"

Gotami carefully avoided Siddhartha's first question. She said, "I think it is important for you to choose the woman whom you want to marry and to get to know that person. But sometimes you may not be mature enough to know what your life is going to be. So, a little bit of counsel from those who know more about life may be helpful," said Gotami.

Siddhartha did not know whether his stepmother was encouraging or discouraging any relationship between him and Yasodhara. What he knew was that his parents wanted him to get married and that he should respect the advice of his parents in choosing a wife.

"Good night, mother," said Siddhartha as he walked away.

He spent the rest of the evening reflecting on his future. "Am I going to lead a life for which I was destined as a result of being the son of a king? Is there any way in which I could change it? Taking a wife is a natural thing. But should it be determined by custom or by predestination? Predestination is a convenient way for custom to justify itself. This is what Narayana's *Purusha-sukta* intends to achieve. No, it is not unnatural for me to take a wife. But I should not allow custom and tradition to interfere with it. If I am to marry, I need to select my wife. She is going to be my friend and partner." He thought about Yasodhara. The more he thought about her, the greater was his conviction that she was the right companion for him.

Gotami was not able to say anything to Suddhodana until the following morning. After Suddhodana attended to his official work, he returned to the family room where Gotami was and inquired:

"Were you able to find out anything about Siddhartha's intentions?"

"Not really. But I suspect they are attracted to each other. Yasodhara was inquiring about Siddhartha when I met her yesterday at the sports festival. Siddhartha was himself curious when I spoke to him about Yasodhara. But he does not say much. I am not even sure whether he has any idea of getting married at all," replied Gotami.

Suddhodana paced up and down the room. He had decided to keep his son in Kapilavatthu without sending him outside for his education. At that time Siddhartha was only a small boy. Can Suddhodana impose his will on Siddhartha once again? It is important for Siddhartha to get married. It is equally important that he gets married according to custom and tradition, where the parents decide whom a son or a daughter should marry. Yet Siddhartha was no blind follower of custom and tradition. Suddhodana decided to test Siddhartha's will.

FIVE

SIDDHARTHA'S DAY STARTED very early. He would be up before everyone else in his household. Sometimes he would take a stroll along the bank of the river Rohini or would go out riding for a few miles, bathe in the river and return in time for breakfast. He was familiar with the sight of men and women, young and old, dipping themselves in the icy cold water of Rohini before sunrise.

On this day Siddhartha was riding along the path that ran parallel to the river Rohini. During the previous night, he reflected on his conversation with his stepmother. He decided to get married, but not the way his parents wanted. He suspected that his father would not like Yasodhara to be his wife. He was not sure what his stepmother's views were. Though she did not indicate her opposition to any relationship between him and Yasodhara, he felt that his father would want to make his own decision in this matter, just as he did with regard to his education. At that time he did not resist his father's decision. Was he going to let his father decide on his marriage too? Marriage is a lifetime commitment. Should he let custom and tradition determine his future all the time? He needed someone to talk to. Yes, Kapila is available. Kapila has little respect for such tradition. He is critical in his outlook. His education in Takkasila has moulded his thinking. He has come under the influence of the Sankhya school. Logical consistency is something he always looks for. He is a very warmhearted person. Kapila would be an ideal person to consult in this matter.

As he rode along, completely immersed in his thoughts, his horse suddenly stopped and refused to move forward. Looking ahead in the vanishing darkness of early dawn, he saw something on the ground blocking his path. Getting down from his horse, he walked up to the object. It was an old man, probably in his eighties, cold like a block of ice, not moving at all.

"Is he dead?" he thought to himself, and a cold shudder ran through his spine. He was frightened. It was the first time he had come across a dead body in a completely unexpected way. He picked up courage and went closer to the man and moved his body a little with his hand. To his surprise and great relief, the man groaned. He was not dead. Siddhartha took off his coat and wrapped it around the man to make him warm. Looking around, he saw some people bathing upstream, and called for help.

Within a few minutes, several men and women reached the spot. He was able to get some spare clothes from them, remove the wet clothes the old man was wearing and cover him up with the warm clothing. Within another half hour or so, the old man regained consciousness, but he was weak. Siddhartha turned around and inquired:

29

"Why should a man of his age and physical condition come here to bathe in the icy cold water at this time of the day?"

Everyone recognised Siddhartha. He was their king's son. For a moment everyone was silent. Finally a middle-aged woman broke the silence.

"Sir, we believe that the water in this river Rohini, originating in the Himalayas, is sacred. If we bathe in it at daybreak, we will be able to wash away all the sins we have committed during the previous day and start a new and fresh life. Having washed away our sins without letting them accumulate, we will be reborn in heaven after death."

"Who taught you to believe in this?" inquired Siddhartha.

"The priest," said the woman. "This person," she continued, pointing at the old man Siddhartha was able to save from death, "himself is a priest who practiced for many years what he preached."

Siddhartha could not suppress his anger as well as his amusement. He remarked, "If one can wash one's sins by bathing in this river and thereby reach heaven, the fishes, tortoises, crocodiles and other aquatic creatures in this river would be the first to go to heaven. I do not think I would want to go there."

He rode away having requested the people gathered around to take the old brahman priest back to his residence. The incident made him realize how wrong tradition could be. He was concerned that he may have to face similar consequences by merely following tradition. He decided to talk to Kapila, and soon after breakfast rode over to his friend's house.

Kapila and his parents were at home when Siddhartha arrived. He was surprised to see Siddhartha so early in the day because the usual time they met was in the afternoons or evenings. Without trying to hide his surprise, Kapila greeted Siddhartha with the words:

"What brings my friend Siddhartha here so early in the morning? Am I going to be showered with some royal favors?"

Siddhartha laughed. So did Kapila's parents. Kapila's father remarked, "In our old age it would be comforting to see Kapila become a court-adviser."

"That's not an impossibility. But right now Kapila and I need to discuss some other matter. Could you excuse us?"

The parents moved inside the house leaving Kapila and Siddhartha in the front yard.

"What is it?" asked Kapila.

"I have to make an important decision. I know what I want to do. But I also want to make sure that I make the right decision. Is it possible for us to go to some place where we can have some peace and quiet to discuss this matter at length?" asked Siddhartha. Looking at his face Kapila knew it was an important matter.

"Surely. Let us ride up to the park by the river. That is a very pleasant place," suggested Kapila.

Within a few minutes they reached the small park full of mango, orange and tangerine trees. There were wooden seats surrounding the trunks of the larger trees, especially those that provided an expanse of shade. Siddhartha and Kapila tied their horses to the low branches of the tree and sat down facing the rippling river flowing by.

"Siddhartha, what is bothering you?" asked Kapila who was rather impatient to get started with the conversation.

"I have a suspicion that my father is planning to get me settled. My stepmother suspects that Yasodhara and I are friends, which is not correct. She told me that Yasodhara inquired about me on the day of the sports festival. I like Yasodhara better than all the other women I have met. My only fear is that my father may arrange something according to his traditional thinking and I may have to live with it for the rest of my life."

"What do you think of Yasodhara?" interrupted Kapila.

"As I said, I like her because often I find her to be open-minded and easy to talk to. She says what she thinks whether people like it or not. She seems to be free from the bondage of tradition."

"So . . . I do see you have a problem," Kapila said lightly. "Do you think your father would not like Yasodhara?"

"She certainly is not his ideal of a woman," responded Siddhartha.

"I think what you should do is to find out Yasodhara's

feelings, and if she is agreeable, try to convince your father that this is the best for you."

"For me, asking Yasodhara is the most difficult part," said Siddhartha, looking at the ground and smiling.

Kapila burst into laughter.

"Poor Siddhartha, reared in Kapilavatthu, like a lion cub brought up in captivity and unable to make its own kill when let loose in the jungle. Visit Yasodhara and her parents. You are the son of the king of the Sakyans. Surely, Yasodhara's parents would be delighted to see their daughter married to you," said Kapila trying to encourage his friend to make a decision.

Siddhartha became thoughtful.

"I don't think it is right for me to exploit my position as the son of Suddhodana to win over Yasodhara, if I want to marry her. Isn't there any other way?" questioned Siddhartha.

Kapila regretted his last comment. Knowing Siddhartha's temperament, he felt he should not have suggested such a course of action. But what else could Siddhartha do? Whether he liked it or not, his position as the son of the king would influence anything and everything he did. Kapila was a determinist. He believed there are substantial relationships between things, between events. A seed cannot produce a different kind of tree, for the tree is essentially in the seed. Siddhartha cannot be anybody else but the son of Suddhodana.

They were silent for a while. Siddhartha listened to the sound of the river Rohini as its crystal clear water tumbled over rocks and flowed down, providing an exotic musical background to the singing of the birds. He gazed into the shallow water and saw how the smaller rocks and pebbles were carried downstream by the strong current giving them a rounded shape as they hit against each other. There was no life in them. He saw some dark ant-like creatures with long legs floating on the water, some of them moving upstream only to be carried down by the current to where they started from. But there were the larger rocks that remained unmoved as the water flowed by. "Does this represent human existence," he asked himself. "Yes, it does. Ordinary uneducated people are like those lifeless rocks and pebbles thrown around and about and against one another, yet all are being pushed down by the strong current of tradition. There are others who try to brave the current, but are beaten back every time. Is it not possible for man to be like the majestic rock that remains unmoved by the powerful current?" He had no answer. He turned to Kapila and said:

"I would like to know Yasodhara's feelings without having to force a decision on her. I should seek her company more often and will have to let my father wait until I know more about Yasodhara. If I have to take a wife, it should be my decision."

Kapila was unhappy that he could not offer his friend any bright suggestions. He was also disappointed over Siddhartha's unwillingness to recognize that in this kind of situation his position in society has an inevitable bearing. Yet he wanted to help his friend. Siddhartha expressed his interest in cultivating Yasodhara's company. Perhaps he could help Siddhartha by finding opportunities for them to meet more often.

SIX

FROM HIS CONVERSATIONS with Kapila, Siddhartha learned more of the ideological changes taking place in the south as well as in the northwest than he could learn from Naradatta, who was intolerant not only of Brahmanism but also of any views regarding moral and spiritual matters. According to Kapila, the kshatriyas were responsible for the religious and social revolution that unseated the brahman clan from the superior position they occupied. Sages like Uddalaka provided a philosophical foundation for such change. Though a brahman by birth, Uddalaka was educated in the north-west, where Brahmanism had much less influence than in the south. As a result, Uddalaka's views were less dogmatic and more rational. He was an intense lover of wisdom, and his life exemplified the fact that one is never too old to learn. Siddhartha had heard how Uddalaka joined his son, when the latter went out for his education, saying, "Wait, we shall both go."

For Uddalaka, "existence" was the primary fact of life. He could not believe that nonexistence was prior to existence. Thinking about the nature of the first "existence," he believed that it was sentient, that it was able to generate a desire or a wish. This was an inherent characteristic of existence. Except for this inherent creative desire, that primordial existence did not possess any of the characteristics of the present world. The present world is an evolution out of this primordial existence with its inherent creative desire. His philosophy, therefore, differed from that of Narayana for whom the fourfold caste system was part and parcel of the primordial stuff out of which the world evolved. Thus the caste system, on the basis of which the brahmans enjoyed a superior status in society, failed to find justification in Uddalaka's thought.

Kapila, as a kshatriya, favored Uddalaka's ideas in many ways. But he could not accept Uddalaka's premise that the original existence out of which the world evolved is unitary or one. Neither was he willing to admit that creativity could be part of dumb material existence. Therefore, he favored the Sankhya view, which was gradually emerging into prominence, that the evolution of the primordial matter was due to the influence of another spiritual substance separate from matter. These two elements could not function independently; they were dependent upon each other, like a blind man and a lame one.

For Siddhartha, all this was interesting speculation. Some of these ideas had the effect of eliminating age-old traditions that the brahman priests were trying to perpetuate. Unfortunately for Siddhartha they made no positive contribution toward solving some of the problems that perplexed him. If everything as it stands now evolved out of one unitary substance, either through its own power, as Uddalaka believed, or through the influence of an external agency, as Kapila recognized, who or what is to be held responsible for the good and bad, wealth and poverty, happiness and suffering that one finds in this world? Kapila would argue that good and happiness are due to the predominance of the more buoyant and luminous elements in the primordial matter, that bad and suffering are the results of the predominance of the mobile and stimulating aspect of the primordial matter, while the indifferent or neutral aspects of human experience are due to the dominance of darkness or inertia in the primordial matter. Siddhartha could not agree with him. What is it that is responsible for the predominance of one over the other? He needed justification. Both Uddalaka and Kapila had failed to provide such justification. So Siddhartha would say to himself:

"I have come to be the son of Suddhodana, the king of the Sakyans. Why I came to be such, I cannot explain with my present knowledge. But the mere fact that I am Suddhodana's son does not entitle me to anything and everything. I need to earn what I want."

Siddhartha was engrossed in such thoughts for a while before he found the next opportunity to meet with Yasodhara. It was at a festival of music held in Kapilavatthu. For the more affluent among the inhabitants of Kapilavatthu, music was a fashionable luxury. They were sent to bed with music and awakened by it. At mealtime or even when they traveled about, the people who could afford it, took with them musicians to entertain themselves. Music was rarely absent from festive occasions, processions, marriages or even funerals. Public musical contests provided useful platforms for musicians to show off their talents and to display their potential.

Having missed the sports festival a few months ago, Siddhartha decided to attend the music festival, primarily in the hope of meeting Yasodhara. He enjoyed music, yet he did not like the way musicians were exploited by the rich. As usual he was accompanied by Kapila.

Yasodhara was with her constant companions, Rohini, a kshatriya woman of sharp wit, and Anopama, the daughter of a wealthy merchant. It was Kapila who spotted these three

35

young women at the music festival. When he saw them, he whispered to Siddhartha:

"Hey, friend, the people whom we are interested in meeting are over there to the left of the pavilion. Do you want to go there?"

Siddhartha was pleased but embarrassed. Deep within him he felt the need to meet Yasodhara. Yet he was frightened of this encounter. Kapila's presence was helpful in overcoming his bashfulness.

Rohini was the first to notice the two young men, Siddhartha and Kapila, walking towards them. She pinched Yasodhara on her arm and directed her attention to the approaching young men. Kapila greeted the young women, but Siddhartha merely smiled at them, trying to hide his embarrassment. Rohini was the first to say something and what she said removed all the tension that was building up within Siddhartha. Teasing Yasodhara, she said, "Yasodhara, here is Siddhartha whom you were inquiring about."

And, immediately she turned to Siddhartha and said smiling, "Yasodhara thinks of you always. She was sorry that she missed you at the sports festival."

"Rohini, how did you know I was unhappy? Did I say any such thing to you?" asked Yasodhara, throwing a frown at her mischievous friend.

"Unexpressed feelings go deeper than those that are expressed, don't they?" asked Rohini.

"You mean to say that by being a benefactress of those ascetics and always singing their praises, you have developed telepathy?" asked Yasodhara. She could not be angry with Rohini, for she knew that her friend spoke the truth. Turning to Siddhartha, she asked:

"In any case, what prevented you from taking part in the sports festival?"

"Kapila and I forgot about the festival. That morning we went to visit people in the village across the river."

"I suppose it is necessary for the son of the king to be in touch with his people," remarked Anopama who had been silent all this time.

"No, I do not want to know about these people because they

are my father's subjects. I wanted to meet them because I am interested in people. I like to know people—know what they think and believe, how they behave, what their aspirations are," replied Siddhartha.

"Wouldn't you like to know what Yasodhara thinks and believes, what her aspirations are?" asked Rohini, continuing with her mischievousness.

Siddhartha looked at Yasodhara. Yasodhara smiled.

"I wouldn't mind," replied Siddhartha, gathering up all his courage.

Everyone laughed. The music competition was about to start. They looked around for some seats, found some and occupied them.

After that conversation, it was natural for the friends of Siddhartha and Yasodhara to let them sit close to one another. Neither Siddhartha nor Yasodhara paid any close attention to the competition. Nor did they engage themselves in a conversation. Being seated close to each other, Siddhartha, for the first time, experienced the pleasant warmth of a female companion. He was, therefore, mute. Yasodhara herself enjoyed the warmth of contact with Siddhartha.

At the end of the music festival, the two men decided to accompany the young women back to Yasodhara's residence. Kapila, Rohini and Anopama walked ahead, allowing Siddhartha and Yasodhara the opportunity for an undisturbed conversation. Siddhartha found that Yasodhara was no longer the talkative and lively person he had seen on earlier occasions. She was quiet, shy and restrained. They walked together for a while in perfect silence, while their friends were arguing and laughing aloud. Siddhartha decided to break the silence.

"Do you think your parents have chosen a husband for you?" asked Siddhartha.

"Even if they have, they have not informed me of it yet," replied Yasodhara, throwing a glance at Siddhartha.

Siddhartha pondered for a moment and questioned her again.

"If they have not done so yet, would you be my wife?"

Yasodhara looked at Siddhartha. Their eyes met. Siddhartha was uneasy, not knowing what Yasodhara's response would be. Yet he noticed the loving affection emanating from her dark blue eyes. In a moment, Yasodhara's shyness disappeared. She regained her old argumentative self.

"What if my parents have chosen someone else to be my husband? Wouldn't you want to speak to them and get them to change their minds?" asked Yasodhara.

"No. I would not want to do that."

"Why not?" asked Yasodhara, in surprise.

"I do not want to force myself on them."

"Yet, would you want to force yourself on me?" was Yasodhara's immediate question, which she also instantly regretted, feeling that Siddhartha would be put off by it.

"No. I would not want to do that either. I do not want you to marry me because I am the son of Suddhodana."

Yasodhara breathed a sigh of relief. She knew what Siddhartha meant. She slowly reached out for his hand and he held it tight.

SEVEN

THE FOLLOWING DAY was a busy day for Suddhodana. Once every three months, the chieftains of the provinces would assemble in Kapilavatthu to meet with him and to hold court. It would be a busy day not only for Suddhodana, but for everyone in his household. The chieftains, each according to his means, would bring with them wheat, rice and other produce from the provinces as part of the king's share. Suddhodana would entertain them with a feast to which the chief officials and their families from Kapilavatthu would be invited. Musicians were there to entertain the guests. There was much merrymaking all around.

All the guests left before nightfall. Suddhodana retired to the balcony overlooking the river Rohini. Siddhartha knew that it had been a rather tiring day for everyone in his household. But he himself had an important errand on his mind.

It was a very pleasant night, with the moon rising above the mountains painting a picturesque landscape of black, grey and silver. Siddhartha came up to the entrance of the balcony and stood there wondering how he was going to break the news of his decision to his father. Suddhodana felt the presence of someone behind him, looked back and saw Siddhartha.

"Son, aren't you tired? These quarterly events exhaust me, but I am satisfied with today's work," said Suddhodana.

"I am not tired yet, father," replied Siddhartha. After a moment's silence, he broke the news. "I understand that you want me to settle down to a married life. I had a discussion with mother and I came to request you to consider Yasodhara as my choice."

Suddhodana had already heard from Gotami that Siddhartha and Yasodhara were attracted to each other. But he did not want to believe that this was true. Yasodhara was not the girl for Siddhartha. He got up from his seat, looked at Siddhartha and asked:

"Do you know Yasodhara well?"

"I think I do," replied Siddhartha.

"Is she a suitable person to be the queen of the Sakyans?" asked Suddhodana, very much agitated.

"Father, I am not looking for a queen. I am looking for a wife," was Siddhartha's immediate reply. "I am sure she will be a fine queen or anybody else she has to be," he added softly. He stood there silent and motionless, with his arms folded, gazing into the moonlit night. The calm outside became intolerable to Suddhodana. It was so quiet that he feared that his son would be listening to the vibrations of his thoughts. He walked away. Siddhartha remained where he was without moving.

Suddhodana came downstairs. One of the guards opened the front door and he walked into the peaceful night, which really gave him no peace at all. He walked along the path that led

39

away from the house and arrived at the gate. Turning back and looking towards the house, he saw Siddhartha's figure on the balcony where he had left him.

Suddhodana returned to his bedroom. Gotami was not yet there. She was still busy with the task of supervising the cleaning up and working with the accountants, seeing that all the things brought by the provincial chiefs were carefully recorded and stored away. He lay down on his bed. He could not sleep. Late in the night, Gotami entered the bedroom. She was exhausted after being hostess and treasurer in one short day. Suddhodana was still awake.

"You are still awake, dear," said Gotami, as she got ready to go to bed.

"Yes, I have to be awake all the time, for otherwise I would not know what happens around here," remarked Suddhodana rather despondently.

Gotami realized that Suddhodana was worried about something. It would not be very prudent to raise any questions at this time and initiate a lengthy discussion. Both were tired. She suggested:

"We are all tired. A good restful sleep, I am sure, will help us to think of the problems afresh. Why don't we get some sleep."

Suddhodana did not object. His body was tired, though his mind was restless. He could not help but fall asleep. But as soon as his physical fatigue was gone, his restless mind woke him up. He had not slept for more than a couple of hours. He got up and went to the balcony. He could not believe his eyes. Siddhartha was standing just where he had left him a few hours ago. Suddhodana was angry. It was the first time Siddhartha had shown his arrogance. But he was also frightened, for Asita's predictions continued to haunt him.

"Siddhartha, why are you still there?" asked Suddhodana.

"I am waiting for you, father," replied Siddhartha.

"How long are you going to wait?"

"As long as it takes me to know of your decision."

"What will you do if I object to your idea?" asked Suddhodana.

"I shall wait until I am able to convince you that my decision to marry Yasodhara is the right one."

"But, what if I were to propose someone else to be your wife?"

"You will have to wait until I am convinced that that person is the right one for me," was Siddhartha's immediate response.

Suddhodana realized the gravity of the situation. He paced up and down the balcony for a few minutes. During that time he mentally reviewed all the facts relevant to the present problem. He noted that Gotami had not said anything negative about Yasodhara or her family, and Gotami was associated with them closely. He felt that Yasodhara was much like Siddhartha—unorthodox. This fact was not such a tragedy after all. He had heard travelers' tales of far away lands where courtiers used high born ladies to control power. Nearer at home, he knew that some neighboring kingdoms had queens who had interfered in the business of government. Neither Yasodhara nor her family would have such ambitions. His household had been peaceful and happy. Yasodhara may prove to be a decent girl. He stopped in front of Siddhartha, and in a very sad tone, spoke to him.

"Alright son, you can go to sleep now. You may have your way. But I certainly hope you are doing the right thing."

Siddhartha regretted the arrogant manner in which he had confronted his father. But he thought he could not help it.

"I shall go now, father," said Siddhartha and immediately retired to his room.

Suddhodana had nothing more to reflect upon. He returned to his bed and soon fell asleep.

Yasodhara's parents did not have to wait long to hear about the impending relationship between her and Siddhartha. As a result of Rohini's talkativeness, Yasodhara's mother, Bimba, learnt of what transpired during and after the music festival. Bimba was delighted by the news. Mahanama, her husband was rather skeptical. Mahanama was not a conservative. In fact, he was a very liberal-minded person. That is one reason why Yasodhara enjoyed more freedom than any other young woman in Kapilavatthu. He would have approved of Siddhartha's critical attitude towards traditional values. But at the same time, he feared that Siddhartha might go to the other extreme of rejecting household life altogether. It was, therefore, for the sake of Yasodhara that Mahanama was very cautious in encouraging such a relationship. But Bimba was elated at the possibility of becoming part of the royal family. Moreover, Siddhartha was a very handsome young man, coveted by many a young woman in the country. Even before getting to know of the relationship between Siddhartha and Yasodhara, Bimba was an admirer of Siddhartha. Once, after seeing Siddhartha participating in a public procession together with his father, she remarked to one of her friends:

"Fortunate are the parents who have a son like him. More fortunate indeed is the woman who will have him as her husband."

For Bimba, it was a dream come true. She was, therefore, ready to do anything to encourage their friendship.

Siddhartha thought he had achieved two things. First he had found out whether the woman he wanted to marry would accept him, not because of his social status, but because she liked him. He trusted Yasodhara for the manner in which she responded to his proposal. Secondly, he had been able to obtain the consent of his father without too much of a struggle. These were important considerations for him. He was realistic enough to think that if Yasodhara's parents agreed to let him marry her, it would be because he was the son of King Suddhodana. He could not have control over everything. Yet he was happy he had achieved something. So he decided to visit Yasodhara and find out whether he would be welcome at her home or not.

When he reached Yasodhara's residence, Yasodhara was with her usual friends, Rohini and Anopama. For Yasodhara it was a surprise, although she knew that some day it would happen. But as soon as Siddhartha was admitted into the main living room in the house, Yasodhara's two friends left her and went inside the house. But before leaving the room, mischievous Rohini could not help throwing a knowing smile at Siddhartha and winking at him. Siddhartha took a seat facing Yasodhara.

"I spoke to my father and obtained his permission to marry you," he said.

Yasodhara smiled. The sparkle in her eyes was visible. In a very soft voice, she asked Siddhartha:

"Did you have to put up a struggle to get your father's consent?"

"I had to, but it was not too bad. Do you think your parents would object to our getting married?" asked Siddhartha.

"My mother suspects something. She likes you very much. I don't know what my father thinks of it. But usually my mother has her way around the house."

There was silence for a moment. It did not last long. Yasodhara's mother walked into the living room. They both got up. Siddhartha greeted her. She took a seat next to Siddhartha.

"I just heard from Rohini that you were here. I am glad that you decided to drop in. I heard that there was a big party at the palace the other day. Did many people come from the provinces?"

She would have continued with her innumerable questions, if Yasodhara, knowing her mother, had not interrupted her saying:

"Mother, shouldn't you ask Siddhartha to sit down?"

"I am sorry, dear," said Bimba. "Please sit down. Yasodhara's father left this morning to visit one of his relations. He should be returning home any moment. Wouldn't you like to stay for dinner?"

"No, thank you," said Siddhartha. "I just wanted to see Yasodhara. I should be leaving soon."

"Well, next time you come, don't be in such a rush. I am sure Mahanama would be pleased to see you. I will tell him that you dropped by."

Siddhartha smiled. Bimba got up, bade Siddhartha good-bye and left the room.

"That's my mother," said Yasodhara in an apologetic tone. "She likes to talk. But she is a very understanding person."

Siddhartha got up from his seat and walked towards the door accompanied by Yasodhara. He took her hand in his. He experienced the same kind of sensation that he had when he first held her hand while returning from the music festival. Once outside the house, Siddhartha gently moved her hand to his lips, kissed it, saying, "We shall get together soon." He left her standing there. After passing the main gate to the house, Siddhartha looked back. Yasodhara was standing there watching him. She waved her hand and he responded with a wave of his hand and rode away.

After Siddhartha left Yasodhara's house, Yasodhara's mother decided to question her daughter about her relationship with Siddhartha.

"Did Siddhartha propose marriage to you?" she asked.

"Yes, he did," replied Yasodhara.

"What did you say to him?"

"Nothing."

"But, don't you like him?"

"I think I like him."

Bimba was surprised.

"If you felt you liked him, why didn't you say something when he asked you for your hand in marriage?"

"Well, I did give my hand to him, although I did not say anything," said Yasodhara smiling.

Bimba was happy, but yet concerned.

"Do you think his father would approve of his marriage to you?"

"That is what he came to inform me."

"Did Suddhodana approve of it or not?" asked Bimba, getting impatient with her daughter.

"Well, Siddhartha has somehow managed to convince his father. It seems that what I have to do now is to get the approval of my own father."

Bimba's face brightened.

"Mother, will you please help me?" pleaded Yasodhara, who had by now fallen completely in love with Siddhartha.

It was evident that Bimba would do anything to promote this marriage. She was ready to plead with her husband to agree to it.

In the evening, Mahanama returned home. He found an unusual cheerfulness on his wife's face. After resting for a while, Mahanama joined the family for the evening meal.

"We had an important visitor today," said Bimba.

Mahanama was not ready for the surprise. But seeing how

44

Yasodhara, who was normally very talkative at family gatherings, had gone mute, Mahanama suspected what it was.

"So there was a royal visit during the time I was gone," he said, looking at Yasodhara who was nibbling at the food on the plate without looking up.

Yasodhara was frightened. She knew her father was a very liberal person. Yet she felt that Siddhartha was not his choice for her. She was not eating her food, but the fingers on her right hand were playing with what was on the plate.

"Is Siddhartha serious about this matter?" asked Mahanama.

"It seems so," replied Bimba.

"I have difficulty thinking of Siddhartha as a family man. Suddhodana is himself worried about Siddhartha not getting involved in the affairs of state. He seems to be a little too irresponsible for a man of his age and status."

Yasodhara's fear was growing within her. She tried her best to conceal it.

"But, isn't that the way with most young men of his age nowadays? Isn't it only a passing phase? But once they are married, they do settle down to their duties and responsibilities, don't they?" asked Bimba, trying to pacify Mahanama.

"Did Siddhartha actually propose marriage to Yasodhara or are you merely imagining things because he visited us?" asked Mahanama.

"Yes, he did propose to Yasodhara," replied Bimba.

Looking at Yasodhara, Mahanama questioned, "Yasodhara, what did you tell him?"

"I did not say anything," replied Yasodhara, still keeping her head bent low.

"But, what about Suddhodana? Is he going to accept Siddhartha's decision?"

"That is what Siddhartha came to inform us today," responded Bimba. "He had discussed his marriage with his father and he has agreed."

"I am surprised that Suddhodana agreed," said Mahanama. "All these years he had been trying to keep Siddhartha under his control. He did not allow Siddhartha to go outside Kapilavatthu for his education. He tried his best to keep him away from all external influences."

"Yasodhara would not be the kind of woman Suddhodana would want for his son. What are your own feelings about this, Yasodhara?" he asked.

She was silent.

Mahanama knew that cupid had completed his work. He was worried, worried for the sake of Yasodhara. He did not trust Siddhartha.

A woman's instinct made Bimba realize that Mahanama was going through a difficult decision-making process. But she also knew that Mahanama was a very considerate person.

"It is getting late now. Maybe we need a little more time to think about it. I am sure you are tired and need to rest, my dear," said Bimba to Mahanama.

Mahanama got up from his seat and went into his bedroom. Yasodhara's food was still on the plate. Her eyes were wet. Bimba walked up to her daughter and, touching her head tenderly, said:

"You need to give your father a little more time to think about it. I am sure everything will work out alright."

And, everything indeed worked out alright for Yasodhara, at least for the time being.

EIGHT

SUDDHODANA MADE ELABORATE ARRANGEMENTS for Siddhartha's wedding. The three residences outside Kapilavatthu, which he occupied during different seasons— the winters, the summers and the rainy seasons—were redecorated for the use of his son and Yasodhara. He was keen on providing Siddhartha with all the comforts in his married life, with the hope that this new life would bring about a change in his attitudes. Realizing that Siddhartha had very little respect for the Brahmanical tradition, Suddhodana decided to minimize the rituals associated with his nuptials. The simple marriage ritual was performed at the Coronation Hall in Kapilavatthu. At the conclusion of the ceremony, Siddhartha and Yasodhara were driven in a horse-drawn carriage to the summer residence of Suddhodana.

It was a lovely residence situated in the mountain slopes north of Kapilavatthu. The garden in front of the house was decked with lotus pools and exotic plants. On either side there were groves of fruit trees. The orchard at the back of the house gradually merged with the jungle vegetation. It was an extremely pleasant spot to live in, especially during the summer when the heat was offset by the sprays of cool water from the fast-flowing streams and miniature waterfalls.

The party consisting of the parents, immediate relatives and friends of the couple arrived at the summer residence late in the afternoon. A plentiful variety of food and drink was available. Entertainment was provided by a group of selected artists. A bevy of pretty young girls provided a fascinating chorus. It was a merrymaking time for everyone, including the landholders of the surrounding village who had come to greet the new couple.

As the day wore on, guests started leaving. Siddhartha and Yasodhara had to remain at the entrance to the house for a while bidding farewell to the guests. The last to leave the house were the couple's parents. Yasodhara walked up to her father, knelt down and holding his feet with both hands, started sobbing. Mahanama, with tears in his eyes, held her by the shoulders, raised her gently from her kneeling position and kissed her on the head. She then went over to her mother, Bimba, who was by now shedding tears of joy mixed with the sadness of separation from her daughter. Next to receive her obeisance were Suddhodana and Gotami. Siddhartha walked up to his father, and lying prostrate, worshipped at his feet. When he stood up, Suddhodana embraced his son, and Siddhartha, with tears in his eyes, whispered to his father,

"Father, I hope I have done the right thing. Please forgive me if I have offended you." From there he went on to pay his respects to his mother, father-in-law and mother-in-law. Nanda, his little brother, was all this time watching the whole scenario. Siddhartha walked up to him, hugged him and gave him a tender kiss on his forehead.

When this final farewell was over, the parents and the members of the immediate families came out of the house and began boarding the carriages to return to Kapilavatthu. Siddhartha and Yasodhara walked with them to the porch outside, leaving the entertainers and the servants inside the house. As they watched their parents leave, a strange sense of loneliness gripped both Siddhartha and Yasodhara. Siddhartha walked up to Yasodhara, placed his right arm over her shoulders and brought her close to him. Yasodhara gently leaned over to him and rested her head against his warm chest feeling a sense of security. She was no longer lonely, nor was he.

During the time Siddhartha and Yasodhara remained at the summer residence, many of their friends visited them. Kapila being Siddhartha's closest friend, was the most frequent visitor. Siddhartha began to realize that it was not possible for him to travel around with Kapila as he used to do. He now had the obligation to be Yasodhara's constant companion. Whenever Kapila left after visiting them, Yasodhara felt that Siddhartha sorely missed his company. In fact, she knew that Kapila was one of few who could provide Siddhartha with any kind of intellectual stimulation. She, therefore, sought to fill that vacuum in his life in order to keep him close to her.

During the evenings, Siddhartha and Yasodhara would step out of the house and take a stroll in the garden surrounding the house. When they returned, they were entertained by the musicians employed by Suddhodana. Sometimes, the girls who constituted the chorus would perform dances in their presence.

Rich people in the kingdom reveled in this kind of entertainment. For long hours in the evenings they would drink intoxicating liquor, and professional musicians, singers and dancing girls would entertain them until they had to be carried to their rooms by the servants in the household. Siddhartha who was not used to such drinking and reveling was gradually getting bored by this routine entertainment. One day, while returning after an evening stroll, Siddhartha asked Yasodhara:

"Do you enjoy the music and dancing that has continued since we came here?"

"Not very much," said Yasodhara, beginning to realize that Siddhartha was getting tired of such entertainment.

"I like music," continued Siddhartha, "it is beautiful. It is natural for a person to be attracted to something beautiful. One can derive a lot of harmless satisfaction. But overindulgence can make you sick. Satisfaction turns to boredom. Why?"

Siddhartha paused for a moment. He questioned Yasodhara again.

"Do you think that these performers themselves enjoy what they are doing? Don't they get tired of it?"

"I am not sure whether they enjoy it themselves. But they probably are not getting tired of it. They take intoxicating liquor while they perform and they probably feel that they can get rid of their tiredness and boredom by doing so. Moreover, they get paid for what they do. One cannot engage oneself in a profession merely for the sake of entertaining oneself."

"That means, if all of us did not want to entertain ourselves in this manner, these poor artists would not have any means of livelihood."

"That's right," replied Yasodhara. "If everyone in Kapilavatthu suddenly stopped drinking and entertaining themselves in this manner, all these people would be affected. They have no other vocation and their families would suffer as a result. But these are people with natural talents. They have been abused and exploited by the rich who think of their own pleasure only. I would also blame the artists for selling their talents in this way. What is needed is restraint and moderation on both sides. It is necessary to safeguard the artists from exploitation by the rich and the artists themselves should not prostitute their talents."

"You are a good teacher, dear," said Siddhartha. "Shouldn't

we make a start? We cannot throw these people out now. Shouldn't we ask them to perform once in three days?"

"Does that mean they do not get their full wages?"

"No," replied Siddhartha, "we will pay them their full wages. But if they are thoughtful people they will at least realize that there are some who appreciate their music, but not in the way they perform it."

"I like that solution," said Yasodhara.

The following day, Yasodhara called the chief servant in the house and instructed him to ask the men and women involved to limit their performances to once in three days. The troupe of musicians and dancers was very disappointed to learn about this. They were under the impression that they were providing good entertainment for Siddhartha and Yasodhara. When they worked at their jobs, they would get exhausted. To overcome the exhaustion, they would take intoxicating liquor. When intoxicated, they would pour all their energies into the performance. At the end of each performance, which would be early morning the following day, they would collapse and fall asleep wherever they were until late morning, thus presenting a rather pathetic spectacle. This was their routine. In order to compensate for their loss of sleep, they would continue to rest in the afternoons. When Siddhartha and Yasodhara restricted their performances, they were thrown completely out of balance. Their routine being interrupted, they had nothing to do during the evenings for two consecutive days. Yet they did not protest through fear they would be earning the wrath of the newly wedded couple. After all, this was the son of their king.

A few days later, Siddhartha asked Yasodhara:

"How do these entertainers feel about having to perform once in three days? Are they having a good vacation?"

"No," replied Yasodhara. "I understand that they are very depressed. They feel that their services are not very much appreciated. Furthermore, they think they are not really earning their wages."

"I am happy that they feel that way. They have to realize that they are exploiting, just as much as they are being exploited. They are hurting themselves, while they are responsible for hurting others. They need to change their attitude with regard to their own professions."

Yasodhara knew that Siddhartha was right. But she decided to drag him into an argument.

"Isn't this the way society functions?" she asked. "See, for example, the kshatriyas fight wars to protect the country. Sometimes, they even have to sacrifice their lives to protect others. For this reason, they are rewarded with the function of ruling the country. Their leaders are the rulers."

Although Yasodhara did not approve of the life of the professional musicians and dancers who found a means of livelihood by catering to the unrestrained desires of wealthy men and women in society, she thought that these professionals did represent a certain inevitable pattern in society.

Siddhartha looked at Yasodhara and smiled.

"Why should there be wars? Who wants to fight wars? Don't you think that wars are a means by which the kshatriyas want to break their monotonous life of pleasure and indulgence, or a means by which they could increase their resources of enjoyment by the annexation of more territory? There are wars because of the desire for power among the kshatriyas. They were encouraged in this by the brahman priests who conceived of a universal monarchy. This was the result of the Brahmanical domination of rulers."

"You speak against the kshatriya clan. But aren't you yourself one of them?" teased Yasodhara, with the hope of finding out what he felt about his own destiny as a kshatriya.

"I am not afraid of self-criticism. Shouldn't I criticize the false assumptions of the kshatriyas because I was born one?"

Yasodhara realized that Siddhartha was speaking his mind. He was deeply concerned about questions of justice and injustice, good and bad. Although she realized that Siddhartha's criticisms of the kshatriyas were justified, she did not accept the idea that each stratum in society should or could completely abandon the various traditional values it had inherited. She was an advocate of gradual change in society, not of its revolutionary upheaval. She remained silent, without trying to continue the argument.

A few days later, they decided to return to their royal residence in Kapilavatthu. Upon their return they were received in the traditional way by the parents of both parties. Siddhartha and Yasodhara took up residence at Suddhodana's palace to enable Siddhartha to participate in the affairs of the state.

NINE

AFTER SIDDHARTHA'S MARRIAGE, his friend Kapila found himself without a close companion. Kapila was not interested in marriage. So it was natural for him to look for a friend with whom he could have the same kind of intellectual companionship that he had with Siddhartha. Naradatta, who became Siddhartha's friend after Kapila left for Takkasila, was a materialist. Though Kapila had met him several times in the company of Siddhartha, Kapila and Naradatta never became close friends.

It was at this time that Kapila met a young disciple of Yajnavalkya. His name was Nalaka. Nalaka had studied in the south and come under the influence of Yajnavalkya. He was interested in the problem of the unity of the individual and universal selves, a doctrine that was presented by Yajnavalkya with great enthusiasm. Nalaka's interest was not merely intellectual. He was keen on experiencing for himself such a unity. Therefore, he spent months in the hermitages of the forests adjoining Kapilavatthu practising meditation. Kapila found that he saw eye to eye on many issues with Nalaka. His major disagreement with Nalaka was on the question regarding the nature of ultimate reality. Kapila had picked up the Sankhya dualism when in Takkasila and had developed it into a systematic philosophy. Nalaka, on the other hand, was involved in spiritual action, in *yoga*. He believed that by following the path of meditation or yoga one could attain liberation and experience for oneself the reality of the transcendent self. He was fascinated by Yajnavalkya's way of explaining the transcendent self in terms of the negation of all duality. Kapila and Nalaka would spend hours debating the questions of duality and nonduality.

After hearing about Nalaka from Kapila, Siddhartha expressed his desire to meet the former. Therefore, the next time Kapila visited Siddhartha, he took Nalaka along with him. They arrived at Suddhodana's residence in the evening and found Siddhartha and Yasodhara seated on a bench in the royal garden. Seeing the visitors approaching, Yasodhara got up and walked back to the house, leaving Siddhartha to talk to his friends. Within no time, Siddhartha developed a liking for Nalaka. He was a very pleasant person, composed and restrained in his behavior. Siddhartha became interested in the spiritual exercises of yoga that Nalaka talked about.

"Tell me something more about yoga," pleaded Siddhartha. "What sort of preliminaries has one to observe? What do you actually do in this kind of meditation and what is your goal?"

The first and most important thing is to look for proper surroundings. The best atmosphere in which such spiritual exercises can be carried out is the forest."

Siddhartha had already learned about the four stages in the life of a brahman. First, a brahman had to be a student of the Vedas; secondly, a householder; thirdly, an anchorite; and finally, an abandoner of all worldly concerns. According to Brahmanism, these represented ways of life to be adopted at different times, usually in that order. One is, therefore, not expected to leave the household life until one is fairly advanced in age and has fulfilled all one's obligations as a householder. But Nalaka was a young man and had not even undertaken the basic responsibilities of a householder, that is taking a wife. Siddhartha was beginning to question the authority and validity of another aspect of the Brahmanical tradition. He needed clarification.

"Is it necessary to retire into the forest to practice this kind of meditation?" asked Siddhartha.

Nalaka went on to give a lengthy explanation.

"It is not impossible to practice meditation while living a householder's life. But what we can achieve by doing so is limited. A hermitage is the ideal environment in which to practice meditation to the highest level of perfection. One does not have to struggle with all the distractions that are normally associated with social or family life. Society is very artificial; we have to follow custom and tradition; we cannot afford to offend anybody by secluding ourselves while living in society. But a hermitage is not such a place; everyone knows that one goes into a hermitage to meditate; people with other kinds of business do not go there. A hermitage is normally in or close to a forest. This provides a natural environment and it is easier for one to develop one's natural capabilities in such an environment."

Siddhartha was beginning to realize that the theory of the four stages in the life of a brahman was an attempt by the brahman priests to counter the ascetic movement, which had gained popularity because of the participation of the kshyatriyas. The ascetics and the wanderers were seekers after truth. During the early stages of these movements there was no specific age at which one should join such a movement. But the brahman priests, realizing that their authority and prestige were being gradually undermined by the achievements and discoveries of these ascetics and wanderers, devised ways to reduce the impact of this movement on their own religion, which emphasized the value of the sacrificial ritual. They needed to keep men and women as householders as long as possible and encourage them to perform the sacrifices upon which the life of the priesthood depended. Hence the theory of the four stages of life which advocated a complete fulfillment of the life of a householder. Siddhartha was pleased that at least some young men among the kshatriyas were ignoring this Brahmanical tradition. But unfortunately he was not in a position to join this band of young men in their search for truth. Yasodhara needed him now, for she was with child.

Before explaining how one undertakes the practice of meditation, Nalaka wanted to explain why one should undertake such a practice.

"Knowledge and ignorance are diametrically opposed, like light and darkness. Wherever there is light, there is no darkness; wherever there is darkness, there is no light. Knowledge is faith and ignorance is doubt. Knowledge is truth and ignorance is falsehood. Knowledge is bliss and ignorance is sorrow. Knowledge is immortality and ignorance is death."

Siddhartha interrupted Nalaka:

"Knowledge and ignorance are found in men. What part of man is associated with knowledge and what is the abode of ignorance?"

"Ignorance is associated with the body and the senses, and knowledge with the Divine Person or the Self in man. This Divine Person, whose breath is life, body is intelligence, form is light and eye is the mind, is the master of the house, the ruler of all. It is like a lonely white swan. During sleep it leaves its cage, the material body, and wanders around as it pleases, enjoying different objects of its liking, and when sleep is over, it returns to its confinement in the body."

"It sounds like a dream state," remarked Siddhartha.

"But, how could this be the Divine Person?" asked Kapila. "It is true that in this dream state, the self seems to have the freedom to move around on its own without being hampered by the body. But all dream states are not pleasant and blissful. There are bad dreams as well as pleasant ones."

"Yes," replied Nalaka, "the dream state does not exhibit the Divine Person in its real form. It is only an intermediary stage. Yet it reveals the ability on the part of the Divine Person to free itself from its confinement."

"How and when does it exhibit its real and true form?" questioned Siddhartha.

"In the state of dreamless sleep," replied Nalaka. "It is a state between the end of dreaming and the state of waking. In this state, the Divine Person frees itself completely from the material world, and therefore experiences no fanciful, terrifying and painful sensations. It transcends everything in the world and becomes whole and serene. It retains no duality. Having attained this unity, the Divine Person thinks its own thoughts, sees its own visions, hears its own voice, smells its own scent, tastes its own bliss. It is the immortal, immaterial Self."

Kapila felt uneasy.

"How could this be the Self?" he asked. "For in such a state, like dreamless sleep, one is not aware of oneself. One cannot speak about oneself, while one is in that state."

"Surely, one cannot speak about oneself in that state. When one wants to speak about oneself, one has to discriminate oneself from others. There is then duality. This immortal Self is beyond description. It cannot be identified with this or that."

"What happens to this Divine Person after the destruction of the material body at death?" asked Siddhartha.

"If the Divine Person is not released completely, it will return to another body after death. Let us consider what happens in dreaming and dreamless states. In the waking state the Divine Person is still there but is in complete bondage. In the dream state, it attains some freedom, but is still associated with forms that are replicas of the gross material things. The dreamless state, wherein the Divine Person exhibits its real nature for a moment, is yet associated with the body. So, after being in a dreamless sleep, a person wakes up and the Divine Person is back again in bondage. Death is like a dream state. Here the Divine Person frees itself from the body. Then it moves around as in a dream and establishes itself once again, this time in a different body. Between such wanderings and its reestablishment in another body, it may fall into such states as dreamless sleep, but so long as it is not completely freed it will not remain in that state for ever. Rebirth is therefore like the waking state."

"Does this mean that the Divine Person, if it is completely freed, will not be reborn?" asked Siddhartha.

"That's right," replied Nalaka. "The Divine Person, when it is completely freed from one body, does not find a foothold in another body. It continues to remain in a luminous, blissful and eternal state with no attachment whatsoever to a material body. It has reached eternality and immortality. It is permanent and without change. It has become one with the Divine Person. It is Brahman."

The conversation was dragging on, but Siddhartha was not ready to give it up yet. He was getting more and more excited. When he first heard of Yajnavalkya's teachings, Siddhartha was not very impressed. The reason was that he got his introduction to Yajnavalkya from Naradatta who was a materialist. But coming from Nalaka, Yajnavalkya's teachings sounded different. Nalaka was not a mere critic nor a mere speculative philosopher. He had been experimenting with these ideas.

"How does one go about freeing the Divine Person completely?" asked Siddhartha.

"That is the purpose of meditation. I go to the hermitage very often to meditate. It is only such spiritual exercises that will enable me to attain freedom and immortality someday. In our waking state we are distracted by our senses. The senses are like horses who would drag us this way and that way unless we are able to control them. Like a good charioteer, we must be able to restrain our senses without letting them loose. Having controlled the senses, we must then try to restrain our mind. The mind can, as in a dream, create its own world and keep us in bondage to that world of mere forms. Further concentration enables us to break through those limiting forms and reach a formless world. In this formless world all limitations are destroyed and one attains perfect peace. It is a world where one transcends good and bad, right and wrong. Constant cultivation of this formless realm will enable us to make it part and parcel of our life."

Siddhartha was fascinated by Nalaka's explanation of the spiritual life. He wished he had more time to discuss various other issues relating to the spiritual life. But it was getting late and dark and time for the two friends to leave. They got up and started walking towards their horses. Siddhartha walked along with them. And when they were about to depart, he said to Kapila:

"We have been visiting villages, speaking to people there

and learning about them. Don't you think we should one day visit a hermitage with Nalaka?"

"If you can obtain Yasodhara's permission, I wouldn't mind," said Kapila with a smile on his face.

And they rode away.

TEN

ON A PREARRANGED DAY, Siddhartha, Kapila and Nalaka were to set out on horseback to visit a hermitage in the outskirts of Kapilavatthu. Yasodhara had no objection to Siddhartha's going there. She knew that Siddhartha loved her dearly and she had no reason to fear that he would leave her and embrace a homeless life immediately.

Siddhartha left the house having kissed his wife good-bye and promising to return soon. Yasodhara walked up to the balcony and waved at him as he galloped away. She returned to the family room and sitting on a comfortable chair worked on a little dress she was preparing for the baby she was expecting in a few weeks. While her fingers worked automatically on the dress, her thoughts were with Siddhartha.

"Should I entertain any fears about Siddhartha leaving me at this point to embrace a homeless life? Siddhartha is not happy with most aspects of the traditional householder's life. He does not like the way the brahman priests are using the faith and confidence of the rulers to achieve their own ends. He does not like the manner in which the rulers are exploiting the people. He not only is intolerant of the rich merchants who take advantage of their wealth which was accumulated through unjust means, but also resents the manner in which they exploit the talents and capabilities of young men and women involved in arts and crafts. Above all, he is saddened by the lack of opportunity for the children of the villagers and the poor servants and slaves in the towns to receive an education. To him they are like beautiful flowers in the forest. Questions regarding truth and justice worry him often. He has compassion for the destitute."

"But," continued Yasodhara with her reflections, "he loves me and he knows that I love him. Someday Siddhartha will leave the household life, but not now. After all, leaving the household life is an important stage in a man's life. But right now he will stay with me."

While Yasodhara was lost in her thoughts, Suddhodana entered the room. In spite of his earlier disapproval of Siddhartha's marriage to Yasodhara, he had begun to like her. He had seen how Siddhartha changed his style of life from a carefree young man to a responsible husband. He had noticed how he spent most of his time with Yasodhara.

"Are you in good health, my dear?" asked Suddhodana.

"I am, father," she replied, trying to get up.

"No, no. Just stay where you are," said Suddhodana, taking a seat facing her.

"Where is Siddhartha?" he asked.

"Siddhartha went out with his friends, Kapila and Nalaka. He said they would be visiting a hermitage. He should be back soon."

Suddhodana could not believe what he had heard. He was shocked. His face turned pale. He gazed intently at the beautiful rug on the floor.

Yasodhara did not say anything. She realized that Suddhodana was upset. After a moment's silence, Suddhodana asked Yasodhara:

"Did you approve of his going to a hermitage?"

"I did not object to it," she said, knowing that Suddhodana would be annoyed with both of them.

"Don't you think that you have acted unwisely in letting him visit a hermitage? After all, Kapila is very pessimistic about life. He has remained unmarried. He has no sense of responsibility. Do you want your husband to be like him?" asked Suddhodana, trying to suppress his anger.

"No. I don't think Siddhartha is influenced by Kapila, although Kapila had been his longtime friend. He is more interested in the views of Nalaka. Siddhartha has turned out to be a greater admirer of Nalaka than of Kapila. He thinks Kapila is a materialist of some sort. In any case Siddhartha is not going to leave me now. He loves me and he knows that I love him. But I do not expect Siddhartha to remain with me all the time. One day he will leave me to embrace the homeless life seeking for the truth. Isn't that the ideal life for man recommended by the brahman priests?"

Suddhodana could not argue with Yasodhara. He knew that it was the ideal life recommended by his own spiritual advisers. But he wanted Siddhartha to stay in household life as long as possible, carrying on the responsibilities of a kshatriya prince.

"I know that Siddhartha does not want the musicians and dancers to come and perform here everyday. But I am going to send them in spite of him," said Suddhodana, assuming that he would be able to change Siddhartha's attitudes by presenting the most beautiful girls in the kingdom to sing and dance before him.

"Siddhartha would certainly be annoyed if the singers and the dancing girls were to appear here every evening. It is adding fuel to fire. Siddhartha sometimes sees these musicians and dancers completely drunk and sleeping on the floor, sometimes fully naked, after a performance. It is upsetting for him to see them in such situations. Please don't do anything to drive him away from me at this time," pleaded Yasodhara.

Suddhodana knew that he was acting in desperation. He said to himself:

"Yasodhara is right. Siddhartha is a very sensitive person. She knows him very intimately. I should respect her wishes. She is a woman of great courage and wisdom."

Suddhodana's affection for his daughter-in-law increased. He got up and walked up to her, kissed her on the forehead and said:

"Yasodhara dear, please take good care of yourself."

And with these words, he left the room.

Yasodhara could not control her sobs. She knew that Suddhodana loved his son and wanted him to be the ruler of the Sakyan kingdom after him. She also knew that Siddhartha did not have the patience to tolerate most of the things he had to do if he were to be the king of the Sakyans. Her love for Siddhartha was so great that she did not want him to be unhappy even for a moment, even if that involved suffering for her. She was willing to sacrifice her happiness, if by doing so Siddhartha would be happy.

Yasodhara was tired. She retired to her room and lay on her bed. She fell asleep. She woke up only after she felt the warm lips of Siddhartha on her forehead. She moved to a side and put her right arm around Siddhartha's neck and brought him closer to her.

"Have you found a suitable hermitage for yourself?" she asked, teasing him.

"No," whispered Siddhartha in her ear. "For the time being, my hermitage is right here. I do not want to leave it as yet."

ELEVEN

SIDDHARTHA WAS PRESENT WHEN the time approached for the arrival of the baby. Some of the most experienced midwives in Kapilavatthu had already been recruited by Suddhodana and were residing at the palace when Yasodhara was ready to give birth to her child. As the pains increased, Yasodhara was taken into a room made ready for her confinement. Siddhartha was in the adjoining room, his anxiety increasing as every moment passed.

He heard Yasodhara's painful and stifled cries as the hours passed. Siddhartha was shaken up. He could not remain in one place. He got up from his seat and started walking up and down the room. After awhile he felt tired. He went back to his seat, but not for long. He got up and started walking again. It was an unending agony for him. Suddenly Yasodhara stopped crying. There was dead silence. Siddhartha's heartbeat stopped. He felt cold. The next moment, there was a lusty cry. It was the baby protesting its entry into the world. Siddhartha fell back on his seat.

Gotami was the first to come out of the room where Yasodhara had given birth to her baby.

"Aren't you proud to be the father of a handsome baby boy?" asked Gotami.

Siddhartha remained silent. The whole experience was a traumatic one for him. He looked at Gotami for awhile and smiled. Gotami did not realize that it was a forced smile.

"Well, now we have to consult Asita regarding an auspicious first syllable for a suitable name for the baby," suggested Gotami.

Siddhartha nodded. "Is it necessary?" he thought to himself. "This is another superstition perpetuated by the brahman priests. They assume that words have magical power. So, a child has to be given a name starting with an auspicious syllable. Otherwise it will harm the child. How our lives have come to be dominated by myth and superstition! When can we get rid of this?"

He was more interested in seeing Yasodhara and the baby than worrying about these questions now. But he had to wait till late evening to see them. It was the most agonizing wait for him. Every minute dragged on like a day during the height of summer. A stream of thought appeared and reappeared in his mind.

How was Yasodhara feeling? Why did she have to go through that pain and agony? People say it is natural for a woman to experience such pain at childbirth. But is nature going to compensate her for that? Is there anything he could do to alleviate her suffering? He did not know. He had to wait until he saw her.

At long last, he was admitted to Yasodhara's chamber. What he saw was incredible. He expected Yasodhara to look pale and sick. She had been suffering from the pain of childbirth for many hours. Yet, when he moved closer to her bed, he discovered a brightness on her face and a sparkle in her eyes that he had never seen before. For him, it was a miracle. The baby was sleeping beside her, carefully wrapped in a spotless white blanket, exposing only his innocent little face. He took a good look at the mother and the baby, walked around and sat on the bed on Yasodhara's right side. Combing her hair with his fingers tenderly, he asked her:

"Are you feeling alright, dear?"

"Yes, I am," replied Yasodhara.

Siddhartha was surprised. He expected her to tell him that she was in great pain.

"I was in the adjoining room and heard you cry in pain," said Siddhartha.

Yasodhara was disturbed. She knew how sensitive Siddhartha was to other people's suffering. He was moved by the suffering of the poor people in the country. He was disturbed to see the conditions of the poor villagers, the servants and slaves working in the houses belonging to the rich, the inconveniences musicians and dancers had to undergo in order to make a living. How great would his suffering be on seeing his dear wife agonizing in childbirth? She felt unhappy that he overheard her crying. She thought it was going to leave an indelible impression on him. She wanted to assure him that her suffering was very brief, compared to the great joy and happiness she experienced after the birth.

"But that was before the baby was born," explained Yasodhara. "Immediately after he was born, I felt a great relief and experienced no more pain. It was like the peace and quiet one experiences after a storm. Even the memory of that painful experience vanished when I heard the baby's crying. Whatever painful experiences I had are gone, are no more. But you seem to be continuing to suffer, aren't you?"

Siddhartha tried to force a smile.

"I felt both happy and unhappy," said Siddhartha.

"But your unhappiness seems to be increasing while your

happiness is gradually disappearing. Isn't that true?" asked Yasodhara.

"Life is full of suffering!" remarked Siddhartha, falling into a rather pensive mood.

"No," argued Yasodhara. "It is full of happiness. But this happiness is occasionally marred by a little unhappiness. That little unhappiness helps to increase the quantity of happiness. Do you know how great my happiness at this moment is?" she questioned, looking at him affectionately.

He acknowledged her feelings with a loving smile, but remained silent indicating thereby that he did not agree with her argument.

Siddhartha was not yet ready to take the baby in his arms. The little thing looked too delicate. He feared that he might hurt the baby, not knowing how to hold him. But he was beginning to feel affection for him. He stood by the bed looking at his son. Yasodhara was watching the expression on his face. It was an expression of affection and compassion. She felt proud for her husband, for her baby and for herself.

Siddhartha left the room. He heard the revelry going on in the house. He felt very lonely. Yasodhara was going to be confined to her room for a few days. His friends did not visit him as frequently as they did before he got married. Yet he did not want to leave the palace and go looking for them. He thought Yasodhara may need him. He should be around.

It was a peaceful night. Yet it did not have much effect on Siddhartha's mind. He had not recovered from the traumatic experiences of the morning. He was walking up and down the path in front of the palace, deeply immersed in his reflections.

"Isn't there a way out of this mass of suffering in the world? The more you look for happiness, the greater is your suffering. People sweat to earn money. The more they earn, the greater is their craving for wealth. The rich spend all their energies looking for more and more wealth and at the same time continue to worry about protecting it. Some want to buy happiness with their wealth. They employ the best of artists to entertain them, pretty girls to sing and dance for them, prostitutes to satisfy their sexual appetites. They lead a life of debauchery, and continue with it because they are not satisfied, hoping that one day they will have satisfaction. Some want to be rulers. When they reach a position of power, they worry about retaining it; they do not want to give it up. They want their progeny to be inheritors of that power, whether they are capable or not, worthy or not. The priests want to dominate everyone's life. They consider their role in society to be enjoined by Brahma. Their children are the only ones considered fit for such a role. Nobody else can do it, even if he is worthy of it or capable of it. Everyone is worrying about something, and everyone ends up in frustration and disappointment. Is there anyone who is really happy in this world? Is there a way to freedom from all this suffering, this anxiety, this frustration?"

Siddhartha remembered the hermitages he had visited in the company of Kapila and Nalaka.

"What about those ascetics who have renounced every comfort, have shunned all pleasures of sense, have given up all material happiness? Do they live a happy life?"

He also remembered the sense of peace and serenity that prevailed in the hermitages.

"The hermitages provide a peaceful atmosphere. How do the ascetics feel about their own way of life? They survive on a minimum of food, clothing and shelter. Their wants are few, requisites minimal. Yet they seek for something. Do they get frustrated if they do not achieve what they want, what they are seeking for?

"There must be a way out of this entanglement! Should man be ever confined to this craving? After all, I am a kshatriya. Shouldn't I embody the kshatriya spirit, 'Better to die in war than to surrender?' This is what I have learnt from Vessamitta."

He was awakened from his dream state by a call from Gotami:

"Son, it is very late now. Don't you think it is time for you to go to bed?"

"Yes, mother," replied Siddhartha, and slowly he walked back to the house. When he entered the bedchamber, Yasodhara was fast asleep, lying on her left side with her right arm wrapped around the little one. Siddhartha stood there like a statue, staring at the mother and son. They both deserved that rest, after what they had gone through during the day. His heart was filled with affection for them. He realized that it was not going to be easy for him to have his own way of life now. He has the responsibility of taking care of this boy. The more he stared at his son, the greater grew his affection for him. Even momentarily, his attention was distracted from the problems of human suffering he had been reflecting about for years. His baby's face, the uncoordinated little arms and legs eclipsed every other thought and aroused desires that Siddhartha had not known before. It caused confusion in him, as a solar eclipse would cause confusion among both man and beast as a result of the sudden change in their routine by such a phenomenon. His son really represented an eclipse, a seizer like Rahu who swallowed the sun and the moon occasionally. He indeed was a miniature Rahu!

Siddhartha nodded kindly at the waiting maid and left the room. The complexity of human existence was far from being understood. He was confused by what he felt. How could a little baby arouse such different thoughts in him? He is Rahula, after all.

TWELVE

KAPILA AND NARADATTA helped Siddhartha to nurture his critical outlook on life. However, it was his association with Nalaka that kindled the spiritual embers that lay dormant in him. His great teacher, of course, was experience.

His marriage to Yasodhara was fulfilling. Though he found that such satisfaction was temporary, he also realized that the gratification of the senses was gradually being replaced by a more sublime form of love and affection. Emotionally he felt one with Yasodhara. Yasodhara's suffering on the occasion of Rahula's birth therefore caused great anxiety in him. He had heard that his mother's death was due to complications at childbirth. It was only at the time when Yasodhara was going through the trauma of childbirth that Siddhartha realized the dangers involved, not before. At the time, he enjoyed the pleasures of married life and he was oblivious to such risks. He felt that if something unfortunate happened to Yasodhara, even the more sublime form of love and affection was going to end and along with it all the satisfaction.

He reflected on the more compassionate love that was instantly generated in him when he first saw Rahula. That compassionate love gradually increased as he watched Rahula grow up and start crawling all over the house under the tender and loving care of the maids. Each time he picked up Rahula and carried him in his arms, he felt the same kind of love and affection for him.

Siddhartha's world of love and affection was expanding. First it was the parents; then Yasodhara entered the scene, and now Rahula. The satisfaction arising from this form of love and affection was indeed superior to that derived from pleasures of sense. Yet it was not going to be everlasting. Once it was threatened because of Yasodhara's suffering. What is there to prevent it from happening again? Human life is not everlasting. It appears to be fragile, like a bubble of water.

"Is there no way to solve this riddle of existence?" he thought to himself. "Isn't there a way one can live happily without having to experience this impermanence and suffering? The brahman priest promises eternal life in heaven as a reward for the sacrificial rituals. Ascetics like Ajita Kesakambali and Makkhali Gosala assume that man has no power to change the course of nature. Others like Yajnavalkya seem to assume that man has the capacity to attain freedom from all suffering and achieve an immortal state. Could there be a state of deathlessness? It seems to be an evil God who created a world full of dissatisfactions, and therefore suffering, with no escape from it. If there were a God powerful enough to create the world, as some believe, he could not be evil. He surely would leave some opening somewhere. There must be a path to freedom somewhere. That trail is probably buried in this thick jungle of ignorance and prejudice, myth and superstition, rite and ritual."

He thought about his love for Yasodhara and Rahula and the need to take care of them. He did not have much of a choice. He had to continue as did his father, Suddhodana, to rule the Sakyan clan.

"But this is not possible," he agonized. "My father, as ruler of this kingdom, has not been able to help many. There is a large population here that is suffering. How could my father help them, when he could not help even his own wife, my mother? How can I help Yasodhara and Rahula? I will be as helpless as my father. There is no other way but to look for a solution to the evils of existence. If I can find it, I will be able to help Yasodhara and Rahula. I will be able to make them happy. I could be a source of pride for my father, or even help him to overcome suffering and anxiety. I will be in a position to contribute to the happiness of all the suffering humanity, and I will at the same time save myself."

Yasodhara knew that Siddhartha was going through a very critical stage in his life. She had no doubts about his love for her, about his love for Rahula. His traumatic experience on the occasion of Rahula's birth had haunted him and he was determined not to be a victim of such suffering again. Yet his love for Yasodhara did not diminish. He was closer to her and concerned about her and the baby.

Suddhodana had been haunted by Asita's predictions throughout Siddhartha's adolescence and even after his marriage. He feared that Siddhartha would give up his princely life for a lonely life in the forest. The situation had apparently changed after Rahula's birth. He had seen Siddhartha and Yasodhara come closer to each other and assumed that Siddhartha was no longer interested in otherworldly ways of life. He felt grateful to Yasodhara and Rahula. He had no way of knowing the actual relationship between his son and daughter-in-law. Rahula became Suddhodana's greatest love. He would even postpone his official duties in order to be with his grandson.

There was nothing that he would not do in order to make mother and child comfortable and happy.

Siddhartha, on the contrary, was becoming more and more aware of the kind of protection Yasodhara and Rahula were receiving from Suddhodana. His fear that they would be severely affected if he were to leave at this time, had kept him back from leaving for the homeless life. But now that fear was being gradually eliminated. He was becoming confident that Suddhodana would care for Yasodhara and Rahula. If he could not find a solution to the trammels of life, he would come back to continue what his father and the kingdom expected him to. If he succeeded in his mission, there was no limit to what he could do not only for his family but for all around him. Either way, his family was not going to suffer. His confidence in the future of Yasodhara and Rahula was slowly opening up an outlet for his spiritual energies.

Yasodhara did not take long to learn about Siddhartha's intentions. He himself did not try to conceal from her his growing interest in a life of asceticism. When she felt that Siddhartha was sometimes in a dilemma as to whether he should remain a householder or adopt an ascetic life, Yasodhara did not hesitate to argue with him, hoping either to change his mind or to postpone his decision. But whenever she realized that Siddhartha was more inclined toward leaving home, she avoided any arguments with him.

Asita Kaladevala, Suddhodana's spiritual guide and Siddhartha's teacher died at the age of eighty-three. As Suddhodana was out of Kapilavatthu during this time, Siddhartha got the opportunity of attending the funeral ceremony. Asita's body, tightly wrapped in a pink-colored cloth and placed on a wooden frame, was taken up to the river Rohini where it was dipped in the water considered to be sacred by the people of Kapilavatthu. Thereafter, it was left on the bank of the river for a while to let the water drip away. A few yards away, a site had been cleared for the cremation of the body. A pile of medium-sized logs, with smaller twigs on top, constituted the pyre. It was not more than three feet in height. After pouring some flammable oil on the wood, Asita's body was placed upon it. A brahman priest, with a torch in hand, circumambulated the funeral pyre, while others of the assembled brahman priests recited portions of the sacred Vedas. After circumambulating the pyre three times, the brahman priest set fire to it.

Siddhartha remained with the all-male crowd of mourners, watching the flames as they engulfed the body. He was sad and depressed; sad at the loss of his teacher and depressed by his inability to understand the mystery surrounding death. Asita was one of the most respected personalities in Kapilavatthu. Yet, his end was not very different from that of any other ordinary person. Was his great personality reduced to nothing by the flames of the funeral pyre? What happened to the so-called indestructible soul? Did it leave the body at death? Was it now moving up to the heaven above with the smoke rising from the funeral pyre? Being disturbed by such thoughts, he could not remain there to witness the conclusion of the funeral rites. He decided to leave for home.

On his way home from the funeral Siddhartha encountered an extremely unfortunate incident. A crowd of people were shouting abuse and throwing rocks and sticks at a woman who appeared almost naked. He hurried up to the scene, and when the people saw him and recognized him, they all retreated and some ran away. A few remained behind. The woman's clothing was dirty and torn into pieces. She could barely hide her nakedness. Siddhartha got down from his horse and with reluctance approached the woman who was lying on the ground. She was hurt by the darts thrown at her by the people. Blood was flowing from wounds on her head.

Siddhartha was furious.

"What has this woman done to be harassed like this?" he questioned those who remained.

"Sir, she goes around the city half-naked and with disheveled hair, muttering all sorts of unintelligible things. It has become impossible for a young girl or a boy to walk on the street. She is a mad woman. We are trying to drive her away from the streets."

"Has any one of you tried to find out why she has gone mad? Have you tried to help her in any way?"

"No, Sir," replied one of the men.

"Don't you feel ashamed of yourself?" asked Siddhartha, his

anger rising. "What if it was your mother or sister or a relative? Would you treat them the same way you do this woman?"

The few who were present could not look Siddhartha in his face. He called a middle-aged man:

"Do you live close-by?"

"Yes, Sir," replied the man.

"Can you get some clothing for this woman?"

"Yes, Sir."

"Also, bring your wife or some women-folk with you."

"I will," said the man, and he headed for his house.

Within a few minutes, he was back with some clothes and was accompanied by his wife.

"Do you think you can help this woman to her feet and get her to put on these clothes?" asked Siddhartha of the woman.

She was not willing to earn the displeasure of the king's son. So she nodded in agreement.

When the woman was well covered, Siddhartha was able to come closer to her.

"Why are you roaming the streets in this manner? Don't you have a home?" questioned Siddhartha.

The woman realized that this young man was a person of great power and majesty. She could not resist answering him.

"I do not have a home. I have nothing to live for," murmured the woman.

"Don't you have a husband? Any relations, mother or father, brother or sister?"

"No, I don't. I ran away with a man I loved. I had a son, two years old. I was expecting my second child and wanted to return to my parents."

She stopped speaking, opened her eyes wide and looked at Siddhartha. Siddhartha could see the sorrow and suffering written in them clearly, though they were completely dry.

"What happened?" asked Siddhartha.

"They are all gone. My husband and I lived far away from my parents. While we were returning to my parents, I began getting pains. My husband went to get some help. He was bitten by a snake and died. Immediately afterwards, it started raining. My little son. . . ," she choked on her words.

71

Siddhartha was getting agitated. He did not want to question her further. But after a moment, the woman continued.

"My little son started running and called for his father. A cruel vulture swooped on him and dragged him away."

This time she could not control her sobs.

"But have your parents rejected you?"

"No," said the woman. "When I returned home, I found the house had burned down and my old father and mother had died in the fire. My second child died before birth. Why was my life spared?"

"Sister," said Siddhartha addressing the woman. Everyone around him was surprised. "Death is something that is not easy to avoid."

"But, why should all these things happen to me only?"

Siddhartha had difficulty answering her question. He knew that her madness was due to her excessive grief. She had completely lost control of herself. He wanted to make her realize that death is not easily avoided. He thought that one day he would find a solution to this problem. Right then he was as helpless as this woman. The only thing that he could do was to try and make her realize that each one of us has to face death. He thought about some means by which he could achieve this.

"Sister, I am the son of King Suddhodana. A week from today I want you to come to the palace. I will try my best to help you. But when you come, you must bring with you a handful of rice from a house in Kapilavatthu where no death has taken place. Will you be able to do that?"

"Yes," said the woman.

Siddhartha turned to the couple who brought the clothing for the woman.

"I want you to take this woman to your house. Get her to clean herself and provide her with some medicine and food."

"You," he said, addressing the man, "should come to the palace tomorrow. I need to compensate you and your wife for your willingness to help this woman."

The man agreed. Siddhartha mounted his horse and rode away. This was too much of an unfortunate experience for him.

"Impermanence and suffering—these are facts of human life," he thought. "A mother or father is bereaved at the loss of a child. So is a child at the death of his or her parents. A brother laments the loss of a sister, a sister of a brother. Is this suffering necessary? Isn't there a way out of it?"

He returned home with the determination that he would convince Yasodhara of his need to look for a solution to the riddles of human life. When Yasodhara saw her husband after he returned from the funeral ceremony, she realized that he was agitated. He was restless and was looking for an opportunity to speak to her in privacy. Rahula was with her, playing. Siddhartha tried his best to avoid noticing Rahula's playful behavior. He remembered what his feelings were when he first saw Rahula. He did not want those feelings to overwhelm him again. It was not good for Rahula; it was not good for Yasodhara. Nor was it going to help him in his search for a solution to the burning questions in life. Yasodhara noticed Siddhartha's discomfort. She signaled one of the maids to take Rahula away. She got up, took Siddhartha's hand and walked toward the balcony. Siddhartha put his arm around Yasodhara's shoulder and drew her close to him.

The sun was setting in the western horizon. The eastern horizon, which in the morning was so colorful with the rising sun awakening everything into life, was gradually being enfolded in darkness and gloom.

"Is this symbolic of my life?" thought Yasodhara.

All her misgivings were confirmed when she heard Siddhartha's soft voice, which came to her like a clap of thunder.

"Dear Yasodhara, may I have your permission to . . ." and Siddhartha could not complete his sentence. He heard Yasodhara's sobbing. His heart sank.

"Yasodhara is hurt," he thought. "There is no way I can leave her now." Yet he could not believe his ears when Yasodhara, choked with her sobs, murmured:

"Yes, dear, I . . . will wait for you."

Siddhartha embraced her. Yasodhara could not contain herself any more. She began to weep. Siddhartha held her until she overcame her agony and regained her composure.

This whole scenario did not go unnoticed in the house. The

maids who were about the place all the time noticed the un-usual behavior on the part of both Siddhartha and Yasodhara. Their gossip did not take long to reach Gotami and, through her, Suddhodana.

A few days later, Gotami confronted Yasodhara with the question:

"Is Siddhartha thinking of leaving for the forest?"

Yasodhara looked at her mother-in-law and smiled.

"It will not be long before Siddhartha leaves us," she replied, in a resigned way.

"Well! Aren't you going to do something to stop him? You are still young. You need your husband. Rahula is still a little baby. Is he going to grow up without a father?" asked Gotami, showing signs of disappointment with her daughter-in-law.

Yasodhara knew that Siddhartha's decision to renounce his home life had not been made overnight. It was years of reflection on problems relating to good and bad, right and wrong, truth and falsehood, impermanence and suffering that led him to make that decision. The water of a river does not flow upstream. If it is blocked, it will find some crevices through which it can escape. Siddhartha had found innumer-able such crevices in life. She knew it would be futile to attempt to hold him back. He would find princely life misera-ble. It was best to let him be free to seek a solution to the problems he was preoccupied with. If he did not find a solution and he decided to return, he would not blame himself for not trying. If he found a solution, everybody would benefit by it. She did not respond to Gotami who was now getting impatient.

"Yasodhara, don't you think you are carrying a heavy respon-sibility for Siddhartha's actions?" she asked finally.

"Yes, mother," replied Yasodhara. "I am responsible for what Siddhartha is doing. I can console myself thinking that I am responsible for his happiness."

Gotami realized that it was futile to argue with Yasodhara. She knew that Yasodhara was very different from many of the young women of her age. Yasodhara was more indepen-dent and intelligent. It was, therefore, time that Suddhodana spoke to his son directly.

When Suddhodana heard that his son was about to leave

home, he rushed to Siddhartha's living quarters. He was followed by Gotami. On this occasion they found Siddhartha and Yasodhara engaged in a casual conversation, with Rahula running around while a maid stood at a corner of the room watching Rahula. As Suddhodana entered the room, Siddhartha and Yasodhara got up from their seats. The maid picked up Rahula and left the room. Siddhartha knew that his father would question him on his decision. Suddhodana took a seat and after him the others settled down to their seats.

"Have you decided to leave the household life?" asked Suddhodana looking at Siddhartha. Suddhodana's face looked gloomy.

Siddhartha did not answer but smiled. Suddhodana and Gotami looked at Yasodhara, expecting one of them to answer. She merely looked at Siddhartha and smiled, as if telling Siddhartha: "It is up to you to answer your father."

Suddhodana was angry. His face turned red. Deep lines appeared on his forehead.

"The kshatriyas have, on previous occasions, left the household life when they had passed their middle age. You are only twenty-nine years old. You are too young to adopt this kind of life. There are other responsibilities that call for your attention now."

"Father, how do we decide when a person is young, is in his middle age or is old? Some die young; they do not have a middle age. Some die during their middle age; they do not know what old age is. Why should a search for a solution to the problems of impermanence and suffering be postponed to one's old age? How can one be sure whether one is going to live that long? You are merely expressing the views of the brahman priest, who wants people to remain in household life as long as they can, so that the priest can get them to perform more and more sacrifices. You are caught up in the net of Brahma, spread by the brahman priest to capture the kshatriyas who were usurping their place in society."

"You are very selfish," said Suddhodana. "You want to go to the forest and be a hermit because you are frightened of your

75

responsibilities. You want to save yourself from all your worries and not care for others who need your help here."

Siddhartha was showing signs of anger. Yasodhara feared the consequences. But before she could say anything, Siddhartha said:

"No. I am not leaving the household life because I want to save myself only. The problems that are worrying me are also worrying many other people in this world, including you. If I can find a solution it will be not only for myself, but also for anyone who would care for it."

Suddhodana knew that when Siddhartha reached a decision, it was after careful consideration of all the pros and cons. But once he made a decision in this manner, he would stay with it to the end. He thought that Yasodhara could not help accepting Siddhartha's decision. That was what Siddhartha did to him when he wanted to marry Yasodhara. Yet, he wanted to throw a last punch at his son.

"How can you hope to help others by adopting the life of an ascetic? Did you ever see an ascetic helping others? Instead they are a burden to society. They spend most of the time in the forest and whenever they want something they cannot get in the forest, they come to the villages. They expect things from the poor villagers without giving them anything in return. What kind of compassionate behavior is that?"

Siddhartha knew that his father was right. The hermits who lived in the forests occasionally came out into the society when they needed something. Pious villagers would supply them with their needs once, twice, thrice, and then the villagers would get fed up and drive them out.

"No. I do not expect to make forest residence a permanent feature of my life. It will only be a temporary phase. If I find a solution to the problems of humanity it will be for the benefit of everyone, for the rich and the poor alike, for those who support my life as an ascetic and for those who refuse to support me. For me, asceticism will not be an end, but only a means."

"Where will you go and when?" asked Suddhodana, trying to suppress his grief.

"I do not know where I will be going, but I know it will be

very soon," replied Siddhartha looking at Yasodhara. She was not ready to face him.

Suddhodana got up from his seat and left the room without saying another word. Retiring to his room, he broke down and cried like a child.

THIRTEEN

IT WAS THE FULL-MOON DAY of Uttarasalha (June-July) that Siddhartha selected for his great renunciation. It had to be a moonlit night, for he wanted to travel as much as possible during the night without having to arouse the curiosity of people whom he would meet on the way. Leaving home at a time when everyone in the household would be fast asleep would prevent any unnecessary commotion. Yet Yasodhara knew that Siddhartha was planning to leave that night. She called one of the stableboys, a favorite of Siddhartha, and said to him:

"Channa, tonight the master is setting out on a long journey. Get the horses ready and ride with him as long as he needs you. When he commands you to return, come back and tell me what happened on the way."

"Yes, my Lady," assented Channa, who was not unaware of his master's plan to leave home for a life in the forest.

Yasodhara retired to bed early in the evening hoping to get up before Siddhartha left. Getting into bed she cried until, through sheer exhaustion, she fell fast asleep. Siddhartha wanted to bid farewell to Yasodhara. But, when he entered her chamber, he found her fast asleep with Rahula at her side.

"Should I wake her up or not?" he thought. "She knows of my departure today. If I were to wake her up, it would be a difficult parting. She should be spared that agony. Or, would she accuse herself for falling asleep at this very important moment in our lives? Would she blame me for running away without bidding her farewell? No. She is intelligent enough to understand why I did not wake her up. In any case, I am leaving home. For the time being it will hurt her, it will hurt my son, it will hurt my parents. But in the long run, everyone is going to benefit, they as well as myself."

He stood there looking at his wife and baby son for a long, long moment. It seemed an endless moment. But finally he turned around and left the chamber. Outside the house, Channa had saddled two horses and was waiting for his master. There was perfect silence in the house, although lights were seen burning in several rooms upstairs. Even the horses did not make any noise, as if indicating that they too were aware of the sadness surrounding this event.

Siddhartha mounted his horse and rode away.

He traveled southward followed by Channa who was carrying a small parcel, containing a robe, a bowl and some other requisites, prepared by Yasodhara. The two of them rode in silence until they reached the outskirts of the city, when Siddhartha felt the urge to stop and take a look at the city he was leaving behind together with his wife, his baby son, his parents and all his relatives and friends—a city in which he grew up with all the pleasant memories of his childhood and youth. Immediately the thought occurred to him:

"I have left my family and my people and I am at the point of adopting a new way of life, a life devoted to searching for what is good. Why should I, at this very important moment in my life, be tempted by the same kind of feelings and sentiments normally associated with the life I am about to abandon? It is not proper for me to be a victim of such temptations."

He continued to move along without trying to stop and look back, but yet the image of Kapilavatthu appeared before his mind with such force and clarity, giving him the impression that the great earth turned around so that he should not have to look back in order to have a glimpse of his beloved country.

By daybreak Siddhartha and Channa passed the border of the Sakyan territory and reached the river Anoma. After crossing the river, Siddhartha shaved his head and beard and changed into the robe Yasodhara had prepared for him. He then made a bundle of his old clothes and handed it over to Channa asking him to return it to his father. Channa with tears in his eyes prostrated before Siddhartha, paying obeisance to his master. Siddhartha dismissed him, thanking him for his assistance.

Channa returned to Kapilavatthu during the early afternoon. He was stricken with grief at the separation from his master. He returned the horses to the stable. Everything around reminded him of his beloved master. It was too much agony for him. Unable to bear it any longer, he left the palace where he had grown up since his childhood, without informing anyone, but leaving the bundle of clothes tied to the saddle on Siddhartha's horse. It was only in the late afternoon that the members of Siddhartha's household discovered the horse and the bundle of clothes Siddhartha had returned.

FOURTEEN

SIDDHARTHA HAD LEARNED from his friend Nalaka about the teachings of the Upanishads. Yajnavalkya's ideas appealed to him. Yet he, like Nalaka, was interested not merely in the ideas expressed by Yajnavalkya, but also in the method by which these ideas could be tested. Nalaka had mentioned to him the names of Alara Kalama and Uddaka Ramaputta as two famous contemplatives who had mastered the techniques of yoga, and who had continued to remain in their own hermitages rather than going out and taking part in philosophical controversies. Siddhartha felt that in his search for a solution to the problems of impermanence and suffering, he ought to meet these teachers first and find out what discoveries they had made. So he decided to make a long trek to Vesali where Alara had his hermitage.

Upon reaching the hermitage, he met Alara and after paying him due respect, said to him:

"Sir, I am Siddhartha. I wish to practice the religious life under your instruction."

Alara looked at young Siddhartha for a moment.

"Where do you come from?" questioned Alara.

"From Kapilavatthu, in the kingdom of the Sakyans," replied Siddhartha.

"You are still young and handsome. Don't you have a family? What made you leave home?" inquired Alara.

"I have a wife and a son. My father is Suddhodana. I had all the comforts in life. But I see very little satisfaction that can be derived from them. Most of the time they end up in suffering and frustration. I am looking for a way out of this mass of unhappiness and disappointment."

Alara had heard about Suddhodana, the chief of the Sakyan clan. He could not believe that Suddhodana's son could adopt a homeless life at so early an age. He realized that this young man was highly motivated about what he wanted to do.

"Siddhartha, I will accept you as a pupil. The knowledge I claim and the theory of the elders I propound are those that have been verified by me. I will instruct you in these. But it is left to you to exert yourself, apply yourself, in order to understand these doctrines for yourself," explained Alara.

"So be it, Sir," replied Siddhartha. He was pleased that the doctrine he was about to learn was not something based on speculation or something accepted on mere faith. This was his first opportunity to undertake an experiment of this kind. All these years he had merely been learning about views expressed by others. His energy and enthusiasm were equal to the task he was going to undertake. Alara began his instruction with the following exposition.

"Meditation, as I practice it, has pacification of the mind as its goal. Objects in the outside world produce attachment and, therefore, agitation. Hence, one should prevent the mind from being disturbed by outside events, external things. This cannot be done easily and quickly. As an initial step one has to eliminate the five fetters. First of these is the view that this body is real. Second is doubt. Third is grasping on to rites and ritual. Fourth is lust for sensuality, and fifth is ill will. Do you think you will be able to eliminate these fetters?" asked Alara.

"Yes, Sir. I should be able to eliminate them without much difficulty," replied Siddhartha, with confidence, because these were the very same things that impelled him to adopt the homeless life.

"If you can eliminate them, you are ready to begin concentration that will lead to the realization of the first stage. Seclusion from sensual desires and unwholesome tendencies will produce joy and happiness of a different kind. You should try to cultivate that joy and happiness born of seclusion while you continue to think and explore. This is the first stage of meditation."

Siddhartha retired to a secluded spot. He had no difficulty in getting rid of the five fetters. He concentrated his mind in such a way as to avoid any sensual thoughts. His mind was temporarily freed from pleasures of sense. But he experienced a different kind of joy and happiness. He thought about it; he contrasted it with the pleasure he had experienced earlier. This was indeed different; this was much superior. He continued to enjoy this joy and happiness born of seclusion from pleasures of sense.

He reported his experience to Alara, and received instruction as to how he should proceed beyond that.

"You reached a state of joy and happiness born of seclusion from sensual desires. You thought about it and reflected upon it and discriminated it from your previous pleasurable sensations. So you were able to understand that it was superior to the pleasurable sensations you had before. If you continue with this thinking, with this discrimination, you will develop an attachment to the new sensations because they appear to you superior. Therefore, now you should try to eliminate such thinking and discrimination. Then you will experience still another kind of joy and happiness."

Siddhartha got the message. He went back to his place of meditation. He concentrated his mind in order to reach the first stage. But as soon as he reached it, he stopped thinking and discriminating. He prevented his mind from roaming all over the new sensations and remained single-minded without thinking and exploring. Instantly, he experienced a joy and happiness born of concentration. He continued to practice this form of concentration until he was able to stabilize it.

"Joy could now be a hindrance for further progress," reminded Alara. "When immersed in it, one becomes unmindful of anything else. Mindfulness is indispensable to seeing things as they are. So attempt to eliminate joy."

Siddhartha followed Alara's instructions and soon reached the third stage of meditation characterized by the purification of equanimity and mindfulness resulting from the elimination of joy. Thereby he was able to remain in an ecstatic state with his entire body pervaded by happiness. And he reached the fourth stage of meditation by eliminating bodily happiness. At this stage, he experienced neither pain nor pleasure, neither joy nor happiness. His mind was composed. With that mindfulness, he was able to gain an outlook of equanimity. His mind became purified, bright, unblemished and malleable, like a lump of clay, well mixed and without impurities, that a potter could use in whatever way he desired. He gained perfect control of his mind.

Alara was impressed by his pupil's ability to master the technique of meditation in so short a time. He was, therefore, ready to initiate Siddhartha into the higher levels of meditation.

"What you have learned so far is the way to get rid of the world of sense pleasures. Your mind is still in the realm of form. It is therefore liable to corruption, unless you are extremely careful. Now you need to get rid of the world of form, and develop your mind to reach the formless world. The formless world is the highest world one can reach. It is the highest state of happiness one can achieve."

"How do I go about eliminating the world of form and

reaching the formless world?" asked Siddhartha. He was pleased with the experiences he already had. Now he was going to be exposed to a completely new world of experience. With his excitement grew his enthusiasm. Enthusiasm increased his energy.

"All forms are finite. The formless is, therefore, infinite. Out of all our experiences in the world of form, the only one that has a semblance of formlessness or infiniteness is space. Thus, your concentration should now be directed at space. When you concentrate on space, it is necessary for you to move around and see whether it is possible to reach the end of space. But remember that before you start practicing this stage of concentration, you have to go through the first four stages of meditation you practiced before."

"Alright," said Siddhartha, and retired to his seat of meditation. It did not take much time for him to repeat the steps by which he was able to reach the fourth stage of meditation. When his mind became supple and malleable, he directed his attention to space. His concentration was powerful and penetrating, but he was not able to reach the end of space. He came out of his state of meditation. He was puzzled.

"Is there an end to space?" he asked himself. "If there is, I should have experienced it. My concentration was strong and penetrating." He was depressed. He returned to Alara and complained.

Alara smiled.

"Did I do something wrong?" asked Siddhartha.

"Yes and no," replied Alara.

"What do you mean by yes and no?" questioned Siddhartha.

"You did not do anything wrong when you realized that space was infinite, that there was no conceivable end. But you were wrong in being puzzled about it. You were puzzled because you assumed that space is like form and has to be finite. You did not realize that the space you were concentrating upon in order to reach the formless was none other than your consciousness of space. Go back and start all over again. When you have reached the state of infinite space, you can develop the next stage of meditation where 'space' turns out to be

83

mere 'consciousness.' When you have done that, see whether you can reach the end of consciousness."

Siddhartha did exactly as he was asked to do. He concentrated on space and tried to reach its end, but immediately moved from there to realize that it was mere consciousness. He directed his attention on consciousness, trying to reach its end and instantly came to the realization that consciousness itself is not a substantial entity that can have form. He had gone beyond the state of infinite consciousness and attained the realization that it was mere nothingness.

He came back and reported this to Alara who was thrilled by his pupil's abilities. In moving his concentration from second to third stage Siddhartha did not commit the mistake he committed earlier. So without his teacher's instruction, he was able to move from the second to the third.

"Well done, Siddhartha," exulted Alara. "You have reached the same level of concentration that I too have reached. I have nothing more to teach you. You are my equal. Join me in instructing others here who are trying to reach the highest."

Siddhartha said nothing. He returned to his little hut where he used to spend the nights. He lay down on the wooden planks that served as a bed, and thought:

"Is this all that I am going to learn from him? What is the purpose of being able to reach such a state of concentration? It is true that when one has reached such a state one has no experience of suffering. But neither does one experience any happiness. One experiences a sense of happiness only when one comes out of that state. But that experience is very temporary. Also, when one returns from that state of experience, having realized nothingness, one tends to think of the material world as an illusion, as nonsubstantial. But that thought is also very temporary. Within no time one gets entangled in the world of the senses. This is not the kind of solution I am looking for."

He returned to Alara's hut, paid his respects to him and sat on the side.

"What is your decision, Siddhartha? Do you plan to stay with us?" asked Alara.

"No. Please excuse my arrogance. This is not exactly the

kind of solution I am looking for. I am grateful to you for accepting me as one of your disciples and instructing me. I have benefited greatly from your instruction. Yet, I would appreciate receiving your permission to leave."

"Siddhartha, you were the best pupil I ever had. I am sorry to see you go. But this is all I can teach you. If you find something superior, please do come back and instruct me. May you reach your goal without any obstructions!"

"May you be happy and have long life!" responded Siddhartha and left Alara's hermitage.

Siddhartha had heard that both Alara Kalama and Uddaka Ramaputta, though living in different hermitages, followed the same techniques of meditation. Yet he wanted to find out what Uddaka Ramaputta's attainments were. He, therefore, visited Uddaka's hermitage, which was not far from Alara's.

Uddaka accepted Siddhartha as a pupil and began instructing him in the techniques; and soon Siddhartha discovered that basically Uddaka gave him the same technique, except that he had taken one more step beyond Alara. Where Alara stopped with the attainment of the state of nothingness, Uddaka had reached the state which he described as "neither perception nor nonperception." What enabled Uddaka to achieve a more advanced state of meditation than that attained by Alara was not different from the method adopted by Alara in abandoning the first two stages. Whereas nothingness was recognized by Alara as a final and absolute state, Uddaka put the state of nothingness itself to test, in order to find out whether it was substantial. Not discovering such a substantial state, he went beyond and discovered that the ultimate state of meditation was neither a form of perception nor of nonperception. In this sense he considered it to be absolute, to be beyond all ordinary knowledge.

Siddhartha left Uddaka too in frustration and moved all the way to the township of Uruvela in Magadha. The kingdom of Magadha was teeming with ascetics and wanderers who were teaching and practicing various religious doctrines. One of the more popular practices among these was an extreme form of self-mortification. Siddhartha thought to himself:

"I have practiced the techniques of meditation under Alara

and Uddaka. Yet the sense of freedom I experienced was confined to the time I remained in that state and briefly afterwards. After some time, my desires and pleasurable sensations began to overwhelm me again. The extreme forms of self-mortification advocated by some ascetics may have meaning. How can the mind be controlled when the body is nourished by good food and the senses are satisfied with pleasant stimuli? How can fire be produced by rubbing a firestick on wet green wood soaked in water? A well-nourished body with pampered senses is like a piece of wet green wood."

While wandering in Uruvela, he came across an isolated mountain situated in the vast plain drained by the river Neranjara. Looking around he saw that the slope of the mountain was studded with caves inhabited by ascetics. He counted at least five of them. They were engaged in the mortification of the body. Siddhartha sat under the shade of a tree, wanting to observe what was going on.

After a few hours, the ascetics engaged in these spiritual exercises emerged one by one from their seats, walked up to the river, washed their faces, hands, and feet, and assembled in one cool spot close to the river. Siddhartha approached them and was greeted by them.

"You have selected a very convenient spot for your spiritual exercises," said Siddhartha, wanting to join them in conversation.

"Yes, indeed," said one of them. "It is a very convenient spot for our spiritual exercises. The river is close by and there is plenty of good clean water. There are some families living on the plains and they are very kind and generous. We have no difficulty in obtaining alms."

"Who are you, your good self, and where do you come from?" asked another ascetic.

"My name is Siddhartha. I belong to the Sakyan clan. I am searching for a solution to the problems of human suffering. Old age, decay, death, impermanence overwhelm everyone. There must be a way out of this; there must be a means to overcome all this."

"Very well! That is what we hope to achieve through our spiritual exercises," continued the ascetic. "Would your good self be interested in joining us?" he questioned, while looking at his other companions for approval. They all nodded their heads in approval.

Siddhartha was pleased. He needed such company. Otherwise he would not know what spiritual exercises to practice.

"Yes, if your good selves may please," was Siddhartha's immediate response. Siddhartha soon came to know their names. They were Kondanna, Bhaddiya, Vappa, Mahanama, and Assaji.

It was late morning—time for the ascetics to go on their alms round. They were in the habit of taking turns in going out for alms. Whatever was collected by one was shared by the others. They did not need a great quantity of food. Being practitioners of mortification of the flesh, they ate little. Sometimes the alms collected by one person exceeded their needs. It was Mahanama's turn to go for alms. This time he invited Siddhartha to come along with him, so that he could familiarize himself with the village where he would have to go for alms in the future.

After returning from the alms round and sharing the very meager meal, one of the first such meals Siddhartha had ever eaten, he spoke to the other ascetics and learned about their spiritual exercises. In the afternoon, he retired to a remote corner of the grove, selected a place he thought was appropriate for his exercises, cleaned it up and settled down.

"My body has to be controlled first," he thought. "At what point do I start? From the head? Yes. That is the seat of all activity. But what is it in the upper part of my body that can be controlled? Under Alara and Uddaka, I learned to control my senses. But that did not help. How do I mortify my head, without having to pull my eyes out or pierce my ears and nostrils with a prick. For that would destroy them permanently. There must be a way of mortifying my head."

He set his teeth and pressed his tongue to his palate. He felt the pressure. He wanted to increase that pressure and he continued to press his tongue to his palate until sweat started flowing from his armpits. He persisted with his effort. Yet his body was not quieted or calmed. Instead, a very severe painful sensation gripped his entire body. But he did not allow the painful sensation to overwhelm his mind. When he finished this exercise, his jaws, throat and ears were sore.

From there he moved to control the part of the body below the neck. He decided to restrain his breath. He restrained breathing in and out from mouth and nose. As he did so, violent sounds issued forth in his ears, and they were like the violent sounds issuing from the blowing of a blacksmith's bellows. Excruciating pain ran through his head, as if a strong man was crushing his head with the point of a sword. He continued, but as he did so, his pain increased, not decreased. Yet he did not let the painful sensation overwhelm his mind.

Next he thought of restraining his stomach. He took food only in very small amounts, as much as his hollowed palm would hold. His body became extremely emaciated. The mark of his seat appeared like a camel's footprint. The bones of his spine appeared like a row of spindles. His ribs stuck out like the beams of an old dilapidated house with a decaying roof of straw. The sparkle of his eyes within the deep eye sockets appeared like the sparkling of water in a deep well. The skin of his head withered like a bitter gourd, cut off raw and left to wither in sun and wind. When he touched the skin of his stomach he was actually touching his spine. So did his stomach cling to his spine. When he touched his limbs, decayed hair fell off his body.

The five ascetics were amazed at the manner in which Siddhartha was practicing austerities. They watched Siddhartha with great interest, hoping that soon he would realize the ultimate goal. Siddhartha was too weak to go about. So the ascetics continued to help him with his needs, bringing him water to drink, and washing him every now and then to keep his body clean of the dust that settled on it.

Siddhartha persisted with his fasting. His body became weaker and weaker, although his enthusiasm grew stronger and stronger. One day, when his body could not take it any longer, he fell prone on the ground. A shepherd boy who was herding his cattle, saw Siddhartha lying on the ground. He ran home and informed his parents that one of the ascetics was dead. The parents, who were pious and devout benefactors of the ascetics, arrived on the scene and discovered that

Siddhartha was still alive. They brought warm milk from the house and made Siddhartha drink it. Siddhartha began to regain his strength gradually and the shepherd family continued to bring him milk as well as other solid foods. His ascetic friends became disappointed with the change in Siddhartha's spiritual exercises and they left him.

Siddhartha continued to remain in the grove until he regained his strength completely. He thought to himself:

"Those ascetics and brahmans who have practiced austerities could not have done so to the extent I have practiced. In truth, I went beyond the practices of my friends who have now deserted me. I was on the brink of death. Yet I did not attain any superhuman knowledge and insight that would give me a glimpse of the ultimate goal free from suffering. This certainly is not the way. Great was the path of the hermits, Alara and Uddaka, in comparison. I have lost the trail and must go back and retrace it."

FIFTEEN

THUS DID SIDDHARTHA SPEND almost six years learning a tradition, giving it up, experimenting with another tradition, going back to an earlier one, until he arrived in Rajagaha, the capital of Magadha.

Living in the outskirts of Rajagaha, one day he went into the city for alms. Having collected the food he needed, Siddhartha was returning to the little grove where he was living. As he walked by, he was seen by King Bimbisara, who was standing on the balcony of his sprawling palace. He called one of his attendants, and pointing to Siddhartha said:

"See that mendicant there! He is very different from anyone I have seen in Magadha. Follow him and find out where he is going. When he reaches his destination, return immediately and let me know."

"Yes, Sir," replied the attendant and hurrying out, he followed Siddhartha until the latter reached a grove in the Pandava hills. Returning to the palace, the attendant informed the king of what he saw. The king summoned a chariot and went to the place where Siddhartha had settled down to partake of his meal. The king waited at a distance until he finished his meal and then approached him.

"You are still very young. Handsome and pleasant as you are, this is not a way of life for you. What is it that drove you to adopt a homeless life? Loss of wealth? Loss in the family? Come back. I will provide you with everything you need. You can help me in the running of the affairs of Magadha. You can enjoy all the pleasures of home life."

Siddhartha gently raised his head. Looking at this person who claimed himself to be the ruler of Magadha and recognizing his status from the way he was dressed, replied in a soft but ringing voice:

"O Your Majesty, I have adopted this life, not because I lost my wealth, but because I have seen how impermanent and unsatisfying those pleasures are that one can buy with wealth. Yes, I have experienced death in my family. Is there any one family where death has not occurred? While realizing that wealth brings no happiness and that mortality is part of man's life, why should I continue to immerse myself in things that give me no permanent satisfaction? I have nothing to do with wealth and all the pleasures of sense that it can bring. I was born the son of Suddhodana, chief of the Sakyans. I am looking for permanent happiness, for what is good, for immortality."

Bimbisara was stunned. He could not believe that this was Suddhodana's son, Siddhartha. Here was one whom he had designs to conquer. Here was the future ruler of the Sakyans whom he had dreamt of subjugating one day. He could not believe his eyes. He wondered whether he was having a hallucination. He looked around and saw his attendants. He reflected on the events of the past few hours and was able to recapture them in their sequence. He said to himself: "In dreams and hallucinations, it is not easy to retrace one's steps. It is not easy to have retrocognition. I am not dreaming. I am not having a hallucination. This is real."

He remained there looking at Siddhartha for a moment and said:

"Sir, when you have discovered the truth and reached your goal, please come back to Rajagaha. I shall be delighted to have you as my spiritual adviser. I shall provide you with everything."

Siddhartha did not say anything. The muscles of his two cheeks moved up producing a streak of a smile.

The king then paid his respects to Siddhartha and departed with his retinue.

Moving in a southwesterly direction, Siddhartha returned to Uruvela where he had practiced self-mortification. Passing the little mountain where he had met the five ascetics, he arrived at a place where an ascetic by the name of Kassapa was performing fire sacrifices. Kassapa's little temple with the fire altar was surrounded by mud huts where his disciples lived. Having learnt from these disciples what was going on, Siddhartha had no interest in meeting with Kassapa and moved closer to the river where he found a little hillock with a large banyan tree providing a cool shade. He went and sat under this banyan tree with his back to the trunk. It provided him with a panoramic view of the river and the surrounding land. He recollected his thoughts about the nature of human existence:

"Man is born in this world. How he came to be born, whence he came, why he came to be born, he does not know. Yet he continues to look for birth, for what is characterized by birth.

"Man is subject to decay. He does not understand why there is decay. Yet he continues to look for what is subject to decay.

"Man is subject to death. He does not know why there is death. Yet he continues to look for what is subject to death, for what is subject to dying and destruction.

"Man is subject to sorrow, to dejection, to lamentation. Yet he pursues what is subject to sorrow, to dejection, to lamentation.

"While being myself subject to birth, it is not proper for me to seek for what is subject to birth. Instead, I should look for what is not subject to birth, for the unborn. While being subject to decay, I should not look for what is subject to decay. Instead, I should look for what is undecaying. While being myself subject to death, to destruction, I should not seek for what is subject to death and destruction. Instead, I should look for the immortal, for the indestructible. While being myself subject to sorrow, to defilement, to bondage, I should not seek for what is subject to sorrow, to defilement and to bondage. Instead, I should seek for the nonsorrowing, the undefiled and the secure state; I should seek for complete freedom."

As he was reflecting thus, the memory of his father's actions, on the occasion of the festival connected with the first sowing of seeds, came to his mind. He remembered how his father's actions contributed to his own suffering as well as to the suffering of his subjects. During the moment Siddhartha was a nonparticipant, he felt relieved, though he was dragged into the same kind of suffering by a mere frown from his father. The best form of life, therefore, should be one that does not lead to suffering for oneself as well as others. Would it be possible for a man to lead such a life? If so, how can one achieve it?

As he remained immersed in these thoughts, he did not realize that the night had passed. The near full moon made the night look like day.

Early in the morning, he saw a beautiful woman accompanied by two similarly handsome young female attendants coming toward him. The three women saw Siddhartha from a distance. They were dumbfounded. They could not believe their eyes. The woman was Sujata, the daughter of a rich merchant. She was in the habit of visiting this majestic banyan tree every morning of the full moon to offer oblations of milkrice to the gods inhabiting the tree. Seeing the handsome figure of Siddhartha under the tree, she assumed that one of the gods had appeared in person to receive her oblations. Yet she was frightened to approach him.

Finally she gathered up sufficient courage and walked up to

Siddhartha and cautiously and respectfully offered the milkrice she had brought with her.

Not knowing the reasons for the visit of the three women and the offering of milkrice to him, Siddhartha suspected that it was Yasodhara who had disguised herself and come here with two dancing girls, with the hope of luring him away. He accepted the offering without looking at them. He did not want to be disturbed by such temptations.

The women left after paying their respects to the deity of the tree. Siddhartha partook of the meal of milkrice, and with his bowl in hand, walked up to the river Neranjara. As the summer season was approaching, the river was being gradually dried up leaving a wide stretch of sand and a stream of water which was merely knee-deep. Crossing the sandy area, he came up to the water which was flowing fairly rapidly. He came to the edge of the water and washed his face, hands and feet. He reached for the bowl, wanting to wash that too. He placed the bowl on the water. It did not sink. Instead, it started moving downstream. He caught it.

"Here again," he thought, "human beings are like this lifeless bowl. They can go only with the stream. Why should all human beings be like this lifeless bowl? Could they not be different? Could they not go against the stream?"

Immediately, his memory of an earlier incident returned to him. He remembered how he had gone to a park in Kapila-vatthu along with Kapila to discuss his relationship with Yasodhara and how he should go about proposing marriage to her. He remembered the thoughts that came to him when he saw the fast flowing stream that carried the small pebbles downstream knocking one against another. The little dark ant-like creatures, struggling to go upstream but thrown back each time they tried to do so, also appeared in his mental picture. He also remembered the rocks that remained unmoved by the fast flowing stream.

What had he been doing all this time, all these six years? It was true that he had left his family and his people behind. But still nothing had changed. He had up to now been moving along with the stream. He had gone to Alara and Uddaka. He had followed the five ascetics in tormenting his body almost to the verge of its destruction. Yet he won nothing. The six years he strived since leaving home had not carried him too far. The thought came to him:

"I cannot depend too much on tradition. I need not follow any teacher. I should be able to find a solution to the problems of existence on my own, on my own striving, on my own exertion."

Looking across the river, he saw a cool and delightful place with a pleasant grove. In the center of the grove was a majestic pipul tree spreading its branches around, its beautiful heart-shaped leaves dangling on their long stems providing pleasant shade. The singing of migratory birds filled the air with delightful natural music. It seemed a quieter place than the one he occupied during the previous night. It was removed from the busy activities of the fire worshippers led by Kassapa. He thought to himself, "This is a fitting place for one's striving. It is indeed a fitting place for me."

He took a few steps into the water which was only knee-deep. The current was strong and the sand underneath was soft. He struggled to remain upright.

He reflected again, "Unlike the lifeless bowl, a human being, with a will, could cross the river or go against the current instead of going downstream."

He visualized his bowl moving upstream with no effort, with ease. "That should be the way I should conduct myself," he told himself.

Crossing the river, he climbed up to the bank, walked up to the pipul tree and sat at its foot with his back to the trunk, facing the East. As he took his seat, he determined not to get up until he had realized the goal for the sake of which he renounced his family, his country and his people. It was an enormous determination, a tremendous undertaking. His whole body trembled as he sat down, giving him the feeling that mother earth herself was trembling.

He needed to develop knowledge and insight. Without being able to understand the mysteries surrounding human life, he could not expect to attain freedom. He sat there in deep reflection. He thought:

"I have learned the techniques of meditation under Alara

and Uddaka. I have not been able to attain any kind of knowledge by doing so. Is it not possible to go beyond what I learned under them?"

He attained the first four preliminary stages of meditation. He persisted and reached the higher stages arriving at the fourth stage of formless meditation characterized as neither perception nor nonperception. He strived and strived and strived. Finally he reached a stage where all perceptions, together with whatever had been felt, ceased completely. It was a state of complete cessation, a state of *nirodha*. He emerged from that state. He had gone beyond his teachers, Alara and Uddaka. Yet he had not found the goal. He had not achieved complete freedom from suffering.

A moment after he emerged from this state, the image of Yasodhara, revitalized by the appearance of Sujata and her two maids, gripped his mind. The whole army of temptations started attacking him. Sense desires, cravings, boredom, hunger and thirst, sloth and torpor, cowardice and uncertainty, malice and obstinacy, praise and blame, gain and honor—all were arrayed against him. He fought them with renewed vigor and achieved a state of calm, of peace and tranquility. In this process, he automatically reached the first stage of meditation characterized by seclusion from sense desires and seclusion from unwholesome elements. His mind became concentrated and gradually he reached the fourth stage of meditation characterized by equanimity and mindfulness. His mind became supple and malleable. Instead of moving in the direction of the cessation of all perceptions and what is felt, he directed his purified and supple mind toward an examination of human life.

With such a collected and purified mind, he remembered his own past. He recollected his manifold past lives, that is to say, one birth, two, three, four, five births, ten, twenty, thirty, forty, fifty births, a hundred births, a hundred thousand births, many ages of the world's dissolution, many ages of the world's evolution. He remembered that he was there so-named, of such a race, with such an appearance, eating such food, with such experience of pleasure and pain, of such life span; and passing away thence, he remembered how he reappeared elsewhere, and all details about that life. In this manner, he remembered his past existences. This was the first knowledge he developed during the first watch of the night.

With that knowledge, he was able to resolve some of the mysteries surrounding his own existence. He thought to himself, "Is it the case with others too?" He wanted to make sure.

So he directed his concentration and purified mind toward the understanding of other beings. With his divine eye, surpassing the eye of the humans, he saw beings passing away and reappearing, inferior and superior, fair and ugly, happy and unhappy, in their new destinations. He understood how beings passed on influenced by their behavior. He saw how beings, having performed evil actions of body, speech and mind, having wrong views, giving effect to wrong views in their actions, on the dissolution of their body after death, reappeared in states of privation, in unhappy states, in perdition, in hell. Likewise, he saw how some beings, having led good lives, reappeared in happy existences, in heaven. In this way, he came to know the decease and survival of other beings. This was the second knowledge he attained and it was attained during the second watch of the night.

These two forms of knowledge provided him with much needed information regarding the nature of man—how he has come to be and how he continues to be. He saw how human suffering comes to be determined by dispositional tendencies, by the incessant craving to organize one's life in such a way as to achieve maximum pleasure. He also realized how human beings, after achieving what they wanted, craved for more, thereby subjecting themselves to dissatisfaction and suffering.

He concentrated his mind and directed it toward understanding the nature of these defiling tendencies. He realized that sensual desire is a defiling tendency, that desire for existence, ignorance and false views are defiling tendencies. He saw how man's dispositions come to be conditioned by likes and dislikes; how the things produced by such dispositional tendencies are unsatisfactory, unsatisfying and lead to suffering, disappointment and frustration; how the elimination of such likes and dislikes, lust and hate, tends to pacify one's dispositions—which is perfect freedom.

As he came to know and perceive these things, he made a determined attempt to pacify his dispositions. His conviction that desire, hate and confusion were the root cause of all suffering was so great that almost automatically his mind came to be freed from all defilements. He was not only free; he also knew that he was free.

Siddhartha had attained freedom from attachment, aversion and confusion; he had attained nirvana. He realized that this is the only kind of freedom one can attain in this life. Any other kind of freedom remains a mere hope, nothing concrete. He also realized that with craving gone, he had eliminated the cause of future births. He knew that he had reached the highest goal of religious life, that there was nothing more to strive for.

He remained seated under the tree for some time, stabilizing his achievements, enjoying the bliss of freedom. His sense of freedom and happiness permeated his entire body producing an aura that was matched only by the splendor of the rising sun. The rising sun awakened everything in nature to produce the most pleasurable sensations such as the melodious singing of the birds, the sweet fragrance of the wild flowers and all the beauty associated with new life. Yet Siddhartha was not overwhelmed by these perceptions, by these sensations. It was as if he were being wrapped around by a seven-hooded snake and yet were able to remain unharmed by it.

SIXTEEN

THE BUDDHA, THE ENLIGHTENED ONE, freed from all defilements, walked up to the river Neranjara, bathed himself in the cool water, cleansed his body and limbs, and walked back to the tree that provided him with shade and shelter during his striving. He stood there in front of the tree gazing at it. It was the tree that gave him comfort, that enabled him to attain his goal. It was the tree of enlightenment, the *bodhi*-tree. He was grateful to this tree. Yet there was no reason to be unnecessarily sentimental about it. He had overcome attachment.

From there he walked up to a banyan tree, not far from the bodhi-tree. He spent some time seated there, reflecting on his freedom, reflecting upon the nature of things. He had overcome his prejudices, his likes and dislikes. Free from prejudices, he saw how things come to be dependent upon other things. He saw no permanent entity underlying things in the world. Everything that is experienced is impermanent, is subject to change, to transformation.

Man comes into the scene. He tries to understand things, how they function. He is not satisfied with mere understanding. He tries to organize them, manipulate them, put them together in the hope of getting the best out of them. Sometimes he succeeds and sometimes he does not. When he does not succeed, he is dejected, depressed, frustrated. When he succeeds, his satisfaction is temporary. He continues to struggle to gain something more. His pursuit is endless. He becomes tired, vexed and dissatisfied. All things that are dispositionally determined are thus unsatisfactory.

That which is impermanent, subject to change and transformation, and that which is unsatisfactory, cannot be substantial, cannot be the essential, cannot be the self, cannot be the soul, cannot be what everybody calls the ultimate.

Such is the nature of the world. That is how the world has come to be. When this exists, that comes to be; on the arising of this, that arises. When this does not exist, that does not come to be; on the cessation of this, that ceases.

A being comes into this world depending upon various conditions. Mother and father provide some of the conditions for his coming to be. He is still a being, not a complete person. Consciousness arises in the being. Mother and father provide the conditions necessary for consciousness to arise. All these together, in harmony, give rise to the person. The arising of consciousness is not spontaneous, it is not uncaused. It is related to past dispositions, to hankering in the past, to grasping in the past. They are the dispositions of a dying person, of a dying person struggling to survive, struggling for existence. These dispositions mold the consciousness of the being that comes to be. They provide the unity of the flowing stream of existence.

A person is born in the world. He is a person because he has a body and consciousness. He has senses. He comes into contact with the outside world through his senses. He comes to have sensations: pleasant, unpleasant or neutral. They become pleasant, unpleasant or neutral because of his dispositions. He is attracted to the pleasant, repelled by the unpleasant, indifferent to the neutral. He grasps on to what is attractive, and rejects what is repulsive. He wants to become this and that according to his attractions, according to his likes, according to his dispositions. He struggles, endeavors, persists. He achieves what he wants to become. He is born to it. Yet he is not satisfied. He aspires for more; he yearns for more. Depression, frustration, suffering and dejection overwhelm him as he continues with his struggle, with his aspirations. This is the mass of suffering.

All this is the result of ignorance. It is ignorance of the fact that persistent craving, continued lust, does not provide lasting satisfaction. Knowing this a wise man makes an attempt to eliminate his craving, to get rid of his lust. He does not grasp on to things in the world, he does not grasp on to a mythical self or soul considered to be permanent and eternal; he does not grasp for views. Nongrasping he remains undefiled by the world. He is like a lotus that grows in the murky water, but rises above the murky water, remaining unsmeared by it. Like the lotus he remains in the world; he is not out of the world. Only he remains unsmeared by the dirt in the world, by lust, greed, hate, aversion, ignorance and confusion.

The Buddha remained under the banyan tree for several weeks thus reflecting on the nature of the human predicament, on how man can help himself to attain freedom from suffering. He enjoyed the freedom he had achieved. At the end of it, he thought to himself:

"I have discovered this path to freedom from suffering with great difficulty, after a life of sacrifice and struggle. People in Magadha are under the yoke of Brahmanism. They are immersed in the Brahmanical teachings. Former teachers like Uddalaka and Yajnavalkya, when they reached Magadha, came under the influence of Brahmanism. Sages like Ajita Kesakambali, Makkhali Gosala and Nigantha Nataputta are not much recognized here. Their teachings, whether they be right or wrong, have been ignored. Brahmans are like parasitical creepers: they depend upon others for new ideas and in no time destroy them after drawing out the sap of vitality in them. It would be an utter waste of time on my part to go around preaching to people here. What if I were to go back to Kapilavatthu where Brahmanism is not so powerful and influential? I would be able to help more people than if I remained here."

Then he remembered that Alara and Uddaka had appealed to him to come back and inform them, if he was able to discover anything new. He thought about them, but soon discovered that they had passed away. He thought about the five ascetic friends who had helped him when he was practicing the mortification of the body.

"They have been of great help to me," he thought. "I should

100

meet them and inform them about what I have discovered and achieved. They were good and intelligent people. They will be able to understand and appreciate what I have to say."

He remembered that after leaving him at Uruvela they made their way to Baranasi. He decided to look for them and set out for Baranasi.

On his way to Baranasi, Buddha sought the cool shade of a tree to rest during midday. An ascetic by name Upaka, belonging to a group known as Ajivikas, saw the Buddha. Assuming that he was a coreligionist, Upaka strayed off the road to speak to the Buddha. Upon reaching him, Upaka noticed that the Buddha was very different from any other ascetic he had seen so far. His faculties were clear and bright; the complexion of his skin was pure and clean; his face was serene and calm, and a strange aura of brightness emanated from his personality.

"Whom do you follow, friend, upon leaving the world?" questioned Upaka. "Who is your teacher and whose doctrine do you profess?"

"I have freed myself from all defilements. With craving gone and mind emancipated through knowledge gained on my own, whom could I claim to be my teacher? Friend, the world is my teacher. I am alone in the world and I shall remain alone in the world."

Being part of a tradition where freedom and security were sought for within the framework of either a supreme being or Brahma, an ultimate reality or Brahman, or a superior teacher or even a tradition, Upaka was unable to understand Buddha's message.

"May be so," said he, nodding his head and continuing on his way.

Arriving in Baranasi after a long trek, Buddha learnt of the existence of a park, known to people as Isipatana, that served as a retreat for the ascetics. It was a very pleasant park with groves of medium-sized trees and bushes providing a haven, not only for the ascetics, but also for harmless wildlife such as the deer who roamed around without being harassed by the people. The presence of ascetics in the park kept away those who would have liked to hunt the deer for pleasure or for food.

It was a pleasant reminder of the ability of man and animal to coexist without fear.

Upon reaching Isipatana, Buddha discovered the five old-time friends continuing with their mortification of the flesh. The five ascetics recognized Siddhartha.

"Here comes the weak-minded Siddhartha, who gave up austerities for a life of abundance," said one of them, calling the attention of the others. "It would not be proper for us to pay any respect to a person who vacillates when faced with the rigors of spiritual exercises."

Yet, as the Buddha came closer to them, they noticed the change in his physical personality. They were mystified by the peace and serenity that was reflected on his face. They realized that it was not the same Siddhartha that they left behind in Uruvela; he was completely transformed. Yet they could not understand his spiritual achievement. In spite of their earlier decision not to pay the Buddha any respect, they could not resist the temptation to get up from their seats when Buddha reached them. One of them took his bowl and robe; another prepared a seat; a third set water for him to wash his feet. When the Buddha settled down on his seat, one of them addressed him:

"Friend, you abandoned the spiritual life of austerities and reverted to a life of abundance. Yet your appearance is different from either a man of austerities or a man of self-indulgence. What makes you so different?"

Buddha smiled.

"Friends, I have discovered the truth about the world. It is deep and profound, difficult to understand, especially by those who are engrossed and entangled in passions and desires. Desire for existence is as harmful as the desire for sense pleasures. Ignorance of the nature of the world is the cause of all such desires. I have eliminated such ignorance and I am enlightened. I am *Buddha*. I have eliminated all desires and I am freed from suffering."

The ascetics were confused.

"How can a person who adopted a life of abundance attain such knowledge and achieve such freedom?" asked one of them.

"There are two wrong views in this world that people grasp on to: the first is eternalism and the other is annihilationism. Ascetics who believe that there is a permanent and eternal self or soul adopt extreme forms of mortification of the flesh hoping, thereby, to free the soul from its bondage to the body. Those who believe that man is destroyed at death advocate a life of abundance, a life of indulgence.

"Friends, there is no permanent and eternal self," continued the Buddha. "The absence of a permanent and eternal self does not mean that man is completely annihilated at death. With the clear and unprejudiced vision I attained as a result of being aloof from sense pleasures, aloof from defiling tendencies, I have discovered the middle position between eternalism and annihilationism. This middle position is dependent arising. It is the nature of the world. It is deep, difficult to see, difficult to comprehend, peaceful, outstanding, beyond speculative reasoning, subtle and to be known by the wise."

"Dependent arising! Dependent arising! What is dependent arising? Never have we heard such a doctrine!" remarked Assaji, one of the ascetics.

"I shall explain it to you, friends. Listen carefully," said the Buddha. "Whatever we have experienced has come to be depending upon various conditions. A sprout has come to be depending upon a seed, upon its fertility, upon the availability of moisture, of the essence of the soil. When the sprout has come to be, we examine the background that gave rise to the sprout and say that such and such conditions gave rise to it. If the sprout did not come to be, we maintain that such and such conditions were deficient and, therefore, it did not come to be. This is the principle of dependence. When this exists, that comes to be; on the arising of this, that arises. When this does not exist, that does not come to be; on the cessation of this, that ceases. Such is the nature of things, the manner in which they have come to be. Such knowledge I call knowledge of things as they have come to be."

"If everything we experience is dependently arisen, how can we attain freedom?" questioned Assaji.

"Dependent arising, I have discovered, does not exclude human dispositions. Human dispositions are also dependently

103

arisen, but that does not mean they are passive. They are active and creative. See the splendor of Kosala. Look at the pleasures enjoyed by the king of Kosala: the royal palace, the pleasure gardens, the lotus ponds, the fountains and all other sources of enjoyment. These are not mere natural occurrences. They are the products of human dispositions. These dispositions are also the causes of suffering, of insatiability, of frustration.

"Friends, this again is a position difficult for the ordinary man to understand, namely, the pacification of dispositions, the abandoning of all clinging, the cessation of all craving, and absence of passion—this freedom."

"But this freedom you speak of is limited, incomplete," remarked Kondanna.

"Yes, you are right," replied the Buddha. "Once a human being has come into existence, the only kind of freedom he can attain is freedom from passion, from hate, from confusion. There is no other freedom he can achieve while living. He cannot free himself from aging, from decay, from disease and from death. Yet he can live without fear, frustration and suffering if he has no passions, if he has no hate, if he has no confusion. This is freedom attained while this psychophysical personality lasts. This is freedom one can have so long as one's faculties—the eye, ear, nose, tongue, body and mind— are not destroyed. But those who crave for complete freedom, while retaining this psychophysical personality, are mistaken. What they want is "freedom" to have permanent and eternal life, to retain their souls in spite of change. This is craving for existence, for permanent life.

"With passions gone, with no more hate and confusion, I have no more clinging to existence. Not clinging to existence, I do not grasp on to life. Not grasping on to life, I will not be reborn after death. Upon the breakup of this fragile body, I will not come to possess a similar body. I will not be reborn. Without being reborn, I will not experience disease, decay and death. This is deathlessness. This is immortality. This is complete freedom. This is cessation."

Assaji was impressed by this new doctrine. "Dependent arising" was unheard of before. He spent a long time reflecting upon it. The more he reflected, the more he was convinced that it truly represented the nature of the world.

Kondanna was interested in knowing how one can achieve this freedom. So he questioned the Buddha:

"Your doctrine of dependent origination is new. It avoids the two extremes of eternalism and annihilationism. It is the middle position. But what is the middle way that leads to such freedom from suffering?"

"A life of self-indulgence, friends, is one extreme. It is low, vulgar, common, ignoble and useless. A life of self-torture is the other extreme. It is painful, ignoble and useless.

"There is suffering in this world. What is suffering?" continued the Buddha. "Birth is suffering; old age is suffering; sickness is suffering; death is suffering. Sorrow, lamentation, dejection are suffering. Contact with what is unpleasant and separation from the pleasant are suffering. Not getting what one wishes is suffering. In brief, clinging to the five aggregates of the personality—form, feeling, perception, disposition and consciousness—as being mine, my self, my soul: this is suffering.

"There is a cause for this suffering. It is that craving, which leads to rebirth, combined with pleasure and lust, finding pleasure here and there. It is craving for passionate things, craving for existence, craving for nonexistence.

"This suffering can be eliminated. It is the cessation of that craving, abandonment of that craving, forsaking that craving, release from that craving; it is nonattachment.

"The path leading to that cessation, to that freedom, is the middle path. It is eightfold, consisting of right understanding, right thought, right speech, right action, right livelihood, right effort, right mindfulness and right concentration.

"The truth of suffering is to be comprehended. The cause of that suffering is to be abandoned. The cessation of that cause is to be realized. The path leading to the cessation of suffering is to be cultivated.

"This, friends, is the truth I discovered about the world. As a result of the realization of this truth, I have attained perfect enlightenment. Knowledge arose in me, insight arose in me that the release of my mind is unshakeable, that this is my last existence and that there is no rebirth for me."

Kondanna was the first to attain enlightenment upon listening to the Buddha. He was the Buddha's first disciple. The four others struggled and strove. They were unable to cast away their belief in a permanent self. Buddha addressed them:

"Friends, this body is no-self. If it were the self, it would not be subject to sickness, and it would be possible in the case of the body to say: 'Let my body be thus, let my body be not thus.' Now, because the body is no-self, the body is subject to sickness and it is not possible to say in the case of the body: 'Let my body be thus, let my body be not thus.' This body, therefore, is not the self because it has no autonomy—similarly, with feeling, perception, dispositions and consciousness.

"What do you think, friends, is this body permanent or impermanent?"

"Impermanent, Sir," said the four ascetics in unison. They had now begun to realize that Siddhartha was no ordinary person. The Buddha smiled, noticing how they had overcome their arrogance in the way they addressed him.

"But is this impermanent body a source of suffering or happiness?" questioned Buddha.

"It is a source of suffering, Sir," replied the ascetics.

"Is it proper to consider what is impermanent, subject to change and a source of suffering as my permanent self, I, my soul?"

"No, indeed, Sir."

"If you really understand that this is the case, friends, you should not grasp on to the body, to feeling, to perception, to disposition and to consciousness as being the self."

"Yes, Sir," replied the ascetics.

"Apart from this body, apart from this feeling, apart from this perception, apart from this disposition and apart from this consciousness, do you have an experience of a permanent self or soul?" questioned the Buddha.

The ascetics were silent. They could not answer.

Buddha continued:

"What you have been asserting as a permanent and eternal self is merely a product of your imagination, an imagination produced by excessive grasping for existence. You were like the men who were enamored of a beauty queen whom they had never seen."

The four ascetics were shaken up and they awoke from their slumber. Reflecting on what Buddha had said, these ascetics, within a short span of time, became dispassionate toward body, feeling, perception, disposition, and consciousness. Becoming dispassionate, their lust faded away. With the fading away of lust, their minds were released from all clinging and they attained perfect freedom.

Now there were altogether six saints in the world—the Buddha and his five disciples. For the first time, he addressed them as "monks."

"Monks, go forth for the benefit of the many, for the happiness of the many, through compassion for the world. Let not two go in the same direction. With this message spread round, the world will be a better place to live in."

SEVENTEEN

WITH THE FIRST DISCIPLES stepping out into the world after their enlightenment, word spread that an ascetic of the Gotama clan, son of a Sakyan, had left his family and embraced the holy life, had attained enlightenment, having discovered, through his own effort, the path thereof. His teachings were excellent and the religious life he advocated was perfect and pure. Ascetics and brahmans flocked to Isipatana to see the Buddha. To many an ascetic who had been wandering about in search of a solution to the ills of life, Buddha's message came as a welcome shower during a prolonged drought.

Having practiced yoga, an important component of the ascetic life, for a considerable length of time, it was easier for these ascetics to understand the teachings of the Buddha and attain peace and tranquility by following his instruction. The reactions of the brahmans were mixed. Some were impressed by Buddha and became his disciples. Others came to him looking for some new inspiration to revive their own religious beliefs, which were receiving a setback as a result of the peoples' eroding of confidence in their ritualism. Householders, both male and female, irrespective of their status in society, came to the Buddha looking for solutions to their household woes.

The rainy season set in and Buddha decided to postpone his visit to Kapilavatthu. Instead, seeing the enthusiastic response to his message, he remained in the South for a while before going back to his homeland.

While Buddha was staying at the Deer Park at Isipatana, Assaji traveled all the way to Rajagaha where he wanted to spread the message of the Buddha. On his first day in Rajagaha when he was going on the alms round in the city, he was seen by a young ascetic named Upatissa, who was a disciple of Sanjaya Bellatthiputta. Sanjaya was a skeptic who was not willing to provide any definitive answer to any kind of question, because he recognized the uncertainty in human knowledge as well as the ambiguity in philosophical explanation. Upatissa and his friend, Kolita, had been disciples of Sanjaya for a long time, but were now getting disillusioned with Sanjaya's teachings. The two friends had agreed between themselves that if either came to know of any new ideas, the other should be informed first, before discussing them with their teacher.

Upatissa was impressed by Assaji's personality, his serenity and deportment, and followed him until Assaji completed his alms round and retired to a quiet spot to partake of his meal. When he had finished his meal, Upatissa approached him and questioned:

"Friend, you look very different from any other ascetic I have seen. Under whom have you gone forth? Who is your teacher and what kind of doctrine do you profess?"

"There is a great monk, friend, the son of the Sakyans, who

went forth from the Sakyan clan. He is enlightened. He is my teacher and it is his doctrine I profess," replied Assaji.

"What does he teach and in what way are his teachings different from those of other great religious teachers?" asked Upatissa.

"He teaches the doctrine of dependent arising. Rejecting a permanent and immutable self, he explains whatever is experienced in terms of dependent arising. His spiritual path is also based on the doctrine of dependent arising. I have followed his path and have eliminated all my passions and desires, and I live in this world like a bird freed from captivity."

Upatissa was excited. This indeed was a new doctrine, unheard of before. He wanted to receive instructions directly from the great monk.

"Where does he live?" asked Upatissa.

"In Baranasi, at the Deer Park in Isipatana," replied Assaji.

"May you be well!" said Upatissa and paying his respects to Assaji, he hurried away to see his friend Kolita. They both decided to leave Sanjaya and go to Baranasi. Sanjaya was heartbroken when he heard that his two best disciples were leaving him. With tears in his eyes, he bade them farewell:

"I regret to see you go. May you be happy under whatever teacher you take refuge!"

Kolita and Upatissa met the Buddha upon their arrival in Baranasi, and became his disciples under the names Moggallana and Sariputta respectively. It was not easy for these two to attain enlightenment under the Buddha because of their mistrust of any form of knowledge, an attitude they had inherited from Sanjaya.

One day Buddha was in the company of Sariputta and Moggallana when a wanderer, named Dighanakha, visited Buddha and got into a conversation. Addressing the Buddha, he said:

"Friend, there are ascetics and brahmans who speculate and propound theories about the nature of everything. In my view a 'theory about everything' is unsatisfactory."

Buddha reflected for a moment. Before his enlightenment, he had come to know how philosophers like Uddalaka and Kapila attempted to explain everything in terms of primordial substances. There were others who reacted to such theories negatively. He looked at Dighanakha, smiled and questioned:

"Dighanakha, you claim that in your view a 'theory about everything' is unsatisfactory. Do you consider your own view to be satisfactory?"

Dighanakha realized that Buddha was trying to lead him from a negative position to a position of noncommitment. He was not pleased with such a noncommittal position. Therefore, he responded:

"Even if my view is satisfactory to me, it would be all the same."

Buddha understood Dighanakha's arrogance. He was careful in analyzing the implications as well as the unfortunate consequences of Dighanakha's assertion. He said:

"Dighanakha, there are two kinds of philosophers. Most philosophers speculate on the nature or essence of everything. Some are satisfied with such speculation, with such theorizing. Therefore, they are enamored by them, attached to them. Others are dissatisfied with such speculation and theorizing. Therefore, they are not enamored by them, not attached to them."

Dighanakha was delighted. He praised the Buddha, saying:

"Good Gotama, you are most enlightened. You commend my view, you recommend my view!"

Buddha could not help smiling.

"Dighanakha, listen carefully. When an ascetic or brahman speculates on the nature or essence of everything and is satisfied with such speculation and theorizing, he obstinately holds on to and insists on it saying: 'This alone is true; everything else is false.' Thereby he becomes a dogmatist. Similarly, when an ascetic or brahman is dissatisfied with such speculation, with such theorizing, he too obstinately holds on to his standpoint saying: 'This alone is true; everything else is false.' Therefore, he too cannot avoid being a dogmatist. Conflict between two dogmatists is not easily avoided; conflict leads to disputes, to quarrels, to suffering. When there is no clinging, when all such views are abandoned, there is peace; there is tranquility.

"All our experiences, Dighanakha, are impermanent, dispositionally conditioned, dependently arisen, of the nature of ceasing, of passing away, of disintegration. A wise man is dispassionate toward things in the world, toward his views about the world. He has no lust; he is liberated. Being liberated he sides with none, disputes with none, and he employs the linguistic usage current in the world without clinging to it obstinately."

Sariputta and Moggallana were standing behind the Buddha fanning him. They were fascinated by Buddha's response to Dighanakha's claim. They were excited about Buddha's way of dealing with philosophical disputes. All these years, under the tutelage of Sanjaya, they had learned to question every kind of knowledge and reject every kind of assertion. They were made to feel that any assertion was inherently wrong and, therefore, contributed to conflicts. Hence the only way to avoid conflicts was to avoid making any assertive statements. In the Buddha's discourse to Dighanakha, the reason for the conflicts in the world was attributed, not to any inherent defect in the descriptive function of language, but rather to the dogmatism with which views are held or presented. It is one's attachment to views that generates all conflicts. Buddha has not only given up attachment to sense pleasures, he also has given up attachment to ideas or views. He is not freed of views, but he is freed from views.

The discussion between Buddha and Dighanakha was an eye-opener for both Sariputta and Moggallana. After listening to Buddha, Moggallana practiced meditation and developed higher knowledge. He became an adept in the first of these consisting of psychokinetic powers. And with the attainment of the last of these higher forms of knowledge, which is the knowledge of the cessation of defilements, he attained sainthood.

But Sariputta was not yet ready for such insight and freedom. He was aware that the Buddha's doctrine of dependent arising was an innovative doctrine. It conformed to all the facts of experience. The nature and behavior of the living saint could be explained in terms of dependent arising. But what about the saint after death? Can anything be truly predicated of him? Is conventional description, linguistic usage

111

adequate to explain the nature of the saint after death? Entertaining such doubts in the inner recesses of his mind, Sariputta was not able to destroy the bonds of existence. Therefore, he decided to question the Buddha regarding the status of the saint.

Having waited for an opportune moment, Sariputta approached the Buddha and questioned him:

"Sir, does the saint exist after death?"

"Sariputta, I leave that question unexplained," replied Buddha.

"Then, does he not exist after death?"

"That too I leave unexplained."

"Does that mean that the saint both exists and does not exist after death?"

"I leave that also unexplained."

"Is it then that the saint neither exists nor does not exist after death?"

"Sariputta, that too is a question that I leave unexplained."

Sariputta was confused. Here is at least one issue on which the Buddha has to admit that language is incompetent to explain the subject matter. Buddha has to adopt the same kind of noncommittal attitude that Sanjaya adopted. He questioned:

"Sir, I assumed that your doctrine is different from that of my former teacher, Sanjaya. But your answer to my question regarding the state of the saint after death is not different from Sanjaya's."

"Sariputta, did Sanjaya adopt a noncommittal attitude to every question that you asked him?" questioned Buddha.

"Yes, Sir."

"There, then, is the difference, Sariputta. I do not respond in this way to every question that is put to me. There are some questions that I leave unexplained. There are others that I will answer after raising counter-questions and clarifying their implications. There are still others for which I give categorical answers. Is that any different from the teachings of your former teacher?"

"Yes, indeed, Sir."

"There are two questions, Sariputta, that one can raise

112

regarding the saint. The first is the question as to what happens to the saint at death; the other pertains to the state of the saint after death. I have provided a categorical answer to the first question. Since the saint has eliminated grasping or clinging to anything, including existence, he has thereby eliminated the cause of rebirth and, therefore, is not reborn. This explanation of mine is in conformity with the dependent arising I have proclaimed. But if you ask me the further question as to what happens to the saint after death, or after he is not reborn, I am not able to answer that question. The reason being that it is an inappropriate question."

Buddha continued with his explanation.

"People who are engrossed with the belief in existence maintain that the saint exists after death in an eternal and blissful state. Those who are enamored with the belief in nonexistence hold that the saint is annihilated after death. Without any means of knowing, I prefer to remain silent on this matter.

"What do you think, Sariputta? When a flame is blown out, when it is gone, is it proper to ask where the flame went, east or west, north or south?"

"It is not proper, Sir, to ask that question," replied Sariputta.

"Why not?"

"Because there is no means of knowing where the flame is. Without the necessary conditions, the flame would not come to be."

"Similarly, Sariputta, a saint who is freed from reckoning in terms of the five factors of personality—form, feeling, perception, disposition and consciousness—can neither be said to exist nor not to exist. When you accept a theory of dependent arising and explain the nature of the living saint in terms of that theory, then you do not ask questions about the saint after death."

"Would you like to know what other questions I would leave unanswered and why?" questioned the Buddha.

"That will certainly help me to overcome my doubts, Sir," replied Sariputta.

"Sariputta, if you ask me whether the world is eternal or not, whether the world is finite or not, whether the soul is identical with the body or whether the soul is different from the body, I will leave all these questions unanswered, unexplained, undeclared. Why?

"Because," continued the Buddha, "in the first place, I cannot answer any one of them on the basis of experience. I have developed extraordinary powers of perception, such as clairaudience and clairvoyance, and I have developed such higher forms of knowledge as telepathy and retrocognition, yet I was not able to perceive the first beginning of the universe, nor have I perceived a permanent and eternal substance in the world or in man. I have not seen an ultimate reality, indefinable and inexpressible. How can one explain what one has not experienced? Shouldn't one remain silent, without having to say, 'It is, but it is indescribable, indefinable'? If one were to explain something without having any experience of it, one would be merely using reasoning with assumed premises. Such forms of reasoning would be based upon one's prejudices, one's likes and dislikes, and would be different from someone else's. Conflict between people holding such divergent theories is inevitable. There is no way in which a decision could be made as to who is right and who is wrong. Therefore, I do not attempt to answer questions relating to matters not empirically given, or which cannot be based on what is empirically given. Not answering such questions, I do not get involved in disputes."

"Secondly, solutions to such problems are not relevant to the solution of many a problem that we face in this world. Whether the world is eternal or not, finite or not, there exists suffering. This suffering is caused. Causes of such suffering can be eliminated. There is a path that leads to the elimination of such suffering."

"Sariputta, let me ask you one more question."

"If you may, please."

"What would you do if you were to be hit by a poisonous arrow? Would you insist that you want to find which direction the arrow came from? Who shot the arrow? What caste is he from? Of what color he is? Is he black, white or brown? Was he born high or low, superior or inferior?"

114

"No, I would not want to wait for answers to such questions," replied Sariputta.

"What would you expect to be done?"

"I would expect the arrow to be removed immediately."

"Why?"

"Because I might die before I find the answers to those questions."

"Just so," responded the Buddha, "the answers to such questions relating to the origin of the universe, and so on will not be relevant to the solution of our immediate problems. In fact, by the time man found a solution to these questions, he would be dead and gone. For all the time man has lived on this earth, he has not yet been able to find satisfactory solutions to these questions. Do you want to waste your time?"

"Not any more, Sir," replied Sariputta, and during the next few days he spent his energies in controlling his passions and desires, and soon attained enlightenment and freedom.

EIGHTEEN

B Y THIS TIME, the Buddha had been able to convert a large number of ascetics and brahmans to his way of thinking. The new message brought hope and solace to a large population that had remained under the yoke of Brahmanical ritualism and superstition. Soon his reputation spread all over the kingdoms of Kosala and Magadha. The success of his mission in Baranasi made Buddha change his mind about going back to his hometown immediately. He spent the first rainy season in Baranasi and decided to go to Magadha.

Returning to the kingdom of Magadha, he went to Uruvela

where he had first met the five ascetics who became his first disciples. During his previous stay in Uruvela he had heard about a matted-hair ascetic named Kassapa, who performed miracles. Kassapa had achieved mastery of psychic powers during the course of his yogic meditation and started performing miracles. Young men who were fascinated by such miracles flocked to him to become his disciples in hope of learning the technique of miracle-making. Brahman householders who identified religion and spiritual life with the miraculous were not only filled with wonder at his achievements, but were also fearful of his powers. He thus enjoyed unquestioned loyalty from his disciples and fear-ridden respect from ordinary brahman householders. His disciples as well as the householders were willing to undertake extensive and expensive sacrificial rituals at his bidding. Sacrifices to the god of fire were prominent among these. The performance of each sacrificial ritual was normally preceded by offerings of worldly goods to Kassapa. Thus he came to amass a fortune, becoming a man of great power and privileges. His capacity to perform miracles and other psychic powers enabled him to enjoy a life of pleasure.

Kassapa had come to know of the Buddha's reputation, but did not pay much attention to it. Upon arriving at Uruvela Buddha decided to visit Kassapa. Kassapa did not appreciate Buddha's visit. He feared that his own reputation with his disciples would be lost if Buddha too possessed such psychic powers and were able to reveal the means by which Kassapa was retaining the faith of his disciples. Therefore, he decided to get rid of Buddha at the earliest opportunity. When, in the evening, the Buddha needed a place to rest for the night, Kassapa offered a small cottage into which he had surreptitiously introduced a venomous snake. Unsuspectingly Buddha retired to the cottage to sleep and he discovered the snake. The Buddha, the enlightened one, was cool and composed. He did not panic. He could not have panicked, for he had gotten rid of all the passions and desires that cause such panic. Buddha settled down to sleep on the floor strewn with dried grass. The snake, not being disturbed, coiled in his own corner of the cottage and remained quiet throughout the night.

In the morning, Buddha woke up and quietly walked out of the cottage, leaving the snake undisturbed. Kassapa, waiting outside the cottage, could not believe his eyes when he saw the Buddha open the door and walk out. His disciples were standing behind him ready to remove the Buddha's dead body. It was greater than all the miracles they had so far witnessed. Kassapa questioned Buddha:

"Friend, what kind of miracle did you perform in order to tame this venomous snake?"

"Kassapa, I have achieved the miracle of taming myself. One who has tamed himself has no difficulty in taming others, whether that be a poisonous snake, a lion, or an elephant, or even the most vicious of men," replied the Buddha.

Kassapa realized that he had been humbled by the Buddha in the presence of his disciples. Sweat flowed from his forehead. He felt ashamed of himself. He realized the implications of the Buddha's remarks, and thought to himself:

"Even a venomous snake, a creature without the ability to think and act, has been friendly toward Buddha, whereas I, the leader of a large congregation of men, have acted worse than the snake in attempting to destroy him."

Overwhelmed by the feeling of shame, he regretted his arrogance and stupidity. Falling prostrate on the ground before Buddha, he pleaded:

"Sir, I was deceived by jealousy and pride. May you instruct me in the art of taming myself."

Buddha taught him the method of controlling the vicious and poisonous tendencies in man. He taught him how to subdue his passions, how to overcome his aversions and his confusions. To Kassapa who had instructed his disciples about the significance of the fire sacrifice as a means of attaining miraculous powers, Buddha delivered a discourse explaining where the real fire is:

"Everything has been on fire, friends. What is everything that has been on fire? Eye has been on fire, friends. Visible form has been on fire. Visual consciousness has been on fire. Visual contact has been on fire. Feeling—pleasant, painful or neutral—that arises with visual contact has been on fire. What is this fire? It is the fire of lust, of hate, of confusion.

The fire of lust, of hate and of confusion has consumed all our senses, our sense objects and our experiences that arise as a result of these senses and sense objects.

"Perceiving that our experiences with the senses have been on fire, a wise man becomes dispassionate toward the eye, to visible objects, to visual consciousness and to visual contact. He becomes dispassionate toward every sense, sense object, sense consciousness and sense contact. Being dispassionate, his lust fades away. With the fading of lust, his mind is liberated. When his mind is liberated, he realizes that his birth is exhausted, he has lived the higher life, done what ought to be done and that there is no more of this to come."

Soon Kassapa, together with his disciples, strived and attained freedom from the three fires burning within. They became saints.

The conversion of Kassapa and his disciples was of tremendous significance. Apart from the success of the Buddha's message in healing the pain and suffering of Kassapa and his disciples, their conversion marked the first crack in the Brahmanical dam that held the waters of religious faith of the people of Magadha. It took some time for the people of Magadha to believe that so powerful a person as Kassapa could be a disciple of Buddha. News of Kassapa's conversion spread like brushfire and it reached King Bimbisara.

"When I saw him some time ago, I suspected that Siddhartha would one day achieve great heights in spiritual matters," said the king to his attendants. "Let us go and see him."

With a large retinue of attendants and brahman householders, the king hurried to Uruvela where Buddha was staying with his disciples. The large congregation of monks wearing yellow robes presented a spectacular sight. The color of the robes matched the brightness and serenity of their faces. An aura of soft light pervaded the entire area, as if thousands of moons were shining in a cloudless night. It was a spectacle the king had never before witnessed.

King Bimbisara approached the Buddha, paid his respects and said:

"Having met you on a previous occasion, I invited you to return to Rajagaha when you had discovered the truth and help me as my spiritual adviser. I was very selfish in my request. Now I find that the world can benefit from your enlightenment. May you please visit my palace with your disciples the day after tomorrow and partake of a meal prepared by me."

Buddha accepted the invitation by being silent.

King Bimbisara returned to the city immediately and made preparations to receive the Buddha and his disciples. Suspecting Buddha's lack of interest in pomp and ceremony, as was evident from the manner in which he humbled a man like Kassapa who previously enjoyed such extravagances, the king decided to avoid any glamorous decorations and ordered the people to wear clean white garments when they came to see Buddha. When the people, clad in white garments, crowded the streets in the morning of the day Buddha arrived in the city of Rajagaha with the large congregation of yellow robed monks, it appeared as if the pure white mist that settled on the ground the previous night was refusing to move up in spite of the appearance of the bright sun on the horizon.

King Bimbisara sent emissaries to receive the Buddha and his disciples upon their arrival in the city and to lead them to his palace. When they reached the palace, the king, followed by the members of the royal household, went out and paid obeisance to Buddha and his retinue who were accommodated in a huge pavilion specially constructed for the occasion. The king served them with the choicest of food prepared in the royal kitchen. When Buddha had finished his meal, the king walked up to him and, kneeling down, said:

"Sir, you have performed the greatest miracle in converting the invincible Kassapa. Pray, tell me, what makes an ideal ruler."

"O King!" replied the Buddha, "an ideal ruler is one who has the welfare of his subjects at heart. He rules the country not by the power of the sword, but in terms of righteousness."

"But, Sir," said the king, "my spiritual advisers who are brahmans inform me that righteousness is to be protected by the sword, and hence we are called kshatriyas, the wielders of the sword."

"Those who justify the use of the sword to protect righteousness assume that righteousness is a law ordained by a supreme divine Being, a creator God whom they call Brahma. For them, that law represents the truth about the world. Man has no power to oppose that divine ordination, that truth about the world. What is opposed to truth is untruth, evil, and therefore, should be punished with the sword, with death."

Brahman priests, who were King Bimbisara's spiritual advisers and who were present on this occasion, looked at each other.

"I have discovered no such truth, O King," continued the Buddha. "The truth that I have discovered about the world is 'dependent arising.' Righteousness is to be understood and explained in terms of 'dependent arising.'"

"Sir, I have difficulty in understanding this 'dependent arising' and this righteousness, and how it can be utilized by a ruler in the administration of a country," remarked King Bimbisara.

"Your difficulties are genuine; your doubts are genuine, O King. It is a doctrine I have discovered by myself. I will explain to you what dependent arising is. Listen carefully.

"Man is neither created by God nor by himself. He has come to be as a result of a complex of conditions. While living in a society, when he commits a crime, he is to be held responsible only in so far as his desires, his passions are involved. Every unenlightened man has passions and desires. They are normally kept under control because of the kind of education he receives from his childhood, and because of the lack of opportunities in society for him to satisfy all those desires and passions. If he does not receive a proper education and if society provides him with ample opportunity, he will certainly let his desires and passions dominate him. In that case, it is not merely he himself that is responsible; his parents, his teachers and also the society in which he lives would be equally responsible for what he does. When his crime is the result of a complex of conditions, why should he be the only one to receive punishment?

"Furthermore, even if punishment becomes necessary, the motivation for that punishment should not be revenge or retribution. Punishment is for the sake of rehabilitation. Therefore, the use of the sword has no justification whatsoever. Capital punishment is generally justified on the grounds that an evil man is incorrigible. I do not believe that man is incorrigible. Man has become evil because of the three roots of evil, namely, passion, hatred and confusion. It is possible for these three roots of evil to be completely eliminated and uprooted. I have achieved such a state and so have most of my disciples who are with me. If the three roots of evil can be eliminated in some individuals, why should it be assumed that they cannot be eliminated in others.

"O King, I do not advocate the destruction of human life, once it has come into being. It is one thing to prevent the arising of a new human life and it is another thing to destroy that which has come to be. Once it has come to be, nobody has a right to destroy it, not even oneself.

"O King, what do you think? Is an action that is harmful to oneself good or bad?" questioned the Buddha.

"It is bad, Sir," replied King Bimbisara.

"Is an action that is harmful to others good or bad?"

"It is bad, Sir."

"Is an action that is harmful to both oneself and others good or bad?"

"I assume that too is bad."

"What then is a good action? What is a bad action?" questioned the Buddha.

"Sir, I will have to admit that a good action is one that leads to happiness of both oneself as well as others, while a bad action is one that contributes to harm of oneself as well as others," replied Bimbisara.

"Well said, O King. That is righteousness; that is the truth I have discovered. This truth is not based on any divine revelation; it is not founded on any divine ordinance: it is based on a recognition that everything that we experience in this world is dependently arisen. It is based on the doctrine that both good and bad are causally conditioned. The elimination of bad is achieved by the elimination of those conditions that give rise to it, while the promotion of good can be realized by the cultivation of conditions that produce it."

"Therefore, an ideal ruler is one who is able to understand

the nature of the world as being dependently arisen and who attempts to promote the good tendencies and eliminate the bad tendencies in himself as well as his subjects."

"Sir, does this mean that an ideal king need not necessarily be a kshatriya?" questioned Bimbisara.

"That's right. A kshatriya becomes a kshatriya, not by virtue of his birth, but by his actions. He is selected to rule, not because he is born to a particular family, but because he is a just person. O King, have you heard of the first ruler of men?" asked the Buddha.

"Yes, Sir. He was called Mahasammata," replied the king.

"Why was he called Mahasammata?" asked Buddha.

King Bimbisara thought for a while. He was familiar with this name, but had never before reflected on the meaning of the term.

"Sir, I assume that *maha* means 'great' and *sammata* means 'agreed upon.' "

"You are right. That is what it means. *Mahasammata* means *mahajanasammata,* that is, agreed upon by the great congregation of people. But was he selected because he was a kshatriya?"

"No, Sir," replied the king. "He was the first kshatriya and others are his descendants."

"How did he become a kshatriya without being born to a kshatriya family?" questioned the Buddha.

Bimbisara did not answer. He was embarrassed. His son and heir to the throne, who was seated next to him, showed signs of anger.

Buddha continued with his explanation.

"He was selected by the majority, because he was just and honest, because he commanded the respect of the majority by his good appearance, his moral integrity, his honesty and his impartiality. Therefore, I maintain that kingship is not a paternal heritage. No one has a right to rule, unless that right is bestowed on him by the people. Therefore, when one is honored by the people with the right to rule, one has to think of the happiness and welfare of all, not merely of the majority who supported him. Passion for those who support one and hate for those who oppose one will not make one a good ruler, even according to the definition of good and bad we have already accepted. Therefore, an ideal king is one who rules the country motivated by his own happiness as well as the happiness of others."

The king was pleased. He realized the greatness of the Buddha, his courage to speak against all dogmas accepted in this society and above all, his compassion for all human life. He fell prostrate before Buddha and said:

"Sir, from now on, please accept me as one of your lay disciples. It is not proper for me to request you to remain here in Magadha all the time so that I can benefit by your noble counsel. Please leave some of your disciples, the worthy ones, here so that myself as well as my people can benefit by their presence. I dedicate this royal Bamboo Grove for your use and for the use of your disciples."

The majority of those present, brahman householders, kshatriyas and people from all walks of life, accepted the new message. One of the significant exceptions was King Bimbisara's son, the crown prince.

NINETEEN

KAPILAVATTHU WAS REJOICING with the news that the Buddha, son of the Sakyans, had attained perfect enlightenment and that his message had spread to every corner of the kingdoms of Magadha and Kasi, inspiring even the most powerful ruler of central India, King Bimbisara, to embrace his teachings. The pride of the Sakyans swelled like the tide during full moon. Yet everyone was disappointed that Buddha had not yet visited his own country. Suddhodana became aware of the feelings of his people. He too wanted to see his son. So he sent Kaludayi, a son of one of his ministers, to Rajagaha with an invitation to the Buddha to visit Kapilavatthu.

Kaludayi, enthralled by what went on in the Bamboo Grove in Rajagaha, almost forgot the purpose for which he had come there. He was amazed at the large gathering of monks living with Buddha, the unending stream of people, ascetics as well as householders, who visited him at every time of the day. He was proud of his Sakya lineage. But on seeing how even such powerful kings as Bimbisara came to pay his respects almost everyday, Kaludayi felt a sense of humility that he had never before experienced. He did not have the courage to go before the Buddha, though he was closely associated with Buddha's family and had had personal acquaintance with Buddha before his renunciation.

Finally, one day, when the Buddha was returning to his small cottage in the Bamboo Grove after delivering a sermon to the monks, he recognized Kaludayi seated at the edge of the crowd and stopped. Kaludayi knew that the Buddha had recognized him. Therefore, he walked up to him, paid homage and remained silent. Buddha questioned Kaludayi:

"What has brought you to Rajagaha, Kaludayi? Are you accompanying your father on an official visit or have you decided to leave the household life and join the congregation of monks?"

"Sir, I was sent by your father to invite you to visit Kapilavatthu. Your family as well as all the Sakyans are eagerly awaiting your visit. This indeed is the proper time to go there."

"Kaludayi, it is too early to set out for Kapilavatthu. Let us stay here until the end of the rains. After that we can all go together. What news do you bring from Kapilavatthu? How is your family? Are my parents well? How did Yasodhara take my renunciation and how is little Rahula?"

"Sir, my parents are well and so are yours. Yasodhara and Rahula are doing well. Your father's love and affection have been a great source of comfort for Yasodhara since you left.

124

Rahula is growing up to be a very handsome boy. He asks about you every now and then."

"I am pleased that my renunciation has not affected Yasodhara and Rahula as much as I thought it would. After all, Kaludayi, we are born into this world alone. It is true that our parents are partly responsible for our being here and therefore have an obligation to provide us with protection and care. But how long do you think it can go on? Moreover, too much protection can be harmful to us. It makes us heavily dependent on others and destroys our ability to deal with problems in life when we confront them. Eventually one has to take care of oneself. Nobody, not even Brahma, the so-called creator, can help us attain perfection and salvation. One is one's own master. Who else can occupy that position?"

"No one else, Sir," replied Kaludayi. What the Buddha said was food for thought for Kaludayi. He reflected on the false sense of security he had enjoyed all this time as the son of Suddhodana's minister. Here was Siddhartha, Suddhodana's own son, speaking about loneliness and the need for working out one's own salvation. With that change in perspective, Kaludayi listened to many a discourse delivered by Buddha during the next few days and became convinced of the truth and relevance of his message. Following the instructions of Buddha, Kaludayi exerted himself and emerged victorious in the elimination of the three roots of evil—lust, hate and confusion. He thus became the first Sakyan to be enlightened following the Buddha.

At the end of the rainy season, Buddha summoned a gathering of disciples and announced his wish to leave for Kapilavatthu along with them. Arahant Kaludayi went ahead in order to inform King Suddhodana of the Buddha's arrival. When Kaludayi arrived at Suddhodana's palace, the king failed to recognize him.

"Your face is familiar to me. Yet I am unable to recognize you. You are not an ordinary ascetic. Pray, tell me who are you?"

"O King, I am Kaludayi whom you sent to Rajagaha to invite your son here. Now I am a son of your son and, therefore, your grandson. Under the peerless Buddha, I myself have gone forth and attained freedom from suffering. Your noble son is on his way to Kapilavatthu and will arrive here soon with a large congregation of monks."

Suddhodana went prostrate before Kaludayi. He was expecting to see his son first. In his imagination he had created a portrait of what his son would look like. Now he was seeing a real portrait of his son through Kaludayi. He was delighted. He paid homage to Kaludayi and immediately made arrangements for him to stay at Nigrodha's Park until the arrival of Buddha and his disciples.

Wandering by stages, Buddha arrived in Kapilavatthu and was met by Suddhodana and a large gathering of Sakyans. Suddhodana was unable to control his emotions. Having walked up to the Buddha, he knelt down and touching his son's feet, shed tears of joy. Seeing their king paying homage to his own son, the assembled Sakyans overcame their pride and arrogance and followed Suddhodana in paying homage to Buddha. Suddhodana conducted Buddha and his disciples to Nigrodha's Park and, in his excitement, failed to make any arrangements for meals that day. When he returned to the palace, he was met by his excited daughter-in-law, who questioned him:

"How is Siddhartha? Has he changed much?"

"He is no more the Siddhartha who was uneasy and unhappy about what went on around him. He is not the same excitable and intolerant person. He is calm, composed and confident. His face is bright and radiant and he seems to have made a marvelous recovery after his strenuous ascetic practices," replied Suddhodana.

Yasodhara was not ready to visit the Buddha. She was frightened of an encounter with her husband from whom she had been separated for almost a decade. She could not visualize what her emotions would be, nor could she imagine what his responses would be. She felt uncomfortable at the thought of visiting him while he was surrounded by his disciples. It was going to be a dreadful experience. She decided to wait until he came to the palace.

That day Kapilavatthu witnessed the most unusual spectacle. Buddha and his disciples, draped in yellow robes, entered the city and moved from house to house, in restrained gait, in order to collect alms. Yasodhara was on the balcony of the palace, buried in her thoughts about Siddhartha, when from a distance she saw Buddha and his disciples going on their alms round. She hurried up to Suddhodana and informed him of what she had seen. Suddhodana became agitated. He realized that no provision was made for Buddha and his disciples to have their meals during the time they were staying in Nigrodha's Park. He rushed to the city, met Buddha and said:

"Sir, the kshatriyas have never gone out begging for food. They have preferred starvation to begging. You are disgracing the kshatriya lineage."

"O King, that kshatriya lineage is yours, not mine. I renounced that lineage long ago. I have nothing to do with that any more. The pride of a kshatriya is no longer with me. Not having such pride, I disgrace none. Mine is a lineage that knows no pride. Brahman, kshatriya, vaishya and shudra—these are distinctions that brahmans themselves make. I am not a slave of brahmans. I am a *buddha*. As all rivers such as Yamuna, Ganga, and Aciravati lose their different designations upon reaching the great ocean, so do all clans and castes abandon their distinctions upon joining the congregation of monks."

King Suddhodana realized the weakness of his own argument and made no attempt to prevent the Buddha and his disciples continuing with their alms round. Instead he invited them to the palace for meals on the following day and departed.

When Buddha arrived at the palace with his disciples on the appointed day to receive the midday meals, Suddhodana, Gotami, Nanda and Rahula were present to receive him. Rahula was confused. He had heard from his mother that his father had left the household life to be an ascetic. Upon seeing the Buddha in his yellow robe, he thought to himself:

"Why did my father adopt this form of life? He had all the comforts in life. Why should he be wearing a yellow robe and going around with a bowl in hand begging for food?"

Though Rahula had attained the same age at which his father had questioned Suddhodana about the meaning and significance of Vedic rituals on the occasion of the festival connected with the first sowing of grain, Rahula had not reached that maturity and independence of thought. All this time his grandfather had played the role of father to him. Now he had found his father. But he regretted his inability to be close to him. He realized that there was a great distance between them. His father did not come out and embrace him. Nor could he go and embrace his father. For him, this agony and suffering seemed unnecessary. It could have been avoided if his father had remained a father to him. Life would have been much more satisfying for him.

After taking the seat prepared for him and when all his disciples had settled down, Buddha noticed that Yasodhara was not present. He looked at Rahula with compassion. Rahula, who was all this time watching his father, immediately took his eyes away from his father and stared at the ground.

It was necessary for the Buddha to dispel doubts in the minds of those assembled regarding the relative value of his life as Siddhartha and his present state as *buddha*. He also realized the confusion in the mind of his son, Rahula. Therefore, at the end of the meal, he delivered a discourse on the three characteristics of existence. Questioning his father who was leading the congregation of Sakyans, he asked:

"O King, what do you think of all the wealth and prosperity that you as king are enjoying? Are they permanent or impermanent?"

Suddhodana thought for a moment and replied:

"Impermanent, Sir."

"In this world of impermanence and change, man seeks for permanent happiness and satisfaction. Do you think, O King, that man can achieve such happiness and satisfaction?"

The king was confused. He questioned the Buddha:

"But, Sir, didn't you yourself leave the household life, a life of comfort and pleasure, in order to attain happiness, in order to attain an immortal state? Have you not attained such happiness, such immortality?"

"I did leave the household life looking for permanent happiness, for immortality. But the happiness and immortality I have discovered is not what I was looking for."

Suddhodana was further confused. He asked:

"What is it that you have discovered?"

"I have discovered the nature of human life; I have discovered the reasons for man's unhappiness and I have found a way out of that unhappiness. And I have achieved immortality, not by eliminating death, but by eliminating the causes that lead to rebirth."

"Sir, for the benefit of all the Sakyans, through compassion for all the Sakyans, please explain what you have discovered," said Suddhodana.

"O King, there are these beings of the animal kingdom, those who are less developed than human beings. Their personalities are more rigid and less flexible. Therefore, when they face the world around them, they respond automatically. But in a human being the personality is more developed and therefore more subtle and flexible. When a man is faced with the world, he does not always respond automatically, without thinking. He makes decisions and these decisions enable him to survive, to organize his life in a world full of hazards. With these decisions he creates his own world. Within the world, which is characterized by change and impermanence, man tries to create his own world. He plans for the future. He craves for happiness and recoils from pain; he desires to extend his life and does not want to die. He accumulates more and more wealth in order to take care of his future. When he is wealthy, he seeks protection from others who have designs on his wealth. He wants protection from robbers, plunderers and those who live on others' sweat. He builds fortresses in order to protect himself. Within that fortress he sets up all the amenities for his pleasure, for his satisfaction. He constructs pleasure gardens, replete with pools and ponds, flower gardens and orchards. He sets up harems to entertain himself and employs musicians, singers and dancing girls. When he grows old, he looks for the best physicians to treat his aging body in order to extend its life span.

"This, O King, is a world created according to one's dispositions. In this way, each man creates for himself his own world according to his own abilities. Beginning with a man who occupies the lowest status in society such as a shudra and reaching up to the greatest monarchs like Mahasudassana, everyone creates his own world according to his dispositions.

"What do you think, O King, are all these things that are conditioned by one's dispositions permanent or impermanent?"

"They are impermanent, Sir."

"Is that which is impermanent satisfactory or unsatisfactory?"

"It would be unsatisfactory if one were to look for permanence in it."

"Is it proper to consider what is impermanent and unsatisfactory as substantial, as your permanent self, as something belonging to you permanently?"

"No, Sir."

"Is it proper to cling to this body, this family, this country as mine?"

"No, Sir."

"Just so, O King, without clinging, without grasping, having pacified all my dispositions, having eliminated all lust, hate and confusion, I have reached the end of suffering, of dissatisfaction. Like the lotus that grows in the muddy water, but which rises above the muddy water and remains unsmeared by it, so I was born in this world, but I have risen above the world and remain unsmeared by it. Just as the lotus, after remaining unsmeared by the water, will wither away, having provided great satisfaction for those who enjoy the beauty of nature, so will I, when my life span is exhausted, pass away after providing solace to those who are intelligent and wise, who seek freedom from suffering."

At the end of the sermon, King Suddhodana overcame his pride and became a "stream entrant," one who has embarked on the spiritual path, destined to be a saint in the future.

While all this was happening, Yasodhara had locked herself in her chamber without having courage to face her husband in public. Buddha rose from his seat and walked up to his father, who himself was on his feet by now. Knowing the difficulties Yasodhara had in seeing him in public, Buddha expressed his wish to see her in her chamber and requested that the king accompany him there. Leaving all his disciples behind, the Buddha, accompanied by his father, mother and son, Rahula, went upstairs. Suddhodana went ahead and reaching Yasodhara's chamber, knocked on her door. In a moment the door was opened and only Buddha with his ability to read the minds of others was able to see really what went on in Yasodhara's mind.

Yasodhara stepped aside after opening the door. Buddha entered the chamber and took a seat. Yasodhara felt as if light appeared in her chamber after years of gloom and darkness. She began to see life in every corner of the room, in every item of furniture and memento. During all these years they had been like dead items to her. She could not control her emotions. The memory of the few years that she spent with Siddhartha unfolded before her mind like a rapidly moving dream experience. Their first meeting at the music festival, Siddhartha visiting her at home, the pungent remarks of jovial Rohini, their marriage and Siddhartha's love and affection during her pregnancy—all these memories came back to her with such emotional force that she fell prostrate before the Buddha, held his feet with both hands and cried until she had expended all her energy and with that all her sorrows.

Buddha remained calm and composed during these moments, realizing that once Yasodhara had the opportunity to cry her heart out, she would return to her normal self. He watched her with compassion. Finally, Yasodhara stopped crying, raised her head and looked at the Buddha. She saw compassion written all over his face. She felt guilty for letting her emotions overwhelm her. A cold shudder ran through her spine. She bent down again, placed her hands and forehead on his feet, paid homage to him and immediately retreated.

Suddhodana, Gotami and Rahula, who witnessed the emotion-charged incident, stood motionless like statues. The tears rolling down their cheeks were the only signs of life in them.

Suddhodana was the first to break the silence.

"Sir, during the years you were gone, Yasodhara lived an ascetic life. Abandoning all pleasures of sense, she confined herself to the palace and rarely went out. Her only source of enjoyment was the sight of Rahula growing up."

"Pleasures of sense, O King, can bring satisfaction, but it does not take long for this satisfaction to turn into dissatisfaction. Dissatisfaction is the inevitable result of grasping or clinging onto things that provide satisfaction. Living the life

131

of a householder one can be satisfied and happy by reducing one's attachment to the things of the world."

Looking at his former wife, Buddha remarked:

"Yasodhara, you had the courage and strength of character to let me leave the household life. With that same courage and strength, you should be able to make your life happy without brooding over the past and longing for the future."

Having uttered these few words, Buddha rose from his seat. Suddhodana, Gotami, Yasodhara and Rahula, each stepped before the Buddha and paid him their respects, whereupon the Buddha walked downstairs and joined his disciples in the main room of the palace.

Buddha's stepbrother, Nanda, was standing with Buddha's bowl in hand when he came downstairs. Without accepting the bowl from Nanda, Buddha walked back to Nigrodha's Park with his disciples. Nanda did not have the courage to return the bowl to Buddha and he walked along with the monks to the park. As Nanda was leaving the palace grounds, his bride-to-be came near him and whispered in his ear:

"Nanda, please come back."

Nanda failed to realize the fear in his bride-to-be until he arrived in Nigrodha's Park. On reaching there, Nanda walked up to the Buddha in the hope of returning the bowl.

Buddha reflected:

"Nanda is a person of weak character. I have seen him grow up from the time he was an infant. He is very much given to pleasures of sense and has little concern for those who serve in the royal household. A self-centered person like Nanda can bring untold suffering to the people if he were to succeed my father as king of the Sakyans. Maybe I should persuade him to leave the household life."

"Nanda," he addressed his stepbrother, "don't you think that someone from the royal household should join the order of monks?"

Nanda stared at the ground. His brother's request came without any prior warnings. He had no time to think of the implications. Out of reverence, rather than inclination, Nanda nodded his agreement.

TWENTY

NANDA'S JOINING THE ORDER OF MONKS caused consternation in the royal household. Although Suddhodana had difficulty understanding the reasons for Buddha's decision to retain Nanda and what prompted Nanda himself to join the order, he remained calm and composed and did not go before the Buddha to question him regarding this matter. Moreover, Nanda was a grown-up man and Suddhodana was not willing to impose his will on him, after the experience he had had with Siddhartha.

The one who was most confused about Nanda's renunciation was Rahula. He went to his mother and questioned:

"Mother, why did uncle Nanda join my father as an ascetic?"

"Your uncle was probably looking for his inheritance from his brother. Perhaps one day you too will look for such inheritance," replied Yasodhara, realizing that the peace and happiness that Siddhartha had won for himself would eventually be shared by everyone in the royal household.

Rahula reflected on his mother's explanation. He thought:

"My father left all the wealth and happiness associated with royalty to look for something better. Now my uncle, Nanda, has done the same thing. I too have a claim to that inheritance."

He expressed his desire to see his father again. Although Suddhodana was not very pleased about Nanda's renunciation, he did not suspect that little Rahula too would join his father. Rahula was too young to be an ascetic. He assumed that Rahula's desire to see his father for the second time was a very natural one. So he let Rahula visit the Buddha at Nigrodha's Park and assigned one of the palace guards to accompany him.

Rahula's visit to Nigrodha's Park accompanied only by a guard of the royal palace surprised many a monk, including Nanda. Under normal circumstances he would have visited Buddha in the company of Suddhodana or Yasodhara. When Rahula walked up to the Buddha unannounced, Buddha thought that Rahula merely wanted to see him and did not expect him to make the kind of request he made.

Upon reaching the Buddha, Rahula said:

"Sir, uncle Nanda has become the recipient of your inheritance. I too have a right to a part of that inheritance. I have come looking for that inheritance."

Buddha smiled. He was not ready to turn Rahula away saying:

"Ascetics like me have no inheritance that is passed on from father to son."

He reflected for a moment.

"Rahula is surely going to inherit the Sakyan kingdom, now that Nanda has joined the order of monks. But what kind of inheritance is he expecting to receive from me? Perhaps he knows that I have nothing to offer in terms of material wealth. Yet, he probably can succeed in attaining the greatest wealth that man can achieve, and that is happiness. It would therefore be wrong on my part to turn him away."

So reflecting, he called Sariputta and asked him to admit Rahula as a novice. Sariputta led Rahula away and having shaved his hair, put a yellow robe on him.

The stunned royal guard could not make any protest. He hurried back to the palace and informed Suddhodana about the incident. Suddhodana could not believe what he heard. First it was Siddhartha, then Nanda and now Rahula. Although he lost his pride when he first listened to the Buddha's sermon, Suddhodana's great delight in seeing the Buddha as an enlightened one was now gradually turning out to be a sort of nightmare. There was not going to be any one person of royal lineage to succeed him as the king of the Sakyans. He hurried up to the Buddha and pleaded that henceforth he should not admit any child into the order without the permission of the parents. Buddha agreed. But it was not necessary to revoke his decision to admit Rahula to the order, for he was the father of Rahula.

The news about the ordination of Nanda and Rahula and Suddhodana's displeasure about it did not take much time to spread among the Sakyans. Their great rejoicing gradually turned into fear as to which family was going to lose a husband or a son next. Asceticism was not something that was popular among the Sakyans. Having realized what the feelings of the Sakyans were, Buddha decided that it was not appropriate for him to remain in Kapilavatthu any longer.

Yasodhara's father, Mahanama, heard that the Buddha was getting ready to leave Kapilavatthu. Siddhartha's leaving his daughter and adopting an ascetic way of life angered Mahanama. But he was consoled by Suddhodana's treatment of his daughter and grandson. Being a liberal in his attitude, Mahanama was now in a position to appreciate his son-in-law's ideas, better than anybody else in Kapilavatthu. So he hurried to Nigrodha's Park and after paying obeisance to the Buddha, questioned:

"Sir, I heard that the monks are preparing a robe for the Blessed One and that soon the Blessed One will be leaving Kapilavatthu. What, Sir, would be the best form of conduct for us who live the life of a householder without being able to leave it?"

Buddha had mixed feelings about the behavior of the Sakyans. They were delighted by the Buddha's success in Magadha and Kasi. It was their pride that made them so elated by his success. When they were themselves confronted by the Buddha, they had different attitudes. They really did not want Buddha's message, although they wanted to revel in his success elsewhere. Mahanama's question provided him with an opportunity to say something relevant to the Sakyans. He addressed Mahanama:

"A believer, Mahanama, has confidence, and is not one without confidence. A believer is one who puts forth effort, not one who is lazy. A believer is one who sets up mindfulness, not one who is confused. A believer is one who has

135

concentration, not one who is unconcentrated. A believer is one who is wise, not one who is ignorant. What do you think, Mahanama? Can one possessed of confidence, effort, mindfulness, concentration and wisdom be a blind believer?"

"No, Sir," replied Mahanama.

"Mahanama, confidence, effort, mindfulness, concentration and wisdom are the five pillars upon which a successful and happy life can be built. Without these, man cannot lead a well-coordinated life. Without them his life would be uneven, rugged, and unsuccessful, and above all, unhappy."

"Sir, how can one who is ignorant come to possess confidence, effort, mindfulness, concentration and wisdom?" questioned Mahanama.

"I understand, Mahanama, that it is difficult for a beginner to attain perfection regarding these five things all of a sudden. It is through a gradual process, a gradual path, gradual practice that he can reach perfection in these matters. There are two conditions of right knowledge: outside information and reflection according to the way things arise."

"Sir, whom should I listen to and how should I reflect?" asked Mahanama.

"First, Mahanama, you should listen to an enlightened one and reflect about him thus: 'Is he a perfectly enlightened one, a worthy one, endowed with both knowledge and conduct, well behaved, able to influence others not by trickery or by psychic power or by claiming to know some mysterious truth about the world, but by the compatibility of his behavior with what he claims to know? When, Mahanama, a person reflects on the enlightened one thus and observes that he is such, his mind is not overwhelmed by lust, by hate and by confusion. His attitude toward the enlightened one becomes straightforward. As a result of his straightforwardness, he is able to understand the meaning and purpose of the teachings of the enlightened one. Such understanding leads to excitement. Excitement produces joy. A joyful mind induces a calmness of body. When the body is calmed, he experiences happiness. A happy person's mind is easily concentrated. Such, Mahanama, is a noble disciple who leads a unified life among those whose lives are diffused, a life of friendliness among those who are full of hate.

"Secondly, you should listen to his doctrine and reflect thus: 'Is this doctrine clearly stated, empirical, not confined to any particular time—verifiable, goal directed, and to be realized individually by the wise?' When, Mahanama, a person reflects thus and observes that it is such, he enjoys all the benefits mentioned earlier.

"Thirdly, you should reflect on the congregation of disciples thus: 'Are the disciples of the enlightened one well behaved, straightforward, endowed with proper conduct? Are they worthy of respect and support? Do they constitute an incomparable source of moral and spiritual inspiration for the world?' When a person reflects thus and observes that they are such, he enjoys all the benefits mentioned earlier.

"Fourthly, you should reflect on your own moral standing thus: 'Is my moral behavior unbroken, without defect, spotless, unblemished, unrestricted, commended by the wise, non-dogmatic and conducive to concentration?' When a person reflects thus and observes that it is such, he enjoys all those benefits mentioned earlier.

"Fifthly, you should reflect on your liberality thus: 'Is my life dominated by avarice, which is the most important cause of the hellish life man creates for himself and others in the world? Do I live restrained regarding my needs? Am I willing to share whatever wealth I have?' When a person reflects thus and observes that he is such, he reaps all those benefits mentioned earlier.

"Finally, Mahanama, you should reflect upon the divine beings thus: 'Whatever divine beings there are, all of them have been born in such heavenly states because they were endowed with such confidence, such morals, such learning, such generosity and such wisdom. Am I possessed of such confidence, morals, learning, generosity and wisdom?' When a person reflects thus and observes that he is such, once again he enjoys all the benefits mentioned above.

"With such reflection, Mahanama, an ordinary man can gradually reach such understanding that he will be able to live a well-coordinated life, making himself as well as others happy in this world."

Mahanama was delighted by the Buddha's discourse. He wanted to question the Buddha about various other matters pertaining to a life of a householder. But looking around, he saw someone else, whom he could not afford to ignore, waiting to see Buddha. So he paid his respects and stepped aside.

Gotami, Buddha's stepmother, approached him holding in her hands a pair of robes neatly wrapped. Addressing Buddha, she said:

"Sir, I learned that the monks are busy preparing a robe for the Blessed One and that the Blessed One plans to leave Kapilavatthu as soon as the robe making is over. This new pair of robes, made of cloth woven by me with thread spun by my own hands was specially prepared for the Blessed One after he left the household life. May the Blessed One accept this pair of robes out of compassion for me."

"Mother, please give the robes to the congregation of monks. When you offer them to the congregation, you will have served both myself and the congregation."

Gotami made her request thrice and all three times Buddha replied the same way. Mahanama, who was standing by realized the reason for Buddha's reluctance to accept the robes for himself. He pleaded with Buddha.

"Sir, please accept the pair of robes presented by Mahapajapati Gotami. Gotami is the Blessed One's maternal aunt who became foster mother upon the Blessed One's mother's death. She nursed and fed the Blessed One during the early years. The Blessed One too had been of great help to her. She took refuge in the Buddha, in the doctrine and in the congregation. Because of the Blessed One she has undertaken to observe the five precepts consisting of not taking life, not misappropriating things, avoiding wrong behavior regarding pleasures of sense, not lying and remaining aloof from states of indolence consequent upon taking intoxicants. She has come to have perfect faith in the Buddha, in the doctrine and in the congregation of monks. She does not entertain any doubts regarding the Buddha's teachings. This offer of a pair of robes is a mere token of that mutual help, mutual assistance."

Buddha's refusal to accept the robes for himself was prompted by his desire to make his followers as well as the benefactors realize that he did not favor the practice of having private property. But Mahanama's comments were sufficient to convince both Gotami and the disciples who were present that her offer of robes would not be looked upon as a special favor bestowed on Buddha. Therefore, he accepted the robes and explained to Gotami the purity of offerings.

"There are four kinds of offerings whose purity and impurity are determined by the donor and the recipient. There is an offering that is made pure by the donor, not by the recipient; an offering made pure by the recipient, not by the donor; an offering that is purified neither by the donor nor by the recipient; and an offering purified both by the donor as well as by the recipient.

"When a donor is a good person and of friendly disposition, and the recipient is a bad person of evil disposition, the purity of the offering is dependent upon the donor, not upon the recipient. When the donor is a bad person with evil dispositions and the recipient is a good person with friendly dispositions, the purity of the offering is dependent on the recipient, and not upon the donor. When the donor as well as the recipient are bad persons, the offering is an impure one. But when both donor and recipient are good persons with friendly dispositions, the offering is made pure by both. Best results are achieved by offerings made pure by both."

Being pleased and gladdened by the Buddha's discourse, both Gotami and Mahanama paid obeisance to Buddha and left. Within a few days, the monks completed the robe making and Buddha left Kapilavatthu headed for Rajagaha.

TWENTY-ONE

YOUNG MEN OF THE KSHATRIYA CLAN who were enthusiastic about joining the band of Buddha's disciples and who were prevented from doing so by their parents were disappointed by Buddha's sudden departure from Kapilavatthu. Among them were Bhaddiya, Anuruddha, Ananda, Bhagu, Kimbila and Devadatta, some of whom were Siddhartha's childhood acquaintances. They were waiting for an opportunity to become part of the new Sakyan tradition, but were frustrated by the Buddha's decision.

They set out from Kapilavatthu leading a four constituent army consisting of elephants, chariots, cavalry and infantry as though moving to the parade grounds. Upon reaching the border, they dismissed the army and, accompanied by a barber named Upali, made their way towards Savatthi. Taking off their insignia and bundling them together, they told Upali:

"Upali, you had better go back. There is enough wealth here for the rest of your life."

On his way back, Upali thought:

"These Sakyans are fierce. They will be angry with me for helping the princes to get away and may even put me to death. These Sakyan princes, who are wealthy and have all the comforts in life, are leaving the household life. How about me? I have nothing but to gain in life by joining the noble Buddha. His lineage is open not only to brahmans and kshatriyas but to everyone. He recognizes no distinctions of caste or creed."

He opened the bundle and hung the valuables on a tree,

saying to himself, "Let him who sees these take them as given." And he went back to the Sakyan princes.

Seeing him returning, they asked him, "Why have you returned?"

"I could not go back to Kapilavatthu. Other members of the army would inform your parents that I have helped you to get out of the country, and they surely would punish me. And so I have come back."

"What do you propose to do?" asked Devadatta.

"With your permission, I will go to see the Buddha, and if he allows me, I too shall go forth."

"You did well not to go home," said Ananda. "The Sakyans are fierce and your life would have been in danger if they came to know that you were instrumental in our leaving Kapilavatthu. Let us all go together and see the Buddha."

They found the Buddha in a place called Anupiya, on the route to Rajagaha. The Buddha was pleased to see the Sakyan princes, who were accompanied by Upali, the barber. They had rid themselves of their princely garments, and so Buddha realized that they had followed him with the intention of joining the congregation. After they paid homage to Buddha, Ananda spoke:

"Sir, we were looking for an opportunity to join the congregation of monks. But the Blessed One left Kapilavatthu too soon. We got out of Kapilavatthu with the help of Upali. We beg of the Blessed One to admit us into the order. It would be appropriate to admit Upali first. Thereby, he will be our senior and we will have to pay our respects to him. By doing so, we will be able to get rid of the Sakyan pride in us."

Buddha was pleased with the attitude of the Sakyan princes. He understood their keenness to overcome their pride and be part of the congregation where status in society did not matter. Buddha considered respecting the seniors to be a good thing. He remembered a story he had learnt from his stepmother when he was a boy, and she was trying to inculcate in him respect for elders in the family. He addressed the Sakyan princes:

"Respecting the seniors is a very good practice. It prevents strife and promotes harmony among people. I remember an

141

old story about three companions who lived somewhere in the Himalayas. They were a partridge, a monkey and an elephant. They lived under the same banyan tree and were very rude and disrespectful and lived without any consideration for one another. They thought: 'If only we could find out which of us is the oldest. Then we could honor, respect, revere and venerate him, and follow his advice.' The partridge and the monkey asked the elephant:

" 'How far back can you remember?'

" 'When I was a calf, I used to walk over this banyan tree so that it passed between my legs and its topmost branch scratched my stomach.'

"Then the partridge and the elephant asked the monkey:

" 'How far back can you remember?'

" 'When I was a baby, I used to sit on the ground and nibble the topmost shoots of this banyan tree,' replied the monkey.

"Finally the monkey and the elephant asked the partridge: 'How far back can you remember?'

" 'In a certain place there was a big banyan tree. I ate one of its seeds and voided it in this place, and this banyan tree grew out of that seed.'

"The monkey and the elephant said to the partridge:

" 'You are older than us. We will honor, respect, revere and venerate you. We will follow your advice.'

"And they lived in harmony thereafter."

From the smiles that appeared on their faces, it was evident that everyone enjoyed the irony. Buddha himself smilingly asked Ananda:

"What do you think, Ananda? Is it proper to ignore a warrior, a serpent or a fire, primarily because they are young and insignificant?"

Ananda thought for a moment and replied:

"No, Sir, it is not proper."

"Why?" asked Buddha.

Ananda had difficulty in answering the question. Though he knew why a snake or a fire should not be ignored on the grounds that they are young and small, he wondered about a young warrior. Buddha himself provided the answer.

"Ananda, one should not condemn or despise a young warrior, on the grounds that he is young. Perhaps this youthful warrior may attain despotic powers and become vindictive. One may be visited by royal vengeance. Even so with a young snake or a small fire. Everything being equal, seniority will be the best criterion to decide who is worthy of respect. But seniority alone does not make one worthy of respect. A person, endowed with moral behavior, concentration and wisdom is worthy of respect, whether he be senior or junior, whether he comes from a high caste or a low caste, whether he is rich or poor."

"That, indeed, is true, Sir," replied Ananda.

The six princes, along with Upali, joined the band of monks and spent most of their time receiving instruction from the Buddha and practicing the holy life. The first to attain enlightenment was Upali, who had developed great faith and confidence in the Buddha. For Bhaddiya, nurtured in comfort and luxury and all the time surrounded by guards and chaperones, this new life devoid of fear and anxiety, suspicion or worry, was such a contrast that he adopted more of the ascetic practices such as living in the forest, surviving only on alms collected by begging and wearing robes made of rags. This fascination with the carefree life prevented him from attaining the goal sooner. But when such fascination gradually wore out, Bhaddiya was able to destroy the bonds of existence and attain freedom. Anuruddha, Bhagu and Kimbila followed Bhaddiya in attaining enlightenment.

Devadatta and Ananda remained disciples without attaining enlightenment. Devadatta saw how the Buddha was respected by everyone around him. Though he liked Buddha very much and had been a childhood companion and also a cousin of Buddha, a deep-seated feeling of jealousy prevented him from concentrating his mind on his own freedom and salvation. Ananda's problem was different. He was so enamored with the Buddha's teaching that, instead of following the Buddha's instructions and attaining freedom from suffering, he continued to remain close to the Buddha so that he could listen to his discourses more often. Therefore, he followed Buddha wherever he went.

When Buddha returned to Rajagaha, he was received with

great enthusiasm and respect by the king of Magadha as well as by the people. During the Buddha's absence, many others joined the order of monks under the tutelage of the disciples whom he had left behind. Magadha was rapidly coming under the influence of the Buddha's message. Many leading brahman teachers were becoming more and more anxious about the fate of their own doctrines in the face of Buddha's teaching that was sweeping across the country.

One such teacher was a brahman named Janussoni. He, like many of his predecessors and contemporaries, was looking for a solution to the problem regarding the essence of everything. It was a question that perplexed many a teacher, and Janussoni decided to find out how the Buddha would deal with this question. Visiting Buddha who was living in the Bamboo Grove in Rajagaha and exchanging greetings, Janussoni asked:

"Friend, some ascetics and brahmans speak of everything. What is your view of everything?"

Buddha reflected upon his discussions with his friends Kapila, Nalaka and others before his enlightenment, and realized how they tried to explain the essence of everything in terms of some substance like primordial matter or eternal self. He knew that these were very speculative views and that Janussoni, the philosopher, was trying to drag him into the web of metaphysical speculation out of which there was no easy escape. Therefore he was very direct with his answer.

"Friend, for me everything consists of the sense organs and their objects—eye and form, ear and sound, nose and smell, tongue and taste, body and tangibility, mind and concepts. Apart from what I can see, hear, smell, taste, touch and conceive of on the basis of such experiences, I am not able to speak of everything."

"What if someone were to say that it is possible to know and see without depending upon eye, ear, nose, tongue and body?" asked Janussoni.

"It is possible for someone to maintain that there can be knowing and seeing independent of the five senses or even the six senses—that a special form of seeing is available where there is no duality of subject and object. I, for my part, have not developed such capacity to know and see. Therefore, I am unable to subscribe to any of their views about the essence of everything. For me, such essences are beyond experience."

"But, friend, these ascetics and brahmans claim that this special way of knowing and seeing is developed by those who have reached the highest state of meditation, of yoga," maintained Janussoni.

"Janussoni, I have reached the highest state of the pacification of mind through concentration, even to the extent of the cessation of all perceptions and whatever is felt, but I have not known or seen any such reality that could be considered the essence of everything. In fact, when I reach such a state of cessation, I do not have any knowledge whatsoever. It is possible for someone to claim that there is such knowledge and seeing, and it is possible for someone to deny that there is such knowledge and seeing. Not having such knowledge and seeing, I cannot assert it. Not knowing whether such knowledge and seeing exist or not, I cannot deny it. In these matters I prefer to remain silent. Remaining silent, I do not come into conflict with the world, although the world may want to conflict with me."

Janussoni did not want to argue with the Buddha; he realized he was not going to get any further answers from him. Therefore, after paying him his respects, Janussoni left the Bamboo Grove.

A disciple of Buddha named Kaccayana, who had been listening to the conversation between Buddha and Janussoni, approached Buddha and questioned:

"Sir, I understand the reason the Blessed One gave to Janussoni for leaving questions regarding 'everything' unanswered. What, Sir, would be a proper view?"

"People in this world, Kaccayana, are engrossed with two views: existence and nonexistence. Before asserting or denying either one of them, one must carefully analyze their meaning and implications. Existence may be understood in several ways. First, it can refer to something that is given in experience. Secondly, it can mean existence itself. Thirdly, it can mean the existence of a substance or essence. What do you think, Kaccayana, are these meanings identical or are they different?"

145

"They are different, Sir," replied Kaccayana.

"Can you give an example to illustrate the first use of the term existence?"

"Yes, Sir," replied Kaccayana. "When we say the eye exists, the object of the eye exists, then we use the term existence to refer to something given in our experience, that is to say, the existence of the eye, the existence of the object of the eye."

"Can you give an example to illustrate the second use of the term existence?" asked the Buddha.

"It is difficult, Sir," replied Kaccayana.

"It is indeed difficult, Kaccayana. What the philosophers do in this case is to abstract existence from the thing about which existence is predicated. They assume that the abstract noun 'exist-ence' implies a reality that is prior or superior to what is expressed by the verb 'exists.' Kaccayana, do you think you can separate existence from a thing?"

"No, Sir. Existence cannot be spoken of independent of a thing that exists."

"Does it mean that since we cannot separate existence from a thing and since existence itself cannot be spoken of, that one should give up talking about a thing as existing?"

"No, Sir. To say, 'This sphere or object exists,' makes perfect sense. But to say, 'This existence exists' makes no sense whatsoever."

"That's right, Kaccayana. This is why one of the earlier sages of the Vedic tradition known to us as Prajapati Paramestin refused to assert either that 'existence exists' or that 'existence does not exist.' I understand that in spite of Paramestin's refusal to assert any one of these two alternatives, one of the more recent sages, Uddalaka Aruni, insisted that 'existence exists.' Unfortunately, Paramestin himself fell into the trap that he was at first trying to avoid. Therefore, he suggested the idea that 'water' may have been the source of everything in this world. He suspected that water was the essence of everything. Thus he avoided the second but recognized the third meaning of the term existence I mentioned earlier."

"But, aren't these two latter meanings related?" asked Kaccayana.

"Yes, they are," replied the Buddha. "When one believes in existence in an abstract sense, it is not very different from the view that says, 'Everything exists,' for both these views lead to the belief in permanence or eternality. When one believes in nonexistence in an abstract sense, it is not much different from the view that holds, 'Everything does not exist,' for both these lead to the belief in annihilation."

"Without falling into these two extremes," continued Buddha, "I speak of things as arising, as changing once they have come to be and as passing away. When one perceives the arising of things in the world, it would be wrong for him to believe in nonexistence. When one perceives the cessation or passing away of things in the world, it would be wrong for him to believe in a theory of existence. Arising of things in the world defeats the belief in absolute nonexistence and passing away of things in the world defeats the belief in permanent existence. The doctrine of the dependent arising of the world represents a middle position between these two extremes. This, Kaccayana, I perceive as the proper view."

One of the disciples in the audience raised the question:

"Sir, how do we get to know dependent arising? What is our source of knowledge?"

"Monks, there are these two kinds of knowledge—knowledge of things through acquaintance and inferential knowledge. Acquaintance provides us with knowledge of things as they arise, of change in things as they have come to exist and of their cessation. When something arises, we see it as arising with the help of other things, conditioned by other things, supported by other things. Whatever change there is in things that have come to be, we see that as being conditioned and supported by other things. Similarly with cessation. This is knowledge of phenomena or knowledge by acquaintance. Whether Buddhas arise in this world or not, this pattern of things, this causal orderliness, this dependence remains. On the basis of such knowledge and such acquaintance, we make inferences regarding the dim past and the future."

"Therefore, monks, dependent arising cannot be separated from the things that are dependently arisen. When one speaks of dependent arising, one should not give the impression that

147

it can be abstracted from the things that are dependently arisen. If one were to do so, dependent arising would not be different from either existence in the abstract sense or existence as implying essence. My advice to Kaccayana would then be contradicted."

Even if the monks had any further questions to ask, they could not do so, for they noticed the arrival of a person of some distinction, accompanied by a large retinue of men and women.

TWENTY-TWO

A RICH MERCHANT OF SAVATTHI named Sudatta, but better known among the people as Anathapindika, "feeder of poor," was in Rajagaha at this time on business. Staying with his brother-in-law, who was himself a rich merchant in Rajagaha, Anathapindika came to know of the Buddha. Upon hearing about the Buddha's reputation, Anathapindika went to the Bamboo Grove and found Buddha involved in a conversation with his disciples. Realizing that his arrival interrupted the conversation, Anathapindika was embarrassed and remorseful. Buddha noticed Anathapindika's discomfort and decided to make him comfortable.

"You have come at an appropriate moment, Sudatta. I have just concluded a very important discussion with my disciples."

Anathapindika was at ease realizing that he had actually not interrupted the discussion. But he was surprised that the Buddha knew his name, which was not known to very many people. He prostrated himself at the feet of the Buddha and said:

"I trust the Blessed One is well. Is there any way I can be of service to the Blessed One and his disciples?"

Buddha realized that Anathapindika meant well when he asked this question.

"Yes, Sudatta, I live well. One who has attained freedom from sense desires, and has no clinging for existence, has no conflicts at heart, has no frustrations. He sleeps well, awakes well, goes about doing what he has to do well. He always lives well."

Buddha knew that when Anathapindika asked him whether he could be of any service to the Buddha and his disciples, he was merely thinking of material help. Therefore, Buddha insisted:

"Sudatta, the best way someone can be of service to me and my disciples is by adopting a life of moral rectitude. I have enunciated this noble eightfold path and one who follows that path not only helps himself, but also helps everyone around him."

Buddha went on to instruct Anathapindika on what he considered to be the best form of life for a householder.

"Householder, there are four kinds of happiness that a householder, enjoying pleasures of sense, may derive from time to time, from season to season."

Anathapindika was excited. He was under the impression that Buddha taught only a way to freedom from suffering which involved renunciation of the household life. But now he was getting a different impression. He questioned the Buddha:

"Sir, what are these four forms of happiness that a householder can achieve?"

"Sudatta, a householder who has come to possess wealth acquired by his own effort, by his own exertion, by his own sweat, by moral means, reflects on his wealth thus: I have acquired this wealth by my own effort, by moral means.' As a result of such reflection he derives great happiness, great satisfaction. This is happiness derived from having sufficient means.

"He experiences the second form of happiness when he enjoys that wealth in the company of those who have acquired

149

their wealth by similar means and also when he participates in meritorious deeds. This is happiness derived from enjoyment.

"Third is the happiness he derives by not being in debt. He reflects: 'I owe nothing to anyone,' and thereby enjoys the happiness of debtlessness.

"And, finally, a householder derives happiness by reflecting on his own blameless life: 'I am possessed of blameless behavior in body, speech and thought.' Thus he enjoys the happiness of blamelessness."

Anathapindika's happiness knew no bounds. He had come to know that the Buddha was perfectly enlightened and that his doctrine was completely new and original. He also had heard that for this very reason Buddha's teachings were disastrous for many a family. Either women lost their husbands or parents lost their sons, because they were leaving the household life to embrace the ascetic form of life under the Buddha. But allaying that fear that many had, Buddha was now conveying the message that even while living a life of sense pleasures, one could be happy and satisfied. This indeed was a middle path. There was no requirement that happiness was restricted to a life of asceticism. Therefore, he said:

"Sir, great indeed is the Blessed One's doctrine. Magnificent indeed is the Blessed One's teaching. From today onward, may the Blessed One receive me as his follower who has taken refuge in him. Sir, may the Blessed One visit Savatthi together with his disciples. Let the people of Savatthi, endowed with faith, be benefited by the teachings of the Blessed one."

Buddha accepted Anathapindika's request in silence. Realizing that the Buddha had no objection to visiting Savatthi, Anathapindika saluted Buddha, rose from his seat and departed. He had accumulated sufficient wealth, sufficient means, and therefore, there was no need to accumulate more, at least at this time. So he cut short his stay in Rajagaha and left for Savatthi. He pleaded with the people on the way:

"Friends, the enlightened one will come by this road. Clean up your gardens, renovate your lodgings, arrange gifts of food."

And those pious people did as he requested them. When Anathapindika arrived in Savatthi he looked around all over the city for a suitable place of retreat for the Buddha and his disciples until he saw a pleasure park belonging to a prince named Jeta. He went to Prince Jeta and offered to buy the park, but Jeta insisted on an excessive price for it. Anathapindika agreed to purchase it, but found that he did not have sufficient funds available. The Buddha's advice that a householder should lead a life of debtlessness prevented him from borrowing money from his friends. Buddha would be arriving in Savatthi any time. He had to have lodgings ready by the time he reached Savatthi. Anathapindika was depressed.

The news reached Jeta that Anathapindika was purchasing the park merely for the use of the Buddha and his disciples and that he was depressed because of his inability to raise all the money he needed to purchase it. Prince Jeta felt remorseful in being so business-like in this matter. He therefore sent word to Anathapindika indicating that he may have the park free if it was for the use of the Buddha and his disciples. Anathapindika was delighted. He hurried up to Jeta's residence with all the money he had. Addressing Jeta, he said:

"O Prince, I do not wish to accept the park free. Although I do not have all the money, I do want to pay for the purchase of the park."

"Alright, Sudatta. You may have the park for half the price I quoted. The other half will be my gift to Buddha and his disciples. Whatever money you have left can be used for the construction of residences for the monks."

Anathapindika was happy. Prince Jeta's liberality had enabled him to participate in the offering of a place of residence for the Buddha. He had found a person who was willing to share his hard-earned wealth. This was the kind of happiness Buddha spoke about.

Anathapindika had dwellings erected, open terraces laid out, gates made, waiting halls put up, fire rooms, storehouses and closets built, walks leveled, bathrooms constructed. To acknowledge his gratefulness to Prince Jeta, he named the park Jeta's Grove.

A few days later, when Buddha arrived in Savatthi, in the kingdom of Kosala, he was received with great respect and honor by Anathapindika and Prince Jeta. The king of Kosala at this time was Pasenadi, who was a brother-in-law of King Bimbisara of Magadha. King Pasenadi had not met the Buddha, but had come to know that he was in Savatthi.

King Pasenadi's chief consort, Mallika, had come to know of Buddha's teachings when she visited her brother, King Bimbisara of Magadha. She became converted to Buddha's teachings through his disciples whom he left in Rajagaha when he left for Kapilavatthu. Every now and then, Mallika would sing in praise of the Buddha and his disciples, although the king himself was not very enthusiastic about the Buddha's teachings.

While the Buddha was staying in Anathapindika's monastery in Jeta's Grove, a citizen of Savatthi who had lost his only son visited Buddha. Noticing that the man was not in his proper senses, Buddha questioned him as to what was worrying him. He replied:

"How could my faculties be in their normal state? My dearly beloved only son is dead. Since his death, I have given no thought to my work or my existence. I keep visiting the place where he was cremated and I do not have any inclination to do anything else."

"It is so, householder," explained the Buddha. "Dear ones who endear themselves bring sorrow and lamentation, suffering, grief and despair."

"Sir, who would ever think so? Sir, dear ones who endear themselves bring happiness and joy."

He was displeased with Buddha's explanation and left. On his way back, he met some gamblers and reported to them what he learned from Buddha. The gamblers said:

"Friend, do not listen to these ascetics who think that everything in this world is full of suffering. It is this perverse view that makes them leave all the pleasant things in the world."

"I agree with your view," said the man, and he went on his way.

This criticism of the Buddha's view eventually reached the royal palace. King Pasenadi told his queen:

"Mallika, I understand that Buddha has made the remark: 'Dear ones who endear themselves bring sorrow and lamentation, suffering, grief and despair.' What does he mean?"

"Dear, if it has been said by the Blessed One, then it must be true," replied Mallika.

The king was angry.

"No matter what this ascetic says, you applaud it. You have become a blind follower of this ascetic."

So saying, he dismissed her in disgust.

Later in the day, when the king's anger had subsided, Mallika approached him and got into a conversation. Their daughter, Princess Vajiri, who was in her teens, wanted to go out with her friends to the jungle behind the palace to collect wild flowers. The king called one of his guards and asked him to accompany them. This provided a good opportunity for the queen to question her husband.

"Dear, why do you want to send one of the guards to accompany Vajiri?"

The king was surprised by this question.

"What do you mean?" he asked the queen. "Do you want to send her with her female friends, without any person to protect them from the dangers in the jungle?"

"Why not?"

"You speak as if you do not care for her," replied the king.

"Dear, is Vajiri so dear to you that if something happens to her it would bring sorrow and suffering, grief and despair?"

"Surely!" said the king.

The queen smiled. The king was embarrassed. He realized his folly. He got up from his seat, paced up and down in deep reflection. He stopped and looked at Mallika and said in a low voice:

"Let's go and see the Buddha and invite him for a meal."

Mallika was happy. Her dream of meeting the Buddha was going to materialize. Pasenadi's sympathy and support was necessary if Buddha's message was to be a success in Kosala. The following day, King Pasenadi went to Anathapindika's monastery accompanied by Queen Mallika and a large retinue. The king paid his respects, exchanged greetings and sat on the side. Queen Mallika's joy was unbounded. In the past, Buddha's teachings had been mere hearsay for her. Now she had the opportunity of listening to him in person. When everyone had settled down, the king asked the Buddha:

"Sir, I understand that the Blessed One has declared: 'Dear ones who endear themselves bring sorrow and lamentation, suffering, grief and despair.' Is there no happiness that one can attain in this world? Is it the reason why the Blessed One has left his home and family and embraced the ascetic life?"

"O King, it is true that dear ones who endear themselves bring sorrow and lamentation, suffering and grief. But that does not mean that everything in this world produces suffering. Indeed there are satisfactions one can derive from having a wife and children. Unless one realizes that all the satisfactions are impermanent and nonsubstantial, these satisfactions can turn into dissatisfactions. One who realizes the nature of satisfactions can continue to live a householder's life without being subject to dissatisfactions. But, by leaving home and family, I have achieved a higher form of freedom and happiness, and this is freedom from continued births."

"Sir, I am grateful to my queen, Mallika, for opening my eyes to the value and significance of the Blessed One's teachings. After visiting Rajagaha a few months ago, she came to have faith in the Blessed One, his doctrine and the congregation of monks. From today onward, may the Blessed One accept me as a disciple. May the Blessed One, together with his disciples, accept my invitation for midday meal tomorrow."

Buddha accepted King Pasenadi's invitation in silence.

With the conversion of King Pasenadi, Anathapindika and Prince Jeta, the kingdom of Kosala came under the influence of the Buddha's teachings. Buddha spent most of his time in Savatthi, in Anathapindika's monastery and it became the regular place of residence for him. Very soon, a rich woman by name Visakha also became converted. She built the Eastern Monastery and offered it to the monks. Thus, Kosala became the land of the Buddha.

TWENTY-THREE

THE NEWS OF SUDDHODANA'S DEATH reached the Buddha when he was in Savatthi. Assuming that he had the responsibility of consoling his stepmother, Buddha decided to return to Kapilavatthu. Arriving in Kapilavatthu accompanied by Ananda and a few disciples, Buddha retired to Nigrodha's Park. He was tired. He needed rest and for a couple of days he remained in the park delaying the visit to his stepmother.

The news of the Buddha's arrival in Kapilavatthu reached Gotami in no time. This news brought great consolation to her. She reflected:

"I am alone in this world now. My dear husband is dead and gone. My stepson whom I cared for as if he were part of my life, left his royal inheritance and adopted an ascetic life. Nanda, who would have carried the royal banner, has joined his stepbrother. And so did my little grandson. My life is rendered purposeless. I need to find a goal of life. Only my son, Buddha, can help me."

She went to Nigrodha's Park. Buddha saw grief and sadness written all over her face. After paying obeisance to the Buddha, she sat on the side and said:

"Sir, it would be appropriate if women were allowed to go forth from home to homelessness under the guidance of the Blessed One."

It took a few moments for Buddha to respond to her. He did not anticipate that she would pose a problem of such magnitude. Therefore, an immediate response was not forthcoming.

155

He reflected on the pros and cons, of the long-term consequences of such an innovative step. His teachings had already caused a revolution in the philosophical, religious, social and political life of the Indians dominated by Brahmanism. The denial of a substantial self or soul, the condemnation of ritualism, the rejection of the caste system and the criticism of the divine ordination of political authority had already created an uproar and resentment among Brahmanical circles. The admission of women into the order would create a still greater disruption in the existing social fabric, and not only the brahmans but even the nonbrahmans, who had come to be influenced by the ideas of the Brahmanical priesthood and who had gotten used to the idea that a woman was indeed the person who keeps a family knit together, would rise against such a step. While recognizing the equality of men and women in matters pertaining to the spiritual life, the Buddha wanted to avoid his teachings becoming so revolutionary and disruptive of the social order. He wanted the situation to be ripe for introducing such changes in the society.

His mother did not directly ask for permission to join the order. Yet there was no doubt in the Buddha's mind about her intentions. There were two different questions he had to solve. One was to help his mother overcome her grief and find some solace in life. The other was the general welfare and duration of the order he had founded. It was a moral dilemma not amenable to an easy solution. Finally, he spoke up:

"Mother, please do not ask for permission for womenfolk to go forth in this dispensation."

She pleaded a second and a third time and received the same response from the Buddha. She was sad and depressed. She left Nigrodha's Park, but there was a determination and calmness on her face. It seemed she had come to a decision.

After Gotami had left, Ananda approached the Buddha and questioned:

"Sir, the Blessed One's mother was sad and depressed by the Blessed One's refusal to let women join the order. Is there any reason why womenfolk should not be admitted to the order? Are they incapable of reaching enlightenment and freedom?"

156

"Ananda, I do not consider women incapable of attaining enlightenment and freedom. But many a male disciple who has already gone forth has not yet reached the goal. There are many who are yet in bondage to desires and passions. Many who join the order in the future too would remain for awhile in bondage before they would be able to free themselves from passions. It is a mere accident that men became my first disciples. Therefore, it is proper that they be provided with the surroundings conducive to their enlightenment and freedom."

Buddha pondered for awhile.

"Ananda, I do not perceive any one form that would overwhelm a man's mind more than the form of a woman. No sound, no smell, no taste, no touch would overwhelm a man's mind more than anything associated with a woman. Similarly, Ananda, I do not perceive any one form that would overwhelm a woman's mind more than the form of man. No sound, no smell, no taste, no touch would overwhelm a woman's mind more than anything associated with a man. Such, Ananda, is the attraction of man to woman and woman to man. Male and female disciples who have not yet attained freedom and have to live together, would be like fire and fuel kept in close proximity."

After a moment's silence, the Buddha continued:

"I have so far not formulated laws that are to be considered binding on those who have joined the order. I have merely indicated the moral principles that my disciples ought to follow on their own initiative. If, at this stage, I allow women-folk to go forth from home to homelessness, it would become necessary to formulate laws binding upon everyone, if the order of monks and nuns were to survive. If not, it would be short-lived."

Ananda remained silent.

Although the Sakyans had very little sympathy for the extreme forms of asceticism practiced by the few ascetics known to them and, therefore, reacted rather negatively toward the Buddha's teaching when he first appeared in Kapilavatthu, the more moderate form of asceticism advocated by Buddha had by now gradually come to be appreciated by them. His teachings that recognized the value of lay life, as well as his social and political philosophy that undermined the authority of the brahman priesthood had gradually penetrated into the Sakyan country. So, when Buddha arrived in Kapilavatthu for the second time, he was received by the Sakyans with greater warmth and sympathetic understanding.

The Sakyans had just completed the construction of a large Convocation Hall when the Buddha arrived there. They invited the Buddha to inaugurate this Convocation Hall. Buddha accepted their invitation. The hall was beautifully decorated for the ceremonial opening. Special seats were prepared for the Buddha and his disciples. When Buddha arrived on the scene, he was received with great honor and respect. The highlight of the ceremony was a sermon by the Buddha.

When the time came for Buddha to address the congregation of Sakyans, Buddha was able to deliver only a brief sermon. He whispered to Ananda:

"Ananda, I am experiencing a severe pain in my back. I need to rest. Could you continue the preaching, elaborating on what I have said?"

Ananda agreed. Buddha retired into a room inside the Convocation Hall to rest. Thereupon, Ananda delivered a discourse on "The Path of a Trainee," explaining in detail how a person should train himself in matters relating to morality, concentration and wisdom. At the end of the sermon, Ananda declared:

"Kshatriyas are the best among those who reckon in terms of lineage. But among gods and men, a person who is endowed with knowledge and conduct is indeed superior."

The Sakyans, pleased by Venerable Ananda's discourse, applauded him.

The after-effects of the severe austerities Buddha practiced for six long years were beginning to manifest themselves in him now. In addition, his extensive travels from country to country, city to city, were also taking their toll on his physical frame. During the next few days, Buddha stayed at Nigrodha's Park, bedridden for the most part. Ananda nursed the Buddha, providing him with all his necessities, such as food and medicine. The Sakyans who had heard about the Buddha's illness visited Buddha at Nigrodha's Park in large numbers.

But Ananda, assuming the role of a protective nurse was at the entrance to the cottage where Buddha was resting and turned away every visitor saying:

"Friend, the Blessed One is ill. He should not be disturbed. He needs to rest. Come back when he has recovered and is in a position to meet you. Please do not worry. All his needs are well taken care of."

After a few days, when the Buddha was recuperating from his illness, his father-in-law, Mahanama, who was by then advanced in years, feeble and walking with the help of a stick, came to see the Buddha. Ananda permitted him into the cottage where the Buddha was and went out to fetch a bowl of rice gruel for the Buddha. When he returned, he heard Mahanama asking the Buddha:

"Sir, sometime ago I heard the Blessed One saying that knowledge comes to those who are concentrated, not to those who are unconcentrated. Does concentration come before knowledge or is knowledge prior to concentration?"

Ananda thought to himself:

"The Blessed One is just recovering from his illness. This Sakyan, Mahanama, is asking him a very profound question. The Blessed One should not be bothered with this kind of question at this time."

In order to interrupt the conversation, Ananda came forward, offered the bowl of rice gruel to Buddha and very politely took Mahanama's hand and led him away. Taking him outside the cottage and settling him down on a bench, Ananda tried to explain the doctrine to Mahanama.

Buddha's stepbrother, Nanda, remained with Buddha ever since he joined the order, while Rahula remained under the guidance of Sariputta. Although many a disciple who joined the order after Nanda was able to follow Buddha's instructions and attain freedom, Nanda made no spiritual progress whatsoever. Buddha was aware of Nanda's indolence and lack of progress. Yet he did not put unnecessary pressure on him. Nanda had to overcome his dilemma gradually. Either he had to accept his decision to follow the ascetic life, which he adopted through respect for his older brother, or he had to give up the ascetic life and return to Kapilavatthu as requested by the lady whom he was going to marry.

Because Nanda was gradually overcoming his dilemma and was getting used to the life of asceticism, Buddha was not willing to let him be on his own. So he requested Nanda to join him when he revisited Kapilavatthu. Buddha was keen that Nanda remain under his own surveillance. He did not realize that taking Nanda back to Kapilavatthu before he attained enlightenment was like trying to drown a tortoise.

Arriving in Kapilavatthu, the monks went out to the homes for alms. Nanda, who was very excited about returning to Kapilavatthu and yet was not able to visit his fiancee, decided to put on the best appearance he could when going around begging for alms. Therefore, he pressed and ironed his robes, anointed his eyes and took a glazed bowl when he went on the alms round, assuming that he would perchance meet his sweetheart. The monks who went along with him noticed his unusual behavior and appearance and reported the matter to the Buddha. Buddha summoned Nanda and reprimanded him saying:

"Nanda, it is not proper for a person who has left home for the life of homelessness through conviction to press and iron his robes, anoint his eyes and carry a glazed bowl. It is proper that such a person should live a life confined to the forest, beg for his food, wear robes made of rags and remain without desiring pleasures of sense. When can I expect such behavior from Nanda?"

Nanda was greatly perturbed. He was sorry that he had offended his most respected brother. He decided to follow his instructions and adopt a life of extreme asceticism, depending solely on alms collected by begging, wearing robes made of rags and trying to control his senses.

Buddha stayed in Kapilavatthu as long as he needed to recover completely from his illness and left for Vesali, the capital of the Vajjian Republic in the southwest.

TWENTY-FOUR

THE COUNTRY OF THE VAJJIS, including eight confed-
erate clans, was to the west and northwest of Magadha.
The Licchavis and the Videhans represented two of the more
powerful clans in this region with their capital cities in Vesali
and Mithila respectively. The ascetic tradition was more influential in this region, with the teachings of the Jain leader,
Nigantha Nataputta or Mahavira being the more predominant.
Ajivikas, another ascetic group, with Makkhali Gosala as their
leader, was also held in high esteem.

The Buddha arrived in Vesali with his disciples and found
lodgings in the Great Wood, so named because this wooded
area was frequented by ascetics. The Licchavis had constructed
several large buildings in this area for the use of the ascetics
and Buddha stayed in one of them called the Pinnacled Hall.

Buddha had never seen such handsome people as the
Licchavis. They were like the gods of the Tavatimsa heaven
descended on the earth. Almost every Licchavi represented
perfection of human form in every aspect.

When the news spread around that the ascetic of the Sakyan
clan who had attained enlightenment was staying in Vesali
many disciples of Mahavira came to visit the Buddha with the
intention of holding debates on various religious and philosophical issues. One of them was Saccaka who was an expert
in debate, erudite and respected by many in Vesali.

One day Saccaka found that a large number of Licchavis
had gathered in the Great Wood for some reason or other. He
went to the Great Wood and announced that he was going to

have a debate with Buddha in the Pinnacled Hall. Many more Licchavis arrived at the Pinnacled Hall to listen to the debate between Saccaka and the Buddha. Approaching Buddha, Saccaka asked:

"Friend I would like to question you on one small aspect of your teachings if you permit me and if you would care to explain."

"Go on, Saccaka, you may ask whatever question you may please," replied Buddha.

"In what way, friend, do you train your disciples?"

"Saccaka, I understand the world to be impermanent and nonsubstantial. The world of human experience which I analyze into body or form, feeling, perception, disposition and consciousness, is impermanent and nonsubstantial. All dispositions, including those things that are determined by dispositions, are impermanent. All things are nonsubstantial. Having understood the world to be such, I train my disciples to perceive the world in this way."

"Friend, I perceive things in a different way. This example occurs to me."

"What is the example that occurs to you, Saccaka?" asked Buddha.

"Whatever living things are, whether they be plants or animals, all of them depend upon this earth for their existence and growth. They have earth as their support. All those who perform various functions depend upon this earth, have earth as their support. Similarly, when a human person accumulates merit or demerit, he does so depending upon his self. He has self as his support, whether that be body or feeling or perception or disposition or consciousness.'

"Saccaka, did you say body or form is your self; feeling is your self, and so on?" questioned the Buddha.

"Yes, friend, I did assert that there is a self and that this self is identical with every factor of the human personality, whether it be body or form, feeling, perception, disposition or consciousness. This is also the view of the majority of people."

"Do not worry about the majority view, Saccaka. You just explain what you yourself believe."

162

"I believe that there is a self and that it is identical with the various factors of the human personality."

"May I question you a little further regarding this notion of the self that you advocate?" asked Buddha.

"Surely, you may ask whatever questions you have. I shall be very pleased to explain to you my position."

"Friend Saccaka, do you think you can tell me a little more about the nature of this self that you recognize?"

"There is no problem at all. It is very clear that this self is permanent, enduring and eternal. It is also the agent of all our actions. It acts and it reaps the consequences. How can we explain the accumulation of merit or demerit if there is no such self? Otherwise, we have to admit that one person does the act and still another reaps the consequences. All acts, as I said earlier, depend on this self. It is the basis or support of all the different acts."

"It seems that this self is very autonomous. It does whatever it wants and reaps all the consequences," said Buddha.

"Yes, indeed, friend."

"Well, Saccaka, let me ask you one more question."

"Please yourself, friend," responded Saccaka.

"What do you think, Saccaka? Does a king such as Pasenadi of Kosala, possess the authority and power in his kingdom to impose capital punishment on murderers, to punish the robbers, to banish those who have to be banished from the country?"

"Yes, indeed, King Pasenadi possesses such authority and power. So do the rulers of any other country. Not merely that. They indeed should possess such authority and power."

"Now, Saccaka. You mentioned that body or form is your self and that self is autonomous. Is it possible for the self to say: 'Let my body be such, let my body not be such'?"

Saccaka remained silent.

Buddha insisted.

"Saccaka, please answer me. This is not the time for you to be silent."

Saccaka maintained his silence.

Buddha insisted a second time.

People in the audience were getting restless with Saccaka's

silence. Saccaka looked around. He saw the anger of the people. So did the Buddha. It was as if a ferocious-looking demon was staring at Saccaka ready to destroy him, a demon with a thunderbolt in his hands waiting to shatter Saccaka's head into pieces if he did not answer the Buddha's question. For it was Saccaka who challenged the Buddha to this debate. Saccaka was frightened. His hair stood on end. He started perspiring. Saccaka even forgot what Buddha's question was.

"Friend, may I know what your question is?" asked Saccaka.

"What do you think, Saccaka? You asserted that body is the self. Do you have any power over that body and are you able to say: 'Let my body be such or let my body not be such'?"

"No, friend."

"Now, watch what you are saying, Saccaka. What you claimed earlier is not consistent with what you say now.

"What do you think, Saccaka? Is body or form permanent or impermanent?"

"Impermanent, friend."

"Whatever is impermanent, is that unsatisfactory or satisfactory, suffering or happiness?"

"It is unsatisfactory. It is suffering."

"Whatever is impermanent, unsatisfactory and is subject to change, is it proper to consider it as mine, as me, as my self?"

"Friend, I admit that it is not proper."

"Such is the training, Saccaka, my disciples receive under me."

Saccaka repented his arrogance and invited the Buddha and his disciples for meals in his house the following day. The Licchavis who were present were greatly impressed by Buddha's teachings and many a young man in the crowd decided to join the Buddha and his disciples.

AT THIS TIME, a wanderer named Vacchagotta was staying close to Vesali, in a monastery known as the "Lone Lotus" meant primarily for wanderers. In Vesali he came to know of the claim made by Nigantha Nataputta that he was omniscient, and that whether he be standing, sleeping or awake he had knowledge and vision set up all the time with regard to everything. Therefore, he called himself a conqueror. Since the Buddha claimed enlightenment, everyone in Vesali assumed that he too was omniscient. Therefore, Vaccha was interested in meeting the Buddha and verifying whether there was any basis for this assumption.

On this particular day, Buddha found that it was too early to go to the city for alms and decided to visit the Lone Lotus to meet some of the wanderers. Vacchagotta was delighted to see Buddha. He assumed that Buddha had read his thoughts and intentions and had therefore visited the Lone Lotus.

"Come, O Blessed One. Welcome, O Blessed One. At last, the Blessed One has decided to visit us. May the Blessed One take this seat that is prepared for him."

Buddha took his seat and the wanderer Vacchagotta sat on the side on a lower seat. He addressed Buddha:

"I have heard that the Blessed One is omniscient and that whether he be standing, sleeping or awake he has knowledge and vision set up all the time with regard to everything. Would this be a true report regarding the Blessed One?"

"No, Vaccha, this is not true. Those who say this indeed misrepresent me. It is a false attribution."

"How should one, then, accurately represent the Blessed One, without misrepresenting him?" asked Vacchagotta.

"I possess threefold knowledge, Vaccha. First is retrocognition. If I so wish, I am able to remember my past experiences starting from the one immediately preceding up to a hundred or hundred thousand existences with all details. The second is clairvoyance. If I so wish, I am able to see, through clairvoyant vision, how other beings are reborn at death, conditioned by their karma or behavior. The third, Vaccha, is the knowledge that in this very life I have achieved freedom of mind and freedom through wisdom by the cessation of defilements. Anyone who accurately represents me will have to say that I merely possess threefold knowledge and nothing else."

Vacchagotta was pleased by what he learned and thanked the Buddha for his visit. Having clarified this misunderstanding regarding his attainments, Buddha left Lone Lotus and went out begging for alms. Having collected whatever food he needed, Buddha returned to the Pinnacled Hall, partook of his meal and retired to his little room to rest for the day.

In the meantime, Buddha's stepmother, Gotami, who had been refused permission to adopt the homeless life under Buddha's dispensation, joined a band of young Sakyan women who were determined to prevail upon the Buddha to let them join the order. Prominent among them were Bimba, Buddha's mother-in-law, and Anopama and Rohini who were Yasodhara's close friends. They shaved their hair, donned yellow robes and set out for Vesali. For these ladies, brought up in luxury and comfort, the long trek from Kapilavatthu to Vesali, was a tiring and tedious one. By the time they arrived in Vesali, their feet were swollen, their bodies were covered with dirt, and they were completely exhausted. Inquiring around, they found where the Buddha and his disciples were staying and went up to the Pinnacled Hall. Ananda was seated on a bench outside the door of the room where the Buddha was resting. He recognized the group of women from Kapilavatthu led by Buddha's stepmother, all in yellow robes. They all looked dirty and tired.

Ananda was shocked. He had been present when Buddha had refused Gotami permission to enter the order. At that time she was disappointed and depressed. Now he saw determination written all over her face. He spoke to them:

"Ladies, you look tired and exhausted. Did you have your midday meal? Is there anything that I can do to make you more comfortable?"

"Venerable Ananda, please do not worry about meals for us. The only way we can have any comfort is by meeting with Buddha and obtaining his permission to join the congregation," replied Gotami.

Ananda requested them to remain where they were and walked up to the door of the room where the Buddha was resting. Buddha was wide awake and he heard the conversation between Ananda and the women. When Ananda appeared at the door, Buddha questioned:

"Ananda, aren't there some important guests who have come to see me?"

"Yes, Sir, the Blessed One's mother, Yasodhara's mother and

many other ladies from Kapilavatthu are here waiting for an opportunity to see the Blessed One."

"Do they still want to adopt the homeless life?"

"They have already done so. They have shaven their heads, donned yellow robes and walked all the way from Kapilavatthu. Their feet are swollen; they are dirty and they look exhausted."

Buddha sat up on his bed, thought for a while, and said to Ananda:

"Ananda, it will not be possible to keep women away from the order any longer. Let them be part of the congregation. But it will become necessary to lay down strict rules for the guidance of both male and female disciples who are not yet enlightened and who are living in the same vicinity."

Ananda was delighted. He immediately left the room. He was pleased that he was able to obtain permission for these enthusiastic women to join the order. Returning to them, he said:

"If all of you ladies are willing to abide by strict rules of discipline, the Blessed One will permit you to join the congregation. Would you agree to such rules of discipline?"

"Yes, indeed, Venerable Ananda. We will abide by any rule if we are allowed to join the congregation," replied Gotami.

Thus came into existence the order of nuns.

Gotami and her friends were pleased. Their fatigue and weariness disappeared instantly. Their faces regained their natural complexion and luster. They retired to a secluded spot, cleaned their bodies, washed their robes and, after resting for a while, assembled in the main hall in the evening to listen to the Buddha.

Anopama and Rohini had difficulty concentrating their attention on the first few occasions they listened to the Buddha. In fact, Rohini tried to keep her eyes away from Buddha most of the time. She was, to some extent, embarrassed by her own mischievous behavior in the past when Siddhartha had been courting Yasodhara. Every time they saw Buddha they were reminded of those past events. It was with great difficulty that they were able to wipe out those memories and concentrate their attention in order to achieve freedom from defilements under the instructions of Buddha.

Upon learning about the presence of the Buddha and his disciples in Vesali and the admission of women into the order, a courtesan named Ambapali, who had amassed wealth by catering to the sensual needs of the rich men of Vesali, decided to visit the Buddha.

Ambapali was sought for by every wealthy Licchavi in Vesali. She was of such perfect beauty that among the Licchavis, who themselves were well known for their handsome personalities, she appeared like the chief goddess among gods. Her dark brown hair, with freckled ends, grew thick and well-ordered. To add to its beauty, it was frequently adorned by exotic flowers. Her eyebrows appeared like the painting by a clever artist. Her eyes shone forth like brilliant gems. Her well-formed and prominent nose, earlobes, and white teeth all added to her charm and beauty. Her well-proportioned breasts earned the envy of every young woman in Vesali. Her slim waist, beautiful thighs, ankles adorned with foot ornaments and lotus-like feet completed an exquisitely beautiful figure, like that of a nymph. While her physical personality provided the highest of visual satisfaction for those who were able to get a glimpse at her, her voice, resembling that of a cuckoo, provided great satisfaction to those who were enamored of natural music.

Her beauty was a great source of anxiety for her retinue. Strong and able-bodied men surrounded her whenever she left her house. Some rich men of Vesali enamored by her beauty lost all their wealth in their attempts to enjoy her company. When she decided to visit the Buddha most people were surprised.

"The ascetic of the Sakya clan will be in trouble this time. Although he has the power of converting almost everyone who went before him, this time it will be Ambapali who will bring about the conversion," remarked some.

Surrounded by bodyguards and her retinue, Ambapali visited the Buddha. Having paid her respects to the Buddha she sat on the side. She observed that among the female disciples who had joined Buddha, there were some who were young and pretty.

"Sir, don't you think it is a crime to admit into the order

young women who have never had the opportunity of enjoying life? Nature has been so bountiful to us that we can have everything we want. Why should young men and women don yellow robes and lead a life of poverty and deprivation?"

"Ambapali, you are very beautiful and attractive. You have all the wealth you want. But how free are you to go around in this world without those guards to protect you? How long do you think you can continue with your present way of life? You are like a crab caught by a fisherman and placed in a pot of water kept over a fire. Until the water starts heating up, the crab feels comfortable and free. But that comfort and freedom is not for long. The world is impermanent and mutable. That is a truth that we cannot afford to ignore."

Ambapali's success in gathering up most of the wealth in Vesali, the insatiable demands of rich men for her company, and her own satisfaction in being able to choose among the men whom she desired prevented her from seeing the world in the perspective in which Buddha saw it.

"Sir, you are handsome too and if you ever wish to enjoy life with me, I will be ready to accommodate you. Let me know when you have changed your mind."

So saying, she left the Buddha, thoroughly disappointed at the manner in which she had, for the first time, been rejected by a man of her desire.

TWENTY-FIVE

NIGANTHA NATAPUTTA, the Jain leader, was at this time living in Nalanda, a small township situated between Vesali and Rajagaha. The Buddha's appearance in Vesali was not looked upon with much favor by the disciples of Nataputta. They found the Buddha to be a formidable opponent, and many Jain disciples who came to debate with Buddha were humbled by him, the first one being the erudite Saccaka.

Having stayed in Vesali as long as he wished, Buddha, accompanied by his male and female disciples, left for Rajagaha. On the way he stopped over in Nalanda and took up residence in a mango grove called Pavarika. Dighatapassi, another disciple of Nataputta, learned about the Buddha's arrival in Nalanda and decided to visit him. Arriving in Pavarika mango grove, he was welcomed by Buddha. After an exchange of greetings, Dighatapassi settled down onto a seat and Buddha questioned him about Nataputta:

"Friend, Tapassi, I understand that, unlike some ascetics like Purana Kassapa, Pakudha Kaccayana and Makkhali Gosala who are known to ridicule karma or moral responsibility, your teacher, Nataputta, is a strong advocate of this doctrine. Tell me something about his doctrine of karma."

"Friend, Nataputta indeed is an advocate of karma. But he prefers to speak of karma as punishment."

"Why is that? What has punishment got to do with karma? When a man commits an evil act of word or deed and if a king or his ministers were to come to know of it, then he will have to face some punishment. But that is because he comes under a law that says that committing such and such act is against the law that is accepted by that society. Such laws are mere conventions. They vary from country to country, society to society. Sometimes a certain act is considered to be a crime in one society and a person committing such an act is punished, whereas a similar act may be rewarded in another society."

"What you say is true, good friend. There are different laws in different societies and different countries. These laws are mere social conventions. But for Nataputta, karma is a law that is common to all societies, all countries, all beings. It is binding on everyone. There is no escape from it. Everything that we experience now, whether it be happiness or suffering, all that is due to our past actions. What we do now will determine our future."

"Does that mean that karma is a law that is external to man—some kind of mysterious force or power that operates independent of man? If that is the case, what difference is there between Nataputta's doctrine of karma and the teachings of those ascetics like Makkhali Gosala who deny karma? A person like Gosala, I understand, believes that man is powerless to do anything through his own initiative, because everything in the world is unalterably fixed."

Tapassi had difficulty in answering Buddha's objection. He thought for a moment. Then his face brightened up.

"Friend Gotama. There is indeed a difference between Nataputta's doctrine and that of Gosala. You see, Gosala denies individual initiative, whereas Nataputta does not. In fact, Nataputta emphasizes the importance of human action. But it is only after a person has committed an act that he loses control over it. It becomes an external force. This law is above all conventional laws, and what man has to suffer under this law is nothing but punishment."

"But, Tapassi, do you mean to say that man has to suffer for everything he does, whether his action is motivated or not, consciously or unconsciously performed?"

"Yes, friend, it is not the motivation that matters. Rather, it is the act itself that matters. Let us say a man steps on an insect even as tiny as an ant. It may be true that he did not see the ant, that he did not step on the ant consciously. But as

171

far as the ant is concerned, it does not matter whether the man is conscious or not. The poor ant loses his life. Nataputta is a very compassionate person, good friend. This is his very noble doctrine of nonviolence."

"I do appreciate Nataputta's unbounded compassion for beings. But I am unable to understand why a man has to suffer for something that he does unconsciously, why he should undergo punishment for an unmotivated action. Shouldn't this act be evaluated from both sides before we try to decide who is to blame, who is responsible? Don't you think that the innocence of man is as important as that of an ant, if not more important?"

Tapassi was silent. Buddha continued his questioning.

"Tapassi, how many different types of punishment does Nataputta recognize?"

"He recognizes three types of punishment—bodily, verbal and mental."

"Which of these is more blameworthy, according to Nataputta?"

"Bodily punishment is more blameworthy," replied Tapassi.

"I thought so," said Buddha. "This is inevitable according to Nataputta's philosophy. I understand that Nataputta recommends extreme forms of behavior such as sweeping the ground in front before you take a step, through fear that you may step on any creatures, or covering your nose and mouth with a piece of cloth to avoid breathing in any insects that may be in the air."

Again Tapassi remained silent.

"Tapassi, I too am an advocate of compassion for other beings and a preacher of nonviolence. But, don't you think that Nataputta's philosophy will make it impossible for anyone to escape punishment? There may be living beings invisible to the naked eye. How can one avoid hurting them when one does not see them? This certainly will make living in this world impossible. Let me ask you one more question:

"How can one ever attain freedom if one accepts Nataputta's philosophy?"

"Friend, Nataputta believes that freedom is attained by a twofold process. First is by punishing oneself for one's past actions without having to wait for such punishment to materialize in the future. This wipes out our past sins. This is the purpose of inflicting pain on oneself, of self-mortification. The other is by refraining from committing any new deeds. This will prevent any influx of new sins, which one will have to expiate in the future. This dual process will enable man to be free and this is what Nataputta has achieved."

"What is the purpose of a life of inaction, Tapassi? Man will not be different from a stone or some such lifeless object," remarked Buddha.

Tapassi was embarrassed. He understood the Buddha's argument.

"Friend, in what way does your teaching differ from Nataputta's?"

"Tapassi, there are many points on which I differ from Nataputta's explanation of karma. First, I do not consider karma to be an inexorable immutable law. Secondly, I do not believe that everything we experience now is due to our past karma, for I find that not all karmas produce consequences. Thirdly, I do not look upon the effect of karma as a form of punishment. And finally, I am willing to attribute responsibility to the doer of an action, only if that action is consciously done. Therefore, in my view, mental action is more blameworthy than the mere physical act."

"Indeed, it seems that your views about karma are very different from Nataputta's. But these differences are stated so briefly that I am unable to understand them. May you explain these points with a little more detail."

"Surely. I shall be very pleased to do so, Tapassi.

"Let us take the first point I mentioned. I do not perceive any fixed laws anywhere. On the basis of our past experiences we observe certain patterns in the way events take place. On the basis of such patterns that we observe, we infer that such and such may be the case in the future. The theory of dependent arising is what I formulated to explain such occurrences. Now, karma constitutes only one factor in this process of dependence. There are many other factors involved. If that is the case, do you think that everything that we experience is due to our past karma?"

"No, good friend, that cannot be," replied Tapassi.

"Therefore, Tapassi, sometimes we have to suffer for things over which we may not have complete control. For example, I may suffer as a result of a change in weather. Is that my past karma?"

"No, I do not think so."

"Sometimes I may have to suffer as a result of a power-hungry king who decides to wage war against my country. That cannot be the result of my past karma?"

"No, it could not be your past karma."

"But if I were to hurt someone else and he were to turn back and hurt me, and I were to suffer as a result, is that due to my past karma?"

"Yes, friend, that indeed is your past karma."

"If the consequences we have to suffer are not all due to our past karma, how can we look upon them as punishments? Moreover, very often people are rewarded for committing evil deeds. For example, if a king's soldier were to inflict losses on the enemies, that soldier is more often rewarded than punished. Don't you think so?"

"Yes, that would be so," replied Tapassi.

"In that case, there are no fixed laws here. Tapassi, there are four kinds of karmas: a karma that is good and leads to good consequences, and a karma that is evil and leads to evil consequences. On the basis of such karmas, one should not arrive at the absolute conclusion that all good karmas lead to good consequences and all bad karmas to bad consequences. Inferring from a particular to a universal, in this manner, is not proper and valid."

"Friend, you said that there are four kinds of karmas. What are the other two kinds?"

"A karma that is good and leads to bad consequences, and a karma that is bad and leads to good consequences. In these cases it is not proper for someone to arrive at the absolute conclusion that there is no connection whatever between karma and consequences, because some karmas are seen to lead to opposite results. Here again it is the wrong kind of inference, that is, an inference from a particular to a universal."

"Without falling into these two extremes, I explain karma

174

as being dependently arisen and the consequence too as being dependently arisen. If, on examining the various factors that lead to a certain event, it is found that a conscious act is involved in the arising of the effect, I maintain that the agent of that act is responsible for that action. Whatever consequences that follow such action will be reaped by the agent as a natural consequence, not as a punishment. Friend Tapassi, I maintain that motivation is identical with karma. An action is an action only when it is motivated, whether that action be of word, deed or thought. This is the doctrine of karma I profess."

"So be it, friend," said Dighatapassi and having saluted the Buddha, he left.

Dighatapassi returned to Nataputta and informed him of his conversation with the Buddha. "Well done, Tapassi! I applaud you for the way you have conducted the discussion. I am pleased that you did not become a disciple of the Buddha. You have represented my teachings correctly."

At this time, another lay disciple of Nataputta, named Upali, was in the company of Nataputta. Having listened to Dighatapassi's report, Upali said to Nataputta:

"Sir, let me also go and meet the Buddha. I will debate with him on the same question. I am confident that I can refute and overwhelm him in such a debate."

Nataputta was pleased.

"Go, Upali. Go and engage the ascetic of the Sakyans in a debate. I am confident that you will be able to win."

Dighatapassi pleaded with Nataputta:

"Sir, do not let Upali go before Buddha. He has the magical power of converting people. I escaped him with difficulty. For some reason or other, he did not push me into providing answers that would have contradicted what I said. Upali is a very faithful follower of Venerable Nataputta. Venerable Nataputta will certainly lose a faithful and generous supporter."

"It is not possible, Tapassi, that a follower like Upali will accept the ascetic of the Sakyans as his teacher. Upali is a convinced disciple and is confident about his understanding of the doctrine. I too have confidence in him."

Upon receiving approval from Nataputta, Upali went straight

to the Pavarika mango grove where the Buddha was staying. Meeting with the Buddha, Upali said:

"Sir, I understand that the erudite Dighatapassi had a good discussion with the Blessed One on the doctrine of karma. What more can one say about the importance of bodily punishment, compared to mental punishment which is nothing."

"Upali, if you wish to have a discussion on this topic, let it be based on facts."

"Yes, Blessed One, I will base myself on facts in any discussion of this topic."

"Householder, your teacher Nataputta is known to be a practitioner of four kinds of restraint with regard to water. But when he moves about in water, he will be destroying many a minute insect. What kind of consequences does Nataputta assign to such actions?"

"Since he is not conscious, he does not attribute much blame to that action."

"If he were to be conscious?"

"Then, it would be blameworthy."

"Wherein does Nataputta include the act of being conscious?"

"Under the category of mental punishment," replied Upali.

"Now Upali be careful. You are contradicting yourself."

Buddha used several examples such as these and led Upali to admit that mental behavior is more blameworthy than mere unmotivated bodily action. At the end of the discussion, Upali realized his inconsistency and sought refuge in the message of the Buddha. Buddha was not very pleased.

"Upali, do what you think is proper. Proper behavior on the part of people like you is important."

"Sir, I am surprised by the Blessed One's attitude. Whenever I became a disciple of any one of the other teachers, he would go around Nalanda proclaiming that I had become his disciple. Now the Blessed One is merely asking me to do what is proper. Sir, I am overwhelmed by the Blessed One's attitude."

"Householder, for a long time your family served as a source of support for Nataputta and his disciples. Please remember that they need your support."

Upali was still more impressed with the Buddha's attitude. All this time he had been receiving wrong reports that the

Buddha had insisted that he be the only one supported by his followers. Now the Buddha was asking Upali to continue serving Nataputta and his disciples, even after he became the Buddha's disciple.

Yet the word spread that householder Upali had become a disciple of Buddha. When this matter was reported to Nataputta, he just shrugged it aside saying that Buddha would have become a disciple of Upali, not vice versa. Tapassi came to inform Nataputta of the same news, and this time Nataputta was a little shaken up.

"Tapassi, go and check whether there is any truth to this story."

Dighatapassi went to Upali's residence. At the entrance to the house he was stopped by the guards.

"Sir, please stay there. From today onward, householder Upali is a disciple of the Buddha. From now onward, the doors of his house are closed to the male and female disciples of Nataputta. They will be open only for the male and female disciples of the Buddha. If you need any food, please remain right there. We will fetch you some."

"Friend, I do not need your food," said Dighatapassi and left Upali's house.

Returning to Nataputta, Dighatapassi informed him of his experience at Upali's residence. The shock was such for Nataputta that he ended up vomiting blood.

TWENTY-SIX

LEAVING NALANDA, THE BUDDHA arrived in Rajagaha where his young son Rahula was staying under the supervision of Sariputta. Buddha and Rahula had not seen each other for several years. When Rahula heard that the Buddha was on his way to the Bamboo Grove he was greatly excited. He set up water for the Buddha to wash his feet, prepared a seat and made ready refreshments. When Buddha had settled down, Rahula went before him and paid him homage. Buddha looked at Rahula. He was no more a boy. He had grown up to be a tall and handsome person. Buddha felt that Rahula was now ready to receive final instruction leading him toward the goal of the religious life. It was not proper for him to continue as a trainee.

"Rahula, how have you fared during my absence?"

"Very well, Sir. Venerable Sariputta has been very kind to me and constantly instructed me in the doctrine."

"Do you enjoy the kind of life you are leading?" asked the Buddha.

"Yes, Sir," replied Rahula.

"Rahula, have you reflected on the kind of life you are leading?"

Rahula was silent.

"What is the purpose of a mirror, Rahula?" asked the Buddha.

"It is for the purpose of looking at oneself," replied Rahula.

"Similarly, Rahula, when you perform any bodily act, you must reflect, as if you are looking at a mirror, whether that bodily action of yours leads to your own harm, harm of others, or harm to both yourself and others. In so reflecting, if you find that it leads to harm for yourself, for others or for both, you must avoid that action as being bad, as being productive of suffering. Similarly with verbal and mental acts.

"But when, Rahula, you perceive that an act of yours, whether bodily, verbal or mental, does not lead to harm for yourself, for others or for both, then you should consider it to be a good action, leading to happiness and therefore, you ought to cultivate it, promote it. So should you train yourself, Rahula."

Rahula received these instructions and following them faithfully, reached perfection with regard to bodily, verbal and mental behavior and in no time attained sainthood.

But his uncle, Nanda, had still not made much progress. Although he had adopted a more ascetic way of life on the advice of his older brother, Nanda had difficulty with it. Leading such an ascetic life without much relish, Nanda gradually became frail and haggard.

One day the Buddha, accompanied by Nanda and other disciples, visited the house of a rich merchant, being invited there for the midday meal. The merchant had a retinue of young girls who were extremely pretty, surpassing even the heavenly beauties. When the Buddha arrived there with his disciples and settled down to enjoy the meal, these pretty young ladies remained staring at the Buddha, astounded by his personality. No one even cared to look at Nanda who by now was reduced to a skeleton. Nanda noticed the lack of any attention for him from the girls.

Returning to the Bamboo Grove, Buddha noticed Nanda's disappointment.

"What is bothering you, Nanda?" questioned the Buddha.

Nanda was quiet. Buddha questioned him a second and third time. Nanda could not remain silent after the Buddha questioned him a third time. He related what he had noticed and did not try to hide his feelings.

"But Nanda, aren't you enamored of the Sakyan beauty?" questioned Buddha without trying to suppress his smile.

Nanda was frightened to say anything that was less than the truth.

"She is no comparison to these girls, Sir. Compared to these, she is like a scalded she-monkey."

"Enjoy the religious life, Nanda. You will attract the attention of ladies who are far more beautiful than these ladies."

Soon the monks learned that Nanda was enthusiastic about the religious life for the sake of gaining the attention of beautiful ladies. His friends in the order treated him as a hireling who had sold himself, since he was leading the religious life for the sake of the pretty ladies.

Nanda was humiliated, ashamed and dismayed by the rumors spreading among his friends. Therefore, he went to dwell alone and withdrawn, diligent, ardent and self-controlled, until he realized the supreme goal of the religious life, namely, freedom from all attachments to worldly pleasures.

Devadatta, who remained in Rajagaha during the time the Buddha traveled in the North, turned out to be a close friend of Bimbisara's son, Ajatasatthu. While Bimbisara was a lay disciple of the Buddha, Ajatasatthu was disturbed by the Buddha's teachings and feared that he would lose the opportunity to become king of Magadha if Buddha's political philosophy became popular in the country. Ajatasatthu, therefore, plotted against both his father and the Buddha. He exploited his friendship with Devadatta in order to attain his devious goals.

For Devadatta, Ajatasatthu's friendship was a great distraction. Ajatasatthu showered material benefits on Devadatta who hardly realized that his friend was gradually dragging him away—away from the goal for which he renounced his family and wealth. Being very innocent by nature, he was corruptible. It did not take long for the other disciples to realize that Devadatta was trapped in Ajatasatthu's vicious net. They reported the matter to the Buddha as soon as he returned to Rajagaha. Buddha condemned Devadatta's behavior, prophesying that he would not only bring harm to himself but would cause suffering for others as well.

At a time when Devadatta was entertaining some displeasure over the Buddha's criticism of his behavior, Ajatasatthu made the suggestion:

"My father is now very old. Yet he is very popular among

his subjects. It is time that he abdicated in my favor. So is the Buddha. He too is now advanced in years. It is therefore proper that Venerable Devadatta, who was Buddha's childhood companion, and therefore the earliest of acquaintances, take over the organization of the order of disciples."

"That sounds very reasonable," replied Devadatta, who by this time had completely forgotten the purpose of the religious life. Therefore, the next time he met the Buddha he presented his request.

"The Blessed One is now old, aged and burdened with years. The Blessed One's health would be affected if he continues to travel around the way he does. It is time for the Blessed One to rest and enjoy the bliss of emancipation. Let him hand over the community of monks to me. I will govern them to the satisfaction of the Blessed One."

This proposal from Devadatta came as a surprise to the Buddha.

"Devadatta, I never considered myself to be governing the community of monks. I was merely a guide, not a governor. Why do you think that someone should govern the community?"

"Sir, the community of monks has grown in leaps and bounds. Not only is there a large section that has yet to attain freedom, there are also women who have joined the order. It is therefore necessary that someone take the responsibility for maintaining order and discipline."

"Enough, Devadatta. Do not aspire to govern the community of monks. Before attempting to discipline others, it would be appropriate for you to discipline yourself," said the Buddha.

It was too much of a rebuff for Devadatta. He could not continue in the community. Neither was he willing to return to lay life. In his folly, he decided to break away from the community and establish his own order.

The following day, Devadatta met Ananda who was going round in Rajagaha for alms and informed him of his intention to found a new order. Ananda reported the matter to the Buddha, who merely said:

"Good is easily done by the noble. Good is not done easily by the evil. Bad is done easily by the evil. Noble Ones cannot commit bad deeds."

181

TWENTY-SEVEN

BUDDHA LEFT RAJAGAHA FOR SAVATTHI. When he arrived in Savatthi and was on his alms round, some people tried to prevent him from taking a certain road. Angulimala, the robber, lived somewhere along that road.

Angulimala's hands were bloodstained. He murdered innocent men and women to satsify a deep-seated yearning to wear a necklace of human fingers. The people of the kingdom of Kosala lived in fear, not knowing when he would strike their city or village.

"Sir, do not take this road. The bandit Angulimala lives somewhere along this road. Many people have been killed by him and others have fled this area."

Buddha was not deterred by their pleas. He realized that Angulimala was not the normal type of robber who killed to rob people of their wealth. He killed people in order to collect their fingers. He was mentally sick and the Buddha could probably save both Angulimala and his victims.

Angulimala was surprised to see the Buddha passing his residence all alone. He thought to himself:

"The strongest of men in Kosala have avoided this road. Even the king's men have kept away from this path. How is it that this ascetic dares to come along unaccompanied? Maybe he is destined to die and provide me with fingers to extend my garland."

Taking his sword, Angulimala went after the Buddha. He was not ready to swing his sword at the Buddha without asking him some questions, for it must have been unbelievable courage that induced the Buddha to come along this path. Going behind the Buddha, he said:

"Stay there, monk, stay there. I want to talk to you."

Buddha continued as if he did not hear Angulimala. Angulimala stopped and yelled at the Buddha at the top of his voice.

"Stop, monk, stop!"

"I have stopped, Angulimala. Don't you want to stop?" asked Buddha as he continued on his way.

Angulimala was confused. He thought:

"These monks, sons of the Sakyans, speak truth and assert truth. But though this monk is walking, he says he has stopped. When I have stopped here, he assumes that I have not. He probably means something."

He questioned the Buddha who continued to go on his way.

"Monk, you say you have stopped and yet continue to walk. When I have stopped, you assume I am walking and have not stopped. What do you mean?"

"Angulimala, I have stopped forever hurting any living being and, therefore, have stopped this continuous roaming and running in samsara, in existence. As for you, with all this violence committed against innocent beings, you will continue to flow along like a rudderless and anchorless boat in a fast-moving stream. Disaster lies ahead for you, unless you are ready to stop now."

Angulimala was shaken up.

"What kind of disaster lies ahead for me?" asked Angulimala.

"You may continue with what you do so long as you are strong and vigilant. But any moment of indolence on your part will spell disaster for you. The king's men are after you and they will one day catch you and punish you for all your crimes. Even if you escape such punishment, you will be haunted by your crimes on your deathbed and that will be your suffering for lives to come."

A cold chill ran down Angulimala's spine. He threw his sword into the ditch by the roadside, took off his necklace of fingers and swung it into the bushes. He fell prostrate before the Buddha and pleaded:

"May the noble one have compassion for me and save me

183

from torments in the future. May I take refuge in the Blessed One."

"Come, monk," said the Buddha.

And that served as the statement of initiation and Angulimala became a disciple of the Buddha. Accompanied by him, Buddha arrived in Savatthi and took residence at Anathapindika's monastery, in Jeta's Grove.

Soon the rumor spread that Angulimala, the robber and murderer, was in Savatthi, hiding among the Buddha's disciples. It was believed that he would, at any time, strike terror into the heart of Savatthi. People were afraid to visit the Buddha and his disciples. They assembled at the palace gates and demanded that King Pasenadi send his army to Jeta's Grove to capture Angulimala.

The king decided to go there himself and accompanied by five hundred soldiers he set out in the direction of Jeta's Grove. People in the city waited in fear for the outcome of the confrontation between the soldiers and the Buddha's disciples. When the king arrived in Jeta's Grove, Buddha asked him:

"Is anything wrong, O King? Have you been attacked by any hostile rulers from the outlying kingdoms?"

"No, Sir. I am not being attacked by any rulers from the outlying kingdoms. I understand that Angulimala has appeared in Savatthi and is hiding in the Jeta's Grove, among disciples of Buddha. Sir, he is a very dangerous person and should be put in chains and gotten rid of."

"But, Your Majesty, if you were to see Angulimala with his hair shaven, donning yellow robes, going forth from home to homelessness, abstaining from killing and stealing, eating only one meal a day, leading a holy and virtuous life, what would you do to him?" asked the Buddha.

"Sir, I would pay homage to him, provide him with alms and arrange for his protection. But, Sir, this is impossible. Angulimala is a man with evil intentions. He has brought disaster on the people of Kosala. How could he turn out to be a virtuous and restrained person?"

All this time, Angulimala was seated near the Buddha and listening to the conversation with his head bent low. Buddha pointed his finger toward Angulimala and said to the king:

"This, Your Majesty, is Angulimala."

The king was frightened. His hair stood on end. Buddha noticed his agitation and said:

"Your Majesty, do not be afraid. There is nothing to fear. Angulimala does not wear the garland of fingers any more."

Angulimala raised his head, looked at King Pasenadi and smiled. It was, indeed, not the smile of a rogue trying to hide his real evil intentions. Instead, it was a smile that depicted, in no uncertain terms, the remorse within for all the innocent lives he had destroyed in the past. It was graceful, unassumed and sincere.

The king's fear and horror subsided. He walked up to Venerable Angulimala and asked:

"Venerable Angulimala is of noble descent, isn't he?"

"Yes, great King," murmured Angulimala, looking at the ground.

"What was the family of Venerable Angulimala's father? What was his mother's family name?"

"My father was a Gagga. My mother was a Mantani," replied Angulimala.

"Let the noble son of Gaggamantani consent to my supplying him with robes, alms food, lodging and medicine."

"There is no great need, O King, for such requisites. I prefer to be a forest dweller, an eater of alms food got by begging, a wearer of refuge rags, restricting myself to only three robes."

The king was moved by Angulimala's humility and restraint. He turned to the Buddha and said:

"It is wonderful, Sir, it is marvelous how the Blessed One subdues the unsubdued, restrains the unrestrained, without resorting to punishment, without resorting to weapons. Sir, may the Blessed One remain in Savatthi as long as it is possible. That would be to our advantage, to our happiness. And now, Sir, may we have permission to leave; we are busy and have much to do."

"It is time now, O King, to do as you think fit."

King Pasenadi paid homage to the Buddha and departed.

One morning, a few days later, Angulimala went into the city for alms. As he wandered from house to house, he heard the cries of a woman inside a house. It was a small house, and whoever lived there appeared to be very poor and destitute. Remaining at the doorstep for a few moments and finding that no one came out of the house to offer him any food, Angulimala suspected that the woman who cried in pain was alone and, therefore, needed help. He peeped into the house and found a woman lying on a contrived bed struggling and crying in pain to deliver her baby. He thought:

"Childbirth is a natural thing. But this woman seems to be in unusual discomfort. Maybe she is a woman difficult to be delivered."

He could do nothing but to rush back to Jeta's Grove and inform the Buddha of this situation. After listening to Angulimala, Buddha said:

"Angulimala, go back to that house. It is possible for you to relieve this woman of her pain by appearing before her and reciting something to distract her from thinking of her painful sensations."

"What should I recite?" asked Angulimala.

"You could say, 'Sister, since I was born I have never purposely destroyed any living being. By that truth, may you and the child have peace!"

"But, Sir, I cannot say that. It is an untruth," replied Angulimala.

Buddha smiled. He was glad that Angulimala was alert.

"Yes, Angulimala, what is false cannot be useful. Uttering falsehood in order to achieve good results is not the proper way for the noble disciples. Still you could say, without contradicting yourself, 'Sister, since I was born with the noble birth of the Aryan disciple, I have never purposely destroyed any living being. By that truth, may you and the child have peace!' "

Angulimala returned to the house and standing before the woman uttered that statement thrice. The woman delivered her child painlessly.

Some people who saw Angulimala coming out of the house, recognized him and thought:

"Disciples of the Buddha do not enter houses without being invited. They collect their alms by standing at the doorstep. The man of this house is not home at this time. He is away in the jungle cutting wood, which is his means of livelihood. This vicious man is again up to mischief, dishonoring even the great Buddha."

They started throwing stones and sticks at him, some of which struck Angulimala and injured him. With his head broken, with blood flowing, with his bowl in pieces and outer robe torn in patches, Angulimala returned to Jeta's Grove and went before the Buddha. Seeing Angulimala's plight, the Buddha said:

"Bear it, Angulimala, bear it. The world is full of ignorant and intolerant people. As such, a bad reputation, once established, is not easily wiped out. A good reputation also is not easily established. Understand this to be the ripening of your karma. Living the holy life, you will soon be able to attain the good reputation and will not be haunted by the evil and suffering consequent on your past behavior. That is the way to freedom from evil karma."

Dwelling alone, withdrawn, diligent, ardent and self-controlled, Angulimala realized for himself with direct knowledge and entered upon and dwelt in that supreme goal of the holy life for the sake of which a householder goes forth from home to homelessness.

TWENTY-EIGHT

WOMEN IN INDIAN SOCIETY during the Buddha's day were second-class citizens. Their lot in the social organization of the kingdoms of Magadha, Kasi and Kosala was unfortunate. In spite of a handful of illustrious women such as Gargi and Maitreyi who actively participated in public debates and discussions, women enjoyed very little opportunity to demonstrate their abilities.

Prejudices against them were many and varied. In the eyes of most, women were mere objects of enjoyment for men. Others believed that their capacities were limited to taking care of the various household chores or rearing children. Many refused to believe that they could attain the spiritual heights that male ascetics were able to reach. No one, of course, believed that a woman could rule a kingdom.

For example, Sela was made to believe that a woman was a mere object of sensual enjoyment, not made for freedom and peace in the world. Soma was told that, with her limited capacity for wisdom, she could not attain the spiritual distinction that men can achieve. Vimala was for a long time duped by the idea that her beauty was what mattered and nothing else. Nanduttara was under the impression that the only religious activities she was entitled to participate in were the worshipping of the sun and the moon. Sona understood that she was born merely to produce children. Mutta was confined to the household by three crooked things: the mortar, the pestle and the crooked husband.

The band of Sakyan women, led by the Buddha's stepmother, Gotami, provided the initiative to change all that. The courage and enthusiasm of women finally enabled them to triumph over the obstacles and seek a place of equality with men regarding moral and spiritual matters.

Yet, there was one major problem the female disciples had to face even after enlightenment. Subha, who enjoyed living in a mango grove (owned by the famous physician, Jivaka) because of the peace and quiet surrounding this grove, happened to be one among many disciples of the Buddha who had to deal with such problems.

One day, when Subha was returning to the mango grove after going on her alms round, she was accosted by a sensuous young man. Subha looked at him and asked:

"Friend, have I wronged you in any way that you stand obstructing my path? I am a disciple of the noble Buddha and I have entered the path of purity. Is there any reason why you should stand in my way?"

"You are young and pretty. What evil have you committed in order to don a yellow robe and go forth like any other ascetic? Discard that silly robe. Your body deserves to be draped with silken cloth from Kasi, not with a dirty rag like this. I cannot think of anyone more lovable than you, dear. Let us enjoy life. It is the first dawn of spring and there could be no better time to enjoy the pleasures of life. The trees are in full bloom and the air is filled with the sweet scent of the flowers. I shall provide you with every comfort, O you beautiful-eyed one. Why let your lovely body wither away like a lotus picked from its natural surroundings?"

"What makes you think that this body, that will eventually lie in a cemetery, has any essence?" asked Subha.

"Few and rare are the things that are beautiful in this world. Your eyes beat them all, O pretty one. Could anyone, having seen them once, ever forget them? Lovely lady, I plead with you to abandon this meaningless life and enjoy the exotic gift of nature you have received. After seeing you I cannot love anyone else."

"Friend, try not to go along a path where there will be no progress. Pursuing a disciple of the Buddha is like asking for the moon or attempting to jump over the majestic Himalayas. I have gotten rid of all attachment to pleasures of sense and I take delight in simple living."

The young man was not put off by such remarks. Subha had difficulty getting rid of him. She thought for a moment. There was only one way in which she could escape his evil intentions.

"Friend, you seem to be enamored by my eyes. Would you be satisfied if I were to pluck out my eyes and offer them to you? Would you then leave me in peace?"

The young man was agitated. He felt that this woman would not hesitate to do what she proposed. Before he could respond to her, she said:

"Friend, I am tormented and harassed by this putrid body. I have no attachment for it. Pleasures of sense are like a sharp-edged sword and the human personality is like an execution-er's block. I have no more delight in it."

"Do not be duped by the fraudulent words of the ascetics. These ascetics leave the household life after enjoying all the

189

pleasures of sense, especially when they are incapable of enjoying them any further. We are born into this life once and it is foolish to throw away this only opportunity for enjoyment," remarked the young man.

"Friend, what you say may be true regarding some ascetics and brahmans who think that one should leave a life of pleasure only when one is advanced in age. But you are mistaken when you attribute such a view to every ascetic. I am a follower of the son of the Sakyans, who makes no such distinction. If one can be happy with a life of asceticism when advanced in age, how could it not possibly bring about happiness for young men and women?"

"But how can you condemn pleasures of sense without ever tasting the joys associated with them?"

"Yes, I can. I have watched those who have given themselves to such pleasures and have seen how they suffer due to their excessive lust. I have witnessed how men and women end up on the executioner's block as a result of their greed, hate and confusion. King Pasenadi has to carry out such executions not because he wants to punish them, but because they themselves are inheritors of their unfortunate actions."

The young man became more and more frightened when reminded that unfortunate consequences await a person of evil actions. He knew that it was futile to try to tempt Subha. He, therefore, made up his mind to leave her alone. But before he left, he said to her:

"Sister, I hope you are right. May you enjoy your way of life!"

When Subha met the Buddha the next time, she reported this incident to him. Realizing the dangers faced by young female disciples who lead a lonely ascetic life, the Buddha advised them to avoid such lonely habitations. He extolled Subha's strength and courage to overcome such temptations and also her manner of dealing with the situation.

Uppalavanna was a young woman of Rajagaha who had joined the Buddha's disciples being disgusted with her lay life where she and her own mother had to live as co-wives of a wealthy brahman. She was present when Subha reported her experiences to the Buddha.

"Sir, should we not use our psychic powers to drive away any such evil ones? We could enter their bellies, or stand between their eyebrows or make ourselves invisible."

"Yes, Uppalavanna. It is possible to do so. But it is not the best way to deal with such situations. Subha did the right thing in creating a fear within the man by indicating the evil consequences he would reap as a result of his vile actions. That produces long-lasting effects. Conversion by means of psychic power will not have such lasting effects. If Subha failed to convince the man of the unfortunate consequences, surely there was nothing wrong in her using her psychic powers to get rid of him. Remember that persuasion is a better method of conversion than showing off your strength."

"I agree, Sir," replied Uppalavanna, who was pleased that the Buddha recognized the ability of women to protect themselves by developing strength of character rather than psychic power.

TWENTY-NINE

PSYCHIC POWER, CLAIRAUDIENCE, TELEPATHY, clairvoyance—these were a few of the wondrous powers some of the ascetics wanted to achieve. Kassapa, who was converted during the early stages of the Buddha's teaching, was one of them. There were innumerable yogins who assumed that these constituted the goal of religious life. These gave them power, wealth and superiority in a society where wondrous and marvelous phenomena were greatly valued. Upajjhayaka was a brahman who had achieved such powers. He rationalized the use of these powers he had gained:

"These are powers which very few people are able to attain. With strenuous practice I have become a proud possessor of these powers. These powers of mine should be used in the service of my king and my country."

Reflecting thus, he went to see the minister in charge of judicial matters.

"Sir, I have developed extraordinary knowledge and I will be able to help you and the king to solve many a crime that is committed in this kingdom."

The surprised minister asked Upajjhayaka:

"How can you be of help to me and the king?"

"You and your majesty take great pains to trace murderers, robbers and other evildoers. Even after you have taken them into custody on suspicion, you are unable to prove them guilty because you cannot provide the necessary evidence. I will be able to use my extraordinary knowledge in order to apprehend the evildoers and also to discover the evidence for their conviction," replied Upajjhayaka.

"That is a noble service, indeed," replied the minister and promised to consult him in the future.

A few days later, when the first case of robbery was reported to the king, the minister decided to test the abilities of Upajjhayaka. A rich merchant of Kosala, who had amassed enormous wealth by unjust means, was robbed of his wife's valuable jewelry by a gang of young men who themselves were victims of the merchant's insatiable thirst for wealth. Upajjhayaka was consulted. He not only provided the names of the robbers, but also led the king's men to the place where the jewels were hidden by the robbers. The minister was overjoyed. He was going to win King Pasenadi's favors not only because of the prompt apprehension of the robbers, but also because of the speed with which the lost items were recovered. He visited Upajjhayaka at home.

"Well done, Sir. You have rendered great service to the king and the country. You have also helped the poor merchant to recover his hard-earned property. The evildoers will be duly punished and you will be amply rewarded."

"Your honor, a robber is a robber, whatever his motive may be. He should therefore be duly punished. I consider it my duty to serve the king and his ministers, whether I am rewarded or not. After all, it is our dharma to do what is considered to be good, whether it leads to good consequences or bad consequences. The law or dharma is supreme. It has to be carried out irrespective of consideration for consequences."

"You are a great sage," replied the minister, who ordered his attendants to provide Upajjhayaka with ample gifts for his services.

The following day, the young convicts were taken in a procession along the streets of Savatthi with their hands and legs chained. At a public park, each one was given ten lashes with a whip and put in jail for several years.

Buddha was returning from an alms round in the city when he heard the commotion of the people gathered in the park. When he returned to Jeta's Grove, one of the monks who had witnessed the punishment meted out to the young men, reported the matter to the Buddha. Buddha made it an occasion to deliver a discourse to the monks on the three forms of dominances.

"There are these three forms of dominances, monks, which one has to reckon with, which cannot be avoided, which a wise man carefully reflects on before committing any action in this world. They are the dominance of the self, the dominance of the world and the dominance of righteousness."

"Sir, in what way do the self, the world and righteousness constitute dominances?" asked one of the monks.

"When you perform an act, whether good or bad, you cannot hide it from yourself. An evil action on your part, even if it be not known to others, will continue to torment you for a long time. Knowing this, a wise one avoids evil actions. This is the dominance of the self.

"Great is the congregation of people in this world. In this great congregation there are ascetics and brahmans who are possessed of enormous powers, who are clairvoyant and telepathic. They can observe you either from near or from far away. They are able to read your thoughts. They will know whether you have done evil or not. They will say to others: 'See that man. He is evil. He is up to such and such evil deeds.' Realizing this, a wise man will avoid committing such evil deeds. This, monks, is the dominance of the world.

"Finally, monks, a person perceives that his associates, who are endowed with knowledge and insight, live a happy and contented life. Realizing this, he too will strive for knowledge and insight. He will refrain from actions that are evil and promote and cultivate good actions. Such is the dominance of righteousness."

On this occasion, a prince named Abhaya, a disciple of the Jain leader, Nataputta, was among those gathered around the Buddha. After listening to the conversation between the Buddha and his disciple and also the Buddha's discourse, Abhaya questioned Buddha regarding statements a person ought and ought not to make, primarily with the intention of finding out whether Buddha would or would not approve of Upajjhayaka's behavior.

"Sir, will the Blessed One speak what is unpalatable and disagreeable to others? If the Blessed One does, then he is not different from any ordinary man. If the Blessed One were to claim that he does not speak what is unpalatable and disagreeable to others, then the Blessed One is not truthful, for the Blessed One has declared that Devadatta is an evil person, destined to suffer for a long time, and this certainly was not palatable to Devadatta."

Buddha realized that this was, indeed, a very difficult question. Prince Abhaya had probably thought of this double-edged question to test the Buddha's wisdom. He looked at Prince Abhaya and smiled. While doing so, he was meditating on an answer.

"Abhaya, a statement we make can have several characteristics. It may be true or false, pleasant or unpleasant to others, useful or useless."

"Yes, Sir. That will leave us with eight different kinds of statements," remarked Abhaya.

"Yes, Abhaya, we will have at least eight different statements."

"Which of these statements will the Blessed One make and which ones will he avoid?"

"If I know that a certain statement is false, useless and

unpalatable to others, I shall avoid making such a statement. If I know that a certain statement is true, but useless and unpalatable to others, that too I shall avoid. That statement which I know to be true and useful, yet unpalatable to others, that I will make depending upon the occasion. If I know that a statement is false and useless and palatable to others, I shall avoid that statement. If I know that a statement is true, yet useless and palatable to others, that too I shall avoid. But if I know that a statement is true and useful and is also palatable to others, I shall assert or make that statement, once again depending upon the occasion."

All this time Abhaya was counting his fingers. Buddha referred to only six kinds of statements.

"Sir," said Abhaya, "what about the statements that are false and useful, both pleasant and unpleasant?"

"You are good at numbers, aren't you Abhaya?"

Prince Abhaya could not help smiling. The Buddha continued:

"Abhaya, it is difficult for me to believe that what is false can be useful. It is for that reason that I avoided any reference to them."

"Sir, it seems that the Blessed One is willing to make statements that are true and useful, whether they be pleasant or unpleasant. But yet the Blessed One seems to make the qualification when he says that even these would be made depending upon the occasion. Why? Does it mean that the Blessed One is not prepared to speak the truth, even though it be the truth?"

"Abhaya, I do not make statements assuming that there are absolute truths," replied Buddha.

"To reject the conception of an absolute truth is also to reject the notion of duty or dharma which many an ascetic and brahman would accept," said Abhaya.

"Abhaya, doing one's duty is a very noble thing. But let it not be forgotten that not all men are enlightened. It is always possible for that noble conception of duty to be utilized by the unenlightened for their own gain and also to cause harm to others."

"Sir, a person like Upajjhayaka was motivated by a noble ideal of duty. If one were to do one's duty, why should one

195

care about anything else? One should do one's duty, even if that were to cause harm to others, whether or not they be one's own kith and kin."

"I care about many things, Abhaya, because I have compassion for beings."

Prince Abhaya was quick to grasp the humanistic attitude of the Buddha and became the third among Nataputta's disciples to embrace the Buddha's teachings.

THIRTY

LIVING AMONG THE KOSALANS, the Buddha traveled the entire length and breadth of the kingdom of Kosala, visiting towns and villages, sometimes invited by the people, and at other times upon his own initiative. During these wanderings, he came to a small town called Kesaputta belonging to a clan called the Kalamas. The Kalamas were frequently visited by many ascetics and wanderers, but had never come under the strong influence of any of them. They were an open-minded group of people. When the news spread that the ascetic of the Sakyan clan was in town, many leading members of the Kalama clan gathered together and invited the Buddha for a discussion. When they met the Buddha, they questioned him:

"Sir, ascetics and brahmans come one after another to Kesaputta. Each one of them expounds his own notions of good and bad, right and wrong. When we mention to them what we have learned from others who have visited us previously, they condemn those views and praise their own ideas.

We are puzzled and are in doubt about all these views. We do not know who speaks the truth and who does not."

"You may well be puzzled, Kalamas. You may well be in doubt. Your doubt has arisen precisely about what ought to be doubted. In your search for what is good and bad, what is right and wrong, you should avoid excessive dependence upon several things."

"Sir, we are anxious to know what they are."

"Complete dependence upon tradition, Kalamas, will not help you to decide properly what is good and bad. Neither will dependence upon report, hearsay and authority of scriptures. Neither are logic and reasoning alone appropriate as a means of arriving at the truth. Reflection upon form, preference for accepted views, mere suitability or even respect for a teacher—these too, on their own, will not provide you with means of reaching a decision regarding good and bad."

"Sir, you have exhausted all the different means of knowledge advocated by the various ascetics and brahmans who have so far visited us. What other ways of knowing are there?" questioned one of the Kalamas.

"When, Kalamas, you know for yourselves that such and such things are blameworthy, are condemned by the wise and are conducive to harm and suffering, then you should abandon them.

"What do you think, Kalamas?" continued the Buddha. "When greed arises in a person, is that conducive to his good or evil?"

"It is certainly conducive to his evil," replied one of the Kalamas.

"Sir, could you explain how a person comes to perform evil by being excessively greedy?" pleaded another.

"Kalamas, how is it that a person comes to destroy life, steal, look for another's wife, speak falsehood or get another to commit such deeds?" questioned the Buddha.

"Sometimes it may be due to greed, and sometimes it may be due to other reasons," replied one of the Kalamas.

"I agree with you that it is not always due to greed that a person commits such deeds. But what other reasons can you think of?" asked Buddha.

"Sir, on some occasions people may commit such deeds because they do not like other persons."

"Yes, you are right. When you say that a person commits such deeds because he does not like another person, that means he is hateful of that person. Isn't that the case?"

"Yes, Sir."

Another of the Kalamas questioned:

"There may be altogether different reasons for a person to commit such deeds."

"Surely. But can you give me one such reason?" questioned Buddha.

"Well, a person may commit such deeds because he is destitute, because he has no means of satisfying himself in this life except by committing such deeds."

"Why should he think that there are no other means of achieving satisfaction?" asked Buddha.

"Maybe, he is ignorant of any other ways of achieving satisfaction."

Buddha was pleased with the questions as well as the responses of the Kalamas. He said:

"Kalamas, you are indeed very intelligent. Now see what you have accepted as reasons for a person to commit deeds such as killing, stealing, looking for another's wife, and lying. There are basically three reasons—greed, hate and ignorance or confusion. Can you think of any other reason?"

"Whatever other reasons we can imagine, all of them can be included under one or the other of these categories."

"Very good, Kalamas! These indeed are the reasons why people commit such deeds. But, Kalamas, are such deeds prompted by greed, hate and confusion conducive to harm and suffering for oneself as well as others?"

"Sir, no decent person will doubt that deeds motivated by greed, hate and confusion lead to harm and suffering for oneself as well as others."

"What is blameworthy, despised by the wise and is conducive to harm and suffering—is that good or bad?"

"It is bad, Sir," replied the Kalamas.

"That means whatever action that is not motivated by greed,

hate and confusion, and which leads to welfare and happiness is good."

"That's right," replied the Kalamas.

"In that case, Kalamas, do not depend entirely upon tradition, report, hearsay, authority of scriptures, logic and reasoning, reflection upon form, preference for accepted views, mere suitability or even respect for a teacher. These alone will not help you to decide what is good and bad."

"Sir, if we do not know that such and such actions will lead to good consequences or such and such actions to bad consequences, how can we decide which to choose?"

"That is a very appropriate question, Kalamas. A man who is completely ignorant is not able to decide what is good and bad, right and wrong. What would you do if you were in such a position?"

"We would have to depend on someone who knows."

"Indeed. Right understanding comes as a result of two conditions. The first is external information and the second, reflection according to genesis."

"Could you elaborate on these two conditions?"

"Surely. So long as we are not familiar with a situation which we need to understand, so long as we have not had an experience of such a situation, it is proper that we depend on someone who has information about it."

"But, Sir, if we do not have any knowledge about a situation, we could be duped by a trickster to believing that what he says is true."

"That's right, Kalamas."

"How, then, can we go about ascertaining the truth about that situation?"

"Kalamas, for a beginner there are at least five approaches to realizing what is true. These are faith, likes, tradition, reflection on form, and preference for accepted views. Unfortunately, these five have a twofold result. Sometimes, what is accepted on good faith may be false, empty without substance, while what is not accepted on faith may be true, real and not otherwise. Similarly with regard to other methods. For this reason, Kalamas, a beginner who is interested in preserving truth should not come to the conclusion: 'This alone is true;

everything else is false!' If he were to do so, he would close all avenues of arriving at truth and would be a dogmatist. Therefore, when one is not certain about a situation, it is always better to suspend judgment."

"Having suspended judgment, how do we go about verifying the truth of what we learn from others?"

"We have already agreed that deeds motivated by greed, hate and confusion are bad deeds. Therefore, it is possible to say that a person who is motivated by greed, hate and confusion is also a bad person. Isn't that right?"

"That's right, Sir."

"If so, it would be appropriate for us to find out whether the person in whom we are going to place our trust and faith is a person motivated by greed, hate and confusion. This can be achieved by carefully examining a person's deed, word, and thought."

"After we discover that a person is a good person or a bad person, what should we do?"

"If you know that a person is bad, you will also know what to do with him, wouldn't you?"

"Yes. We should not trust him or have faith in him. But does this mean that we place all our trust in a good man and accept everything that he says?"

"No, Kalamas. You can trust him, but you need not accept everything that he says. After placing trust in a good person, it is not necessary for you to accept everything he says merely on the basis of faith. We all need teachers. That does not mean that we should accept everything that the teacher tells us, merely because we trust him. At this very crucial point, we must try to verify for ourselves whether what we have accepted on good faith is true or false. The second condition I mentioned to you earlier becomes very important at this stage. Reflection according to genesis is the only way in which you will be able to know whether what you have accepted on faith is true or false."

"Sir, what is reflection according to genesis?" asked one of the Kalamas.

"Seeing things as they have come to be, Kalamas, is reflection according to genesis. Let me question you, Kalamas.

When things arise in this world, do they arise on their own or do they depend on various other factors?"

"Sir, as far as we know, nothing arises in this world on its own. Everything has come to be depending on other things."

"If everything that we have experienced so far is dependently arisen, will it be possible for us to know things as they are without the conditions that give rise to them?"

"No, Sir. That would not be possible."

"Therefore, Kalamas, look back and see how things have come to be. So far they have arisen dependently. A careful examination of how things have come to be will enable us to avoid what is evil and promote what is good. Avoiding what is bad and promoting what is good—this, Kalamas, is the message of buddhas."

The Kalamas thus became faithful followers of the Buddha.

THIRTY-ONE

PATRONIZED BY KING PASENADI, Buddha spent the last few years of his life in Savatthi. When the king died, Buddha decided to move on to Rajagaha. He was almost eighty years old now. Arriving in Rajagaha, the Buddha learned that Ajatasatthu had dethroned his old father and crowned himself as king of Magadha. Ajatasatthu too learned of the Buddha's arrival in Magadha, but his dislike of the Buddha's liberal views prevented him from visiting the Buddha.

Ajatasatthu wanted to assure himself that he was the undisputed ruler. Because of the way he had ascended the throne, he feared that someone might attempt to usurp the throne or that the more powerful of the adjacent confederates, such as the Vajjis, would annex Magadha. He wanted to find out whether such a thing could happen to him. So he summoned his chief minister, Vassakara, and said:

"Vassakara, I understand that the Buddha has arrived in Rajagaha and is staying at Vulture's Peak. He is possessed of all the psychic powers as well as supersensory knowledge. It is possible that he may know whether there is anyone who plans to wage war against Magadha. Inform him that I wish to attack the Vajjis and destroy them. See what he has to say and come and report it to me."

Vassakara agreed. Visiting the Buddha at Vulture's Peak, Vassakara exchanged greetings with him and when all the pleasantries were over, he informed Buddha of King Ajatasatthu's intention to wage war against the Vajjis. Buddha thought that it was not necessary for Ajatasatthu to inform him of his intention to wage such a war against the Vajjis. He realized that it was a mere pretence on the part of Ajatasatthu to know whether the Buddha recognized his sovereignty and whether Ajatasatthu was safe in his position, which he had attained by foul means. Therefore, instead of answering Vassakara, Buddha addressed himself to Ananda, who was standing behind, fanning him.

"Ananda, have you heard whether the Vajjis hold frequent and well-attended meetings?"

"Yes, Sir, I understand that they do so," replied Ananda.

"Have you heard whether they assemble in concord, rise in concord and do their duties as Vajjis in concord, whether they do not unnecessarily tamper with the laws they have enacted in concord, whether they honor, respect and revere the more enlightened and experienced Vajjis, whether they let their women and girls live without fear of harassment, whether they uphold religious tolerance and freedom?"

"They do indeed, Sir," replied Ananda.

"As long as they do so, Ananda, the Vajjis will remain strong and invincible. They will not easily decline or deteriorate as a nation."

Buddha turned to Vassakara and said:

"Vassakara, once I was living in Vesali, in the Sarandada Monastery. At that time I preached to the Vajjis these seven

202

things that prevent the decline of a nation. As long as they follow these moral principles, it will not be easy for any other nation to conquer them."

"Sir, it seems that it would not be easy to bring about destruction of the Vajjis if they were to follow a single one of these moral principles, let alone all seven. It would be foolish on the part of King Ajatasatthu to wage war against them. He will never get the better of the Vajjis by fighting, unless he buys them over and sows seeds of dissension among them."

Without questioning the Buddha any further, Vassakara paid obeisance to the Buddha and left. Ajatasatthu who was informed about Buddha's views was greatly agitated. He pondered over his problems:

"Buddha's influence on my father almost deprived me of my legitimate inheritance. Now he is providing advice to those Vajjis and other groups who do not care for royal lineage. He is destroying the kshatriya clan which was ordained by Brahma to rule the earth. A heretic like this should be gotten rid of before things become worse."

He knew that Devadatta was angry with the Buddha for refusing to let him lead the order of monks and nuns.

"Devadatta is the only person who will stand up against the Buddha," he thought. "He was rebuffed by the Buddha and, therefore, should be willing to get rid of him. My authority in Magadha will never be firmly rooted so long as the Buddha lives and his teachings are respected by the people."

He spoke to Vassakara:

"Can you think of some plan to bring the Buddha into disrepute in the eyes of the Magadhans?"

"That would not be easy, Your Majesty," replied Vassakara.

"I know it is not easy. But it is not impossible. Maybe the Buddha's cousin, Devadatta, can help."

Shrewd as he was, Vassakara did not take long to concoct a plan.

A few days later, Vassakara saw Ajatasatthu and informed him of his plan.

"Your Majesty, the Buddha is not very popular either among the brahman priests or among the ascetics. It is possible that his unpopularity among them would be utilized to our advantage."

"The Buddha may be unpopular among the brahman priests, but how is it that he is not favored by the ascetics?" inquired Ajatasatthu.

"Many an ascetic thinks that the Buddha is leading a life of luxury. Wherever he goes, people build comfortable lodgings for him and his disciples and serve him with the choicest of food. The ascetics who lead an austere life have been completely overshadowed by the Buddha. It may be possible that this displeasure on the part of the ascetics could be used to discredit the Buddha."

"How do we go about achieving this?"

"We have Venerable Devadatta's support, don't we?" asked Vassakara.

"Surely. But what can Devadatta do? He himself is not highly regarded by the people."

"Venerable Devadatta could be made the advocate of asceticism. For the ordinary man, seeing is believing. He is more fascinated by what he can see with his naked eyes than by what is given to his intellect. The Buddha may be an ascetic in spirit, but he does not appear to be an ascetic in practice. Let Venerable Devadatta propose a more austere way of life than what is practiced by the Buddha and his followers. Even some of his own disciples who have not attained enlightenment may favor such a form of asceticism."

"Vassakara, you indeed have a brilliant mind. What more can I expect from my chief minister? I shall personally go to meet Venerable Devadatta."

Ajatasatthu was delighted with Vassakara's proposition and was immediately off to see Devadatta. At this time, Devadatta was living with a company of disciples separated from other monks and nuns. Seeing his royal friend and patron from a distance, Devadatta went forward to meet him.

"What brings His Majesty here? Could I be of any service to His Majesty and his people?" asked Devadatta.

"Yes, indeed, Venerable Devadatta. I am concerned about the spiritual values and traditions of our nation. The brahman priest has always been a great source of spiritual strength for the householder. The ascetic tradition has catered to the spiritual needs of those who have fulfilled all their social obligations and were ready to retire into the forest. But these noble traditions have been threatened by the Buddha, who not only leads a life of luxury, but encourages his disciples also to do so. Unlike other noble ascetics like Nataputta, the Buddha is leading a very suspect life. It is only a person like Venerable Devadatta who can change this unfortunate situation. Maybe Venerable Devadatta ought to suggest to the Buddha the need to recommend to his disciples a truly ascetic way of life. Buddha will not be able to reject such a request and still maintain the popularity he enjoys now."

Devadatta reflected for a moment. On an earlier occasion he made a proposal to the Buddha instigated by the prince, who now was the king. Unfortunately, that proposal was more of a self-serving one, and Devadatta really could not find fault with the Buddha for rejecting it, although he was angry at the manner he came to be rebuffed by the Buddha. But the present suggestion by Ajatasatthu pertained more to the doctrine and discipline. If the Buddha refused to accommodate Devadatta, he could become unpopular not only among outsiders, but even among some of his own disciples.

Devadatta readily agreed. With five of his friends, Devadatta visited the Buddha. It was a rather surprise visit and the Buddha did not have time even to think what Devadatta's purpose might be, and, therefore, remarked rather sarcastically:

"Devadatta, what prompted you to visit with us? Have you another proposal to make?"

Devadatta and his friends were taken aback.

"The enlightened one knows beforehand why we are here," thought Devadatta. "It is indeed difficult to escape his omniscience. In any case, I should make my proposal and I am sure, in spite of all his powers, he will have difficulty in rejecting it."

"Sir, the Blessed One has always enjoined a life of asceticism. But many a monk today leads a life of luxury. It is not in keeping with those who have renounced pleasures of sense to lead such a life. Now, here are five points that the Blessed

One may enjoin his disciples so that they could attain the goal sooner and preserve the purity of the ascetic tradition."

"What, Devadatta, are the five points you have in mind?" asked Buddha.

"Sir, there are five appropriate forms of behavior that a person who has renounced home life should adopt. He should be a forest dweller for life and avoid any form of social life. He should be dependent upon food collected by begging and not accept any invitation. He should wear robes made of rags instead of those provided by householders. He should live under trees instead of occupying comfortable lodgings. Finally, he should never eat meat or fish, but should subsist entirely on a vegetable diet. Such ought to be the austere life to be adopted by those who have renounced household life. Such a life would not only bring the spiritual goal closer and sooner, but also would make it more admirable in the eyes of the people."

"Enough, Devadatta," replied the Buddha. "Let there be no popularity contest. If a monk has attained freedom from defilements, I do not see any reason why he should confine his life to a forest. Like a lotus that remains unsmeared by the water in the lake, an enlightened disciple is able to live in society without harming himself and still to be of great service to humanity. Devadatta, what purpose is served by the most beautiful flower that blooms in the forest and fades away in the forest?"

Devadatta looked at his friends. None of them showed any interest in answering the Buddha. Buddha continued:

"I do not wish to see my disciples who have attained freedom from all attachments wither away like forest flowers. People in the world need their help. They should devote their lives to the service of humanity."

Buddha thought for a moment.

"But, if a monk is not freed from attachment, is not enlightened, if he wishes to be a forest dweller, let him be one. Yet, if forest dwelling is distracting to him, if it does not help him to attain the goal of the religious life, let him live in the village or township. Even so with regard to the other three points you have raised. Regarding the last point, I have allowed monks to eat fish and meat that is pure in three respects—when it is not seen, or heard or suspected to have been killed for one personally."

"Sir, if there are to be no definite rules to be followed by the disciples, how can they be expected to attain enlightenment and freedom?" asked Devadatta.

"Devadatta, the adoption of fixed rules of discipline will enable man to attain freedom only if everything in the world, including human life, is governed by fixed laws. But I see no such fixed and unalterable laws in the world. Not seeing such invariable laws and seeing things as they have come to be conditioned by various factors, I declare the world to be in a process of becoming. How then can I prescribe inviolable laws of discipline for the monks?"

Buddha rested for a moment.

"Devadatta, suffering in this world is due to the dispositional tendencies of man. These dispositional tendencies are variously conditioned. Happiness can be achieved by the pacification of all dispositional tendencies and if the dispositional tendencies are variously conditioned, there should also be different paths to such happiness and freedom. Therefore, Devadatta, I consider the goal to be one and the path thereof to be manifold."

Having listened to such a discourse, Devadatta's friends could not help abandoning him and joining the Buddha. Devadatta returned to his monastery alone. Heartbroken at the loss of his friends, loss of his reputation and at the realization that he had committed crimes against his noble cousin, Devadatta was taken ill and in a few days passed away.

When informed about the death of his cousin, the Buddha sympathetically observed:

"Monks, Devadatta is an example of a well-motivated man falling into the snares of an evil-minded man. Therefore, I exhort you to shun the wicked and cultivate the company of the noble ones."

THIRTY-TWO

L EAVING RAJAGAHA, THE BUDDHA moved northwest accompanied by a large following of disciples, including Ananda. Visiting several small towns on the way, he arrived in Vesali, the capital of the Licchavis, where he stayed for a brief period on his way to Rajagaha from Kapilavatthu. Arriving in Vesali, he took residence in a mango grove that, by this time, had come to be a possession of the famous courtesan, Ambapali.

Ambapali heard that Buddha had arrived in Vesali and that he was living in her mango grove. She hurried to see the Buddha, this time accompanied only by a handful of middle-aged women. Buddha saw her from a distance and noticed the change in her retinue. When she approached him, he asked her:

"Ambapali, where are those able-bodied handsome men who accompanied you as bodyguards wherever you went?"

Ambapali looked down in embarrassment. Her beauty was gone. Wrinkles had appeared on her face, like the lines left on the desert sand after a storm. Her dark hair had turned completely gray. The flowers she was wearing added no beauty to it. Her eyes appeared in their deep sockets like water in a deep well. Her previously well-proportioned limbs retained no such proportion. After a moment, she picked up her courage and said:

"Sir, I do not need those guards any more."

"Why, Ambapali?"

"Nobody is interested in my body now. If no one desires it, there is no need to protect it."

"But, Ambapali, people were all the time running after it and you were trying to make those people crave for it more and more by placing guards around it."

Ambapali was silent.

"Ambapali, you were as responsible as they were for your problems. They were given to pleasures of sense and so were you. If you had not encouraged them, they would not have been seeking your company the way they did. See my disciple Subha. She was a pretty young woman and was followed by many pleasure seekers. But no one dared to place a hand on her even when she was living alone in the forest. Compare yourself, with all your frustrations and depressions, with Subha who has led a happy and peaceful life all along."

"Sir, I deeply regret the ignorance and arrogance I displayed when I met the Blessed One on that previous occasion. May I be pardoned for my sins and may the Blessed One accept me as a disciple."

"Yes, Ambapali, it is not too late for you to make yourself happy and contented."

Ambapali invited the Buddha and his disciples to have the midday meal at her residence the following day; she paid obeisance to the Buddha and left.

On the way, she met a band of Licchavis coming to see the Buddha. They stopped her and questioned her.

"Ambapali, have you seen the Buddha?"

"Yes, friends, I have seen him for the first time," replied Ambapali.

Some in the crowd were surprised by her statement.

"Ambapali, we all know that you met the Buddha when he visited Vesali on an earlier occasion. At that time, everyone believed that you would convert the Buddha and make him change his way of life. But now you say that you have seen him for the first time."

"Yes, friends, I have seen the Buddha for the first time and he has accepted an invitation to a meal at my house for the morrow."

So saying she went on her way. The Licchavis could not believe what they had heard. They thought:

"How is it that the Buddha, when he was young, was not attracted to Ambapali. It seems that in his old age he has lost his strength of character and has accepted an invitation to visit her."

They proceeded to the mango grove and met the Buddha. Having paid him obeisance, the Licchavis sat on the side and addressed Buddha:

"Sir, it is our good fortune that the Blessed One decided to visit Vesali again. The Licchavis of Vesali have got together to welcome the Blessed One and his disciples and may the Blessed One accept their invitation to midday meals tomorrow."

"Friends, I cannot accept your invitation for tomorrow. I have agreed to accept meals from Ambapali."

The Licchavis were very upset. Their leader thought to himself:

"This Ambapali has beaten us again. Maybe we could get the Buddha to change his decision."

"Sir, this Ambapali is vile and is not to be trusted. She has lost her hold on the young men in Vesali and she is very angry with the people. We met her on the way and she informed us that she met the Blessed One for the first time. Yet all of us know that she saw the Blessed One on a previous occasion and tried to seduce the Blessed One. She probably is out to take revenge on the Blessed One for the rebuff she received on that occasion. Please do not accept her invitation."

"No, Licchavis, she was not lying when she said that she saw me for the first time. Indeed, she told you the truth. When she came to see me on the previous occasion, she was so enamored and obsessed with her own beauty that she failed to see me. Licchavis, he who sees the truth about the world I have discovered and explained, he sees me. Ambapali has become my disciple."

The Licchavis were surprised.

"Sir, we are at a loss and we cannot understand how such a vile and crafty woman was able to understand the deep and profound teachings of the Buddha."

"Ambapali had no difficulty in understanding the change

that has taken place in her personality. Licchavis, you your-selves have taught her a lesson. When she was young, you adored her and sought her company. You were willing to sacrifice everything in your possession in order to enjoy her company. But you do not appear to be interested in her any-more. Why? What makes you reject and condemn something that you craved and adored for years?"

The Licchavis remained silent.

"That is what Ambapali has realized," continued the Bud-dha. "She has come to realize that impermanence makes no discrimination. The most powerful, the most beautiful and the most pleasurable come to an end—are rendered powerless, ugly and a source of suffering. It is time for you to understand that this is the nature of life. Licchavis, do not place the blame entirely upon Ambapali. Ambapali has repented her ignorance and arrogance and has achieved peace of mind. Having lost the opportunity to enjoy Ambapali's beauty, you are haunted by deprivation, by jealousy, by hate. These do not contribute to your welfare and happiness. You seem to have forgotten the customs and traditions that made the Vajjian confederacy great. It may not take long for the evil forces to overwhelm you."

The Licchavis, who were a part of the great Vajjian confed-eracy, were agitated. They apologized to the Buddha and taking leave of him, immediately returned to Ambapali's res-idence and pleaded with her:

"Ambapali, let us participate in the preparation of tomor-row's meal for the Buddha and his disciples. Let us make it an occasion for the entire Licchavi clan led by you to host the great sage."

"Yes, indeed, friends," agreed Ambapali, who thenceforward utilized her enormous wealth to support not only the Buddha and his disciples, but also the sick and the poor among the Licchavis.

THIRTY-THREE

THE BUDDHA STAYED IN AMBAPALI'S mango grove as long as he chose to and said to Ananda:

"Come, Ananda, let us go to the village of Beluva."

"Even so, Sir," replied Ananda, and made arrangements to leave Vesali. Immediately after the Buddha's arrival in Beluva, the rains set in. Therefore, he remained in this small town together with his disciples until the rainy season was over.

After he took up residence in Beluva for the rains, a severe sickness attacked him with violent and deadly pains. He bore them without complaint, mindful and conscious. Until the Buddha recovered from his illness, Ananda kept constant vigil over him.

Soon after recovering from his illness, Buddha came out of the sickroom and sat on a seat made ready for him. Addressing Ananda, he said:

"Ananda, I am grateful to you for taking care of me during my illness. You look very tired. Did you rest during the time I was sick?"

"Sir, all these years I have been used to seeing the Blessed One in good health and comfort. Indeed, when the Blessed One was overwhelmed by illness, I felt as if my body were quite rigid. My vision was blurred and my mind was confused. However, I comforted myself thinking that the Blessed One would not pass away without making any pronouncement regarding the community of disciples."

"Ananda, what does the community of disciples expect of me?"

"Sir, as long as the Blessed One is living it is possible for the disciples to approach the Blessed One and get their problems solved. Who would be in a position to help them when the Blessed One is gone?"

"Ananda, I have taught the doctrine and discipline without secret and public versions. I have not kept anything from you. I am not a close-fisted teacher. Neither did I, at any time, think that I was governing the community of disciples and that the community was dependent upon me. The need to make a pronouncement about the community would arise only if I had done so."

Buddha remained silent for a moment, showing signs that he could not continue to speak at length as he used to without resting. After a moment he continued:

"Ananda, ignorant and empty people assume that they are rulers, that others can survive only by depending upon them. On the contrary, the enlightened ones are mere guides, not rulers or authorities. Not having assumed such authority, I have nothing to pass on to a successor.

"Now I am old, Ananda. I have reached my eightieth year. My body is like an old cart that can only carry on with the help of makeshifts. I am not free from bodily pain. With such painful experiences I remain calm, but sometimes I need to attain the state of cessation of perception and what is felt in order to remain at ease. Very soon, Ananda, I shall be gone.

"Since attaining enlightenment, Ananda, I have depended on myself, had myself as a refuge. Similarly, Ananda, each one of you should make an island for yourself, be your own refuge, and not depend on any other for refuge. Make the doctrine your refuge, not anything else. I shall not appoint anyone as my successor, as an authority. Let the doctrine that I taught you and the discipline I recommended to you be your guide, your authority."

"Sir, how does one go about making the doctrine one's refuge?" asked Ananda.

"The four states of mindfulness I have taught you should serve as your guide, as your refuge. A disciple should abide contemplating body as body, ardent, fully aware and mindful, having overcome covetousness and grief in the world. Simi-

213

larly, he should abide contemplating feeling as feeling, mind as mind, mental objects as mental objects. Either now or when I am gone, a disciple who trains himself thus will make an island unto himself."

During this time, Sariputta, one of the chief disciples of the Buddha, who had been living mostly in Magadha, was taken seriously ill and in a few days passed away. A young disciple by name Cunda collected Venerable Sariputta's bowl and robes and set out looking for the Buddha. Finally he arrived in the village of Beluva and was met by Ananda.

Ananda was greatly moved by the news. He announced the sad news to the Buddha.

"Sir, the Venerable Sariputta has passed away. When I heard the news, my body became rigid, my vision failed and my mind was confused."

"What do you think, Ananda? When Venerable Sariputta died did he take away with him the code of virtue, the method of concentration, the means of understanding, the way of deliverance, the knowledge and vision of deliverance?"

"No, Sir. But I cannot help thinking how helpful he was to his fellow practitioners—advising, informing, instructing, urging, rousing, pacifying and gladdening them, how tireless he was in teaching them the doctrine."

"That is true, Ananda. But, haven't I already told you that there is separation and parting from all that is dear and beloved? How could it be that what is born, has come to be, is dispositionally determined and is subject to fall, should not come to an end? This is not possible. Sariputta was, indeed, like the main branch of a tree. That great branch has fallen. So will the tree. That is why I have advised you to make an island for yourself, a refuge unto yourself. Exhort yourself, Ananda, do not relax."

Buddha was a little too weak to leave Beluva, so he remained there a bit longer. During this time the news of the passing away of another of his famous disciples, Moggallana, was brought to him.

That afternoon, he came out of his little cottage and sat in the open air. The disciples gathered round him. They too had come to know of the passing away of Venerable Moggallana.

214

Some of the young disciples who had yet to attain nirvana and who had previously been instructed by both Sariputta and Moggallana were present. All of them were sad and despondent. Some had swollen eyes. The atmosphere at the gathering was very different from anything that had prevailed before. There was complete silence.

Noticing the silent community of monks and nuns, Buddha said:

"It seems that this assembly is very empty. The assembly is empty because Sariputta and Moggallana are not there. There is nowhere one can look and say: 'Sariputta and Moggallana are living there.' '

"Yes, Sir," responded Ananda. "The congregation is empty. It is empty as a result of the passing away of Venerable Sariputta and Venerable Moggallana. I cannot imagine how it would survive in the absence of the Blessed One."

"Ananda, there were many disciples who passed away before Sariputta and Moggallana. How is it that the community did not feel the same way as they do now?"

Ananda knew why the Buddha was asking that question. Yet he replied:

"Sir, unlike many other disciples, Venerable Sariputta and Venerable Moggallana have been of great service to the community. When the Blessed One was away they served as our teachers, our guides."

"Yes, Ananda, naturally the community will feel the loss of these two great teachers. Yet, Ananda, it should serve as a lesson to those disciples who have not yet attained enlightenment. They should realize that not only the greatest and the mightiest will come to an end, but also that suffering is the inevitable result of dispositional conditions. Look, Ananda! You did not feel as sad at the passing away of other monks and nuns as you did at the demise of Sariputta and Moggallana. You were favorably disposed towards Sariputta and Moggallana. If not for your dispositions, you would not have been so affected. Ananda, strive for the pacification of dispositions. Then only will there be an end to suffering."

215

THIRTY-FOUR

FROM BELUVA, THE BUDDHA made his way to a village called Bhanda. Returning from his alms round and having partaken of his meal, the Buddha addressed Ananda and said:

"Ananda, there are these four bases of psychic power. They are concentration of purpose, of will, of thought and of investigation. If anyone has developed and cultivated these bases of psychic power, he will be able to overcome illness and live a full life span. Ananda, I have developed and practiced these bases of psychic power and, therefore, if I so wish, I could live a full life span without letting illness overwhelm me."

Ananda, who was already depressed by the demise of Sariputta and Moggallana and was now worried about the impending demise of the Buddha, lacked the attention and concentration to request Buddha to live a full life span. Realizing that Ananda was not in control of himself, Buddha reflected upon the state of the community of disciples and realized that it was well-established and that it could continue even in his absence. Therefore, he made up his mind not to prolong his life by the use of psychic power.

A few days later, Buddha walked into an assembly of disciples unannounced. Everyone was silent. No one thought of asking the Buddha any questions, assuming that by doing so he would be tiring the Buddha who was now very weak and in constant pain. Buddha understood the sentiments of the disciples. He said to them:

"You are unusually quiet, monks and nuns. You are overwhelmed by the demise of loved ones. I have insisted that it is the nature of all dispositionally conditioned things. They arise and pass away. A realization of this will enable you to overcome sorrow and suffering and attain perfection. Strive with diligence. Do not let indolence overcome you."

Buddha waited for a moment, and continued:

"Ripe is my age and there is very little life left to me. Soon I will leave you and depart. I have made my own refuge. Monks and nuns, be diligent and mindful. Be virtuous. With thoughts well-concentrated, keep constant watch over your hearts. Those who live diligently in this doctrine and discipline will overcome the round of rebirths and make an end of suffering."

After making these remarks, the Buddha got up and walked back to his cottage.

Those monks and nuns, including Ananda, who had not as yet attained freedom, were stricken with grief. Some began to shed tears. Finally, Ananda addressed the community:

"Friends, I understand that anyone who has developed and cultivated the four bases of psychic power will be able to overcome illness and prolong life up to a maximum period. The Blessed One is foremost among those who have cultivated such power. Therefore, the Blessed One should be able to live longer. I will make an appeal to the Blessed One to use his powers to live as long as he can."

"Very well, Ananda. That indeed is a very good proposition. Please, Ananda, approach the Blessed One and make that request," replied the monks and nuns.

Ananda waited for a good opportunity and approached the Buddha.

"Sir, it is the feeling of the community that the Blessed One should extend his life by using psychic powers."

Buddha reflected for a moment. He thought to himself:

"Is it proper for me to extend my life in this manner? What would the consequences be if I were to do so? Would the community be benefited or would it be harmed?"

After weighing the consequences thus, he spoke to Ananda:

"Ananda, it would be possible for me to live a full life span by overcoming the effects of my illnesses through psychic power. I made that suggestion to you on an earlier occasion.

You were silent then. But now you are requesting me to do so. Your request at this time is not proper, Ananda. It is motivated by your desire for my company, your dislike of losing my company. If I were to accede to your request, it will bring great harm both to you and to the community."

After a moment's silence, the Buddha continued:

"If I were to prolong my life, it should be done for different reasons. It should be to help the community to overcome attachment and aversion, not to promote them. It is time, Ananda, that you as well as others who have not attained freedom from attachment and aversion, strive for such freedom. Ananda, I feel that my life will continue only for another three months. At the end of three months, I will be laying down this body of mine and attain perfect freedom. You may announce this to the community."

So saying, Buddha dismissed Ananda. When Ananda reported to the community everything Buddha had said, many of the unenlightened members of the community were annoyed with Ananda.

"Ananda, you are at fault for not requesting the Blessed One to prolong his life when he discussed that possibility with you. It is unfortunate, Ananda. It is our loss."

"Friends, when the Blessed One mentioned about that possibility of his extending his life span, I was under the influence of the evil forces. I was overwhelmed by passion, by desire, by attachment. These are the same evil forces that are prompting you to make this request to the Blessed One now. The blame falls on all of us. We have spent so many years with the Blessed One and we have failed to be his true disciples. We have not made any attempt to overcome our passions, our desires and our attachments. Let us, even at this late stage, strive for that supreme goal."

Ananda, heavy at heart, left the congregation of disciples to attend to the Buddha's needs.

After a few days, Buddha decided to move further north. He left the village of Bhanda and reached a small town called Pava. Arriving in Pava, he and his disciples took up residence in a mango grove belonging to a goldsmith's son, named Cunda.

218

Cunda was delighted to hear that the Buddha and his disciples were living in his mango grove. After visiting the Buddha, Cunda invited the Buddha and his disciples for the midday meal on the following day. Although not in very good health, Buddha agreed to partake of a meal in Cunda's house, in order to please him.

Cunda's happiness knew no bounds. He got the best and the choicest food prepared for the occasion. One of the dishes consisted of tender meat of the wild hog. It was normal on such occasions for the host to serve the Buddha first and then proceed to serve others. People in the household would bring each dish and hand it over to the chief host who would serve the first ladleful to the Buddha and the dish would then be passed on to others who would go round serving the rest of the disciples.

When Cunda came up with the dish containing hog's meat, the Buddha asked Cunda as to what it contained. Upon realizing that it was hog's meat, Buddha felt that this kind of meat would not be easily digested, especially by his disciples who were not involved in strenuous physical exercises. The only way in which anyone of his disciples could overcome the effects of such a diet was by the use of psychic powers. Neither had the majority of his disciples who were with him developed such powers, nor did he want even those who had such powers to get used to such habits. Therefore, he called Cunda and said:

"Cunda, you have taken such great pains to prepare this food for me and my disciples. But this particular dish is not suitable for them. Only an enlightened one can partake of it and survive. Therefore, if you wish, you may serve it to me. But do not serve it to the disciples."

Cunda was embarrassed. But yet he was pleased that at least the Buddha was in a position to partake of it. At the end of the meal, Buddha gave a sermon on the significance of liberality as a means of overcoming one's passions and desires and left Cunda's residence.

Upon returning to his lodgings, Buddha was again overwhelmed by a severe illness. Once again he bore it without complaint, mindful and fully aware. The night passed by. He had little sleep. The only time he could rest was when he attained to the state of cessation of perception and what is felt.

Remaining in bed and attaining such a state in order to overcome the pain he was experiencing until he passed away was not the Buddha's way of life. Therefore, on the following morning the Buddha called Ananda and informed of his interest in proceeding to Kusinara, a small town not far from Pava.

On the way, Buddha left the road and took shelter under a tree. Addressing Ananda, he said:

"Ananda, please fold my outer robe in four and lay it out. I am tired and I need to lie down."

Buddha rested for awhile. When he got up he felt very thirsty. Buddha knew that this severe thirst was partly due to his illness. He called Ananda and informed of his need to drink some water.

Taking Buddha's bowl Ananda went up to the river that was flowing by. The water was muddy.

"Probably a caravan of carts has crossed the river at the ford above stream," thought Ananda. "It would not be proper for the Buddha to drink this water. I should go upstream and try to reach a place where the water is clean and cool."

It took so long for Ananda to fetch some clean water that in the meantime the only way Buddha could avoid any discomfort was by attaining the state of cessation.

During the time Buddha remained under the tree absorbed in the meditative state of cessation, there was a torrential downpour accompanied by thunder and lightning. The disciples took shelter under trees during this heavy rain. Buddha was still in the meditative state when the rain ceased.

A follower of Alara Kalama, a person named Pukkusa, who came by on the road from Kusinara to Pava, saw the Buddha remaining unmoved by the lightning, the thunder and the heavy downpour. He waited until the Buddha emerged from his meditative state and said:

"Sir, I am a follower of the teachings of the great sage Alara Kalama. Although I was not a direct disciple and have never met Kalama, I admire his teachings and try to attain the goal he preached. I have heard that once when Venerable Kalama was absorbed in meditation, five hundred carts passed by quite close to him. But when someone questioned Venerable Kalama a little later as to whether a caravan of carts passed by, he replied that he did not either hear or see any. It is marvelous, Sir, that Venerable Kalama could remain unmoved by the noise of five hundred carts. But, Sir, it is indeed a greater miracle that you were able to remain unmoved by events like thunder, lightning and torrential rain. Were you a direct disciple of Venerable Kalama?"

"Yes, friend, I was a disciple of Kalama for a short time. Not being satisfied with his teachings, I left him. After leaving him, I attained, on my own exertion, wondrous and marvelous powers greater than those attained by Kalama. The ability to remain unmoved and unaffected by thunder, lightning and rain is certainly not the greatest of these powers I have attained."

"Sir, what greater powers can any mortal attain? Pray tell me," pleaded Pukkusa.

"Friend, thunder, lightning and rain are not the worst forces of nature man has to confront in this world. Desire, hate and confusion are far greater and more destructive. If a person can remain unaffected by these, not merely when he has attained to the meditative state of cessation, but when he is wide awake, when all his sense faculties are open, that I consider to be the greatest power any man can achieve. That is what I have attained and that is the goal of the religious life that I advocate."

By this time, Ananda had returned with a bowl full of clean water. Buddha drank the water, quenched his thirst and continued on his way to Kusinara.

THIRTY-FIVE

BUDDHA REALIZED THAT HIS STRENGTH and energy would take him only up to Kusinara. Therefore, he informed Ananda that Kusinara would be the last city that he would be able to visit. Ananda and other disciples who had not attained enlightenment were grieved. Speculations among them were rampant.

One of the disciples told another:

"Cunda is responsible for the Blessed One's illness. He should not have served the Blessed One that hog's meat when the Blessed One mentioned that it was not a suitable meal for ascetics like us."

The other replied:

"But I understand that the Blessed One asked Cunda to serve him with that dish and prevented us from being served with it. So how could Cunda be held responsible?"

"Does it mean that the Blessed One partook of that meal knowing that he would become ill as a result of it? Why did the Blessed One do such a thing?" questioned a third.

While they were engaged in such speculation, Ananda appeared on the scene. One of the monks asked Ananda:

"Venerable Ananda, we are puzzled by the Blessed One's behavior. Who should be held responsible for the Blessed One's illness? Is it Cunda or is it the Blessed One himself?"

"Friends, it is true that the Blessed One knew that partaking of Cunda's meal would lead to his illness. On the contrary, if he had refused that meal he would have caused remorse and regret in Cunda. But he was prepared to accept that meal and then to try to minimize the consequences. The Blessed One could eliminate the evil effects of that meal by the cultivation of the four bases of psychic power."

"If one can overcome the destructive effects of such a meal by cultivating the four bases of psychic power, why wouldn't the Blessed One allow others to do the same?"

Ananda was amused.

"Friends, you have failed to realize that the Blessed One is the greatest, incomparable teacher in the world. He knows very well that those who have not attained the goal by eliminating desire, hate and confusion will use psychic powers, when they have developed them, for wrong purposes. Many evil deeds have been perpetuated by people who have developed psychic powers and who have not attained freedom from desire, hate and confusion. Therefore, he has discouraged the use of psychic power. As to why he himself used psychic power in order to overcome the painful effects of Cunda's meal, he may have an explanation. I assume that the Blessed One realized that his life was coming to an end. Refusing a meal prepared by a faithful follower because it leads to one's temporary discomfort was not looked upon by him with favor. He has emphasised the need to understand situations as they have come to be, taking all relevant factors into consideration. Reflection according to the way things arise has been declared the best way of understanding situations and dealing with them. There are no fixed laws or rules in terms of which everything is to be evaluated. This, monks, is the middle path."

While this discussion was going on the Buddha himself appeared on the scene. Everyone was silent. After making himself comfortable on a seat that one of the monks prepared by folding a robe, the Buddha questioned the disciples:

"Monks, you were engaged in a very important and lively discussion. May I know what the topic of the discussion was?"

Ananda spoke up.

"Sir, how does the Blessed One look upon the meal provided by Cunda as a result of which the Blessed One became gravely ill?"

"Ananda, it is possible that someone might provoke remorse

in the Goldsmith's son, Cunda, saying: 'It is no gain; it is loss for you, Cunda, that Buddha passed away after getting his last alms food from you.' This is not proper, Ananda. Ananda, there are two kinds of alms food that have equal consequences and equal ripening and their consequences and ripening are far greater than any other's. What are the two? They are the alms food that after eating, a person discovers the supreme enlightenment and the alms food that after eating, that person attains final nirvana, laying down the psychophysical personality which many cling to as the self or soul. Cunda has performed a deed that will be to his happiness for a long time."

Everyone in the audience was silent. Buddha finally asked:

"Monks, is there anyone among you who wants to raise any questions? If so, it is time for you to raise such questions now. Do not regret later that you failed to question me while I was still alive."

The disciples continued with their silence until Ananda decided to raise one question:

"Sir, is there any difference between the Blessed One and those disciples who have attained knowledge and freedom?"

"No, Ananda. As far as attainments are concerned there is not the slightest difference between me and the disciples who have attained knowledge and freedom. We are equals. The only difference between us is that I have discovered the path and others have followed me on that path to reach the ultimate goal of knowledge and freedom that any Buddha may have achieved in the past and will achieve in the future."

Emotionally overwhelmed, Ananda sang praises of the Buddha:

"The Blessed One is the greatest of teachers, the almighty and the supreme leader of gods and men. There is no teacher comparable to the Blessed One in the whole world. Sir, it is not possible that any disciple in the community can have any doubts, any questions regarding the teachings of the Blessed One."

"Ananda, you seem to be overly confident about the attitude and understanding in the community. The disciples are not raising any questions through respect for me, not because they do not have any questions."

One of the monks in the congregation, realizing that the Buddha understood their attitudes, broke the silence and asked:

"Sir, how are we to treat women?"

"Do not see them."

"If they are seen, how should we treat them?" asked the monk.

"Do not address them."

"If they do address us, how should we treat them?"

"Be mindful."

A female disciple in the audience noted that the Buddha's answer was specifically to the question raised by a monk who had not attained freedom. Therefore, she decided to question him about the specific behavior of the unenlightened female disciples toward the male disciples.

"Sir, how should an unenlightened female disciple behave toward unenlightened male disciples?"

"You should treat them the same way as the unenlightened male disciples should treat you."

After awhile the Buddha and his disciples arrived in Kusinara. They took up residence in a grove of *sala* trees. Buddha was tired and weak. He realized that his last moment was approaching. He called Ananda and requested a couch to be made ready between two large sala trees that provided a good shade. When his request was done, Buddha laid himself down on the right side with one foot overlapping the other. He was fully mindful and aware.

Ananda too realized that the Buddha's life was coming to an end. He went inside a dwelling, stood leaning against a door and wept. Another monk noticing Ananda's behavior walked up to him and questioned:

"Venerable Ananda, why are you weeping?"

"Friend, I am still only an initiate whose task has yet to be completed. My teacher is about to attain final nirvana. What can I do?"

Buddha noticed the absence of Ananda. He called one of the disciples and asked:

"Where is Ananda? I have not seen him for awhile. This is very unusual."

"Sir, Venerable Ananda remains inside a dwelling, weeping."

"May you go and call Ananda," requested the Buddha.

When Ananda arrived, the Buddha said to him:

"Enough, Ananda, do not lament. You have been of great help to me, and by being so, you have been of great service to all my disciples, including those who have attained enlightenment. This is indeed the time when you must act with courage. Have I not repeatedly told you that there is separation and parting from all that is near and dear? Whatever has come to be is liable to destruction. Ananda, you have long and constantly attended me with acts of loving kindness, helpfully, gladly, sincerely and without reserve. Your life has so far been a great success. Keep on endeavoring and very soon you will attain knowledge and freedom."

Ananda, thus consoled, was able to speak up. With tears still in his eyes, Ananda pleaded with the Buddha.

"Sir, Kusinara is a very small town. The Blessed One should not attain final nirvana here. There are other great cities like Campa, Rajagaha, Savatthi, Saketa, Kosambi and Baranasi. Let the Blessed One attain final nirvana in any one of these towns. More people would be able to honor the Blessed One in those towns."

"Ananda, do not speak thus. It is not proper to condemn this town because it is small. Who knows? In time to come this could grow into a great city and those other great cities may come to be nothing. Tonight, Ananda, during the last watch of the night, I will attain final nirvana."

The word spread around in no time among the people of the Malla country that Buddha had arrived in Kusinara, one of their smaller cities, and that this night Buddha would attain final nirvana. Many people gathered from all parts of the country to pay homage to the saint of the Sakya clan. One of them was a wanderer by name Subhadda.

Subhadda approached Ananda and informed him of his desire to see the Buddha.

"No, friend. It is not the time to disturb the Blessed One. The Blessed One is tired," replied Ananda. Subhadda insisted and Ananda continued to refuse.

Buddha heard their conversation. He told Ananda:

"Ananda, do not try to keep out Subhadda. Let him come

and see me. Whatever questions he has, he will ask them only for the sake of knowledge, not because he wants to cause trouble. He is a man of experience and whatever I tell him he will quickly understand."

Subhadda was allowed to go before the Buddha who was lying on his couch.

"Sir, I beg the Blessed One's pardon for questioning at this moment when the Blessed One is tired."

"Go on, Subhadda. Ask whatever question you may have," replied the Buddha.

"Sir, there have been these monks and brahmans, each with his community, each with his group of disciples, each a renowned and famous teacher reckoned by many as a saint— leaders like Purana Kassapa, Makkhali Gosala, Ajita Kesa-kambali, Pakudha Kaccayana, Sanjaya Bellatthiputta and Nigantha Nataputta, who claimed direct knowledge and insight. Did all of them possess knowledge and insight or did some and others not?"

"Subhadda, leave aside the question as to whether a teacher has attained or has not attained the direct knowledge that he claims. I shall explain to you the doctrine. Listen carefully."

"Even so, Sir," replied Subhadda.

"Subhadda, in whatever doctrine and discipline the noble eightfold path is not found, that doctrine and discipline is empty of true disciples. It is on the basis of the behavior of the disciples that the value of any doctrine and discipline lies. If these disciples live rightly, the world will not be devoid of saints, of accomplished ones."

The wanderer Subhadda was delighted.

"It is magnificent, Sir, it is indeed magnificent. This, indeed, is the best standard by which a doctrine and discipline can be evaluated by one who has no way of determining whether the founder of that doctrine and discipline had direct knowledge or not. Sir, may I be admitted as a disciple of the Blessed One?"

Buddha called Ananda and requested that Subhadda be admitted to the community. Thereby, Subhadda became the last of the disciples admitted by the Buddha.

Buddha thereupon summoned all the disciples who were around, and spoke to them:

"Disciples, when I am gone you may think that the word of the teacher is a thing of the past. But you should not regard it so. The doctrine I taught you and the discipline I instituted should serve you as your teacher after I am gone."

Buddha was silent for a moment. Finally, he said:

"I declare to you, my disciples, that all dispositions and all those things that are determined by dispositions are liable to dissolution. Attain perfection through diligence."

This was the Buddha's last statement.

Instantly, Buddha closed his eyes, entered the states of meditation he had practiced all his life and reached the state of cessation of perception and what is felt.

Ananda said to the disciples assembled: "The Blessed One has attained final nirvana."

Anuruddha, who had joined the community along with Ananda, and who had already attained knowledge and freedom, insisted:

"No, Ananda. The Blessed One has not attained final nirvana. The Blessed One has merely attained to the state of cessation."

Emerging from the state of cessation, the Buddha gradually returned to the first stage of meditation. From there he moved again up to the fourth stage. Finally, moving out of the meditative state, he opened his eyes, surveyed the world that lay before his eyes and breathed his last.

REFERENCES

All references are to the editions of the Pali Text Society unless otherwise stated.

CHAPTER ONE

The story of Siddhartha begins with the ceremony connected with the first sowing of seeds. It is based upon the reminiscence of Buddha as recorded in the *Maha-saccaka-sutta (Majjhima-nikaya* 1.246). The reference is to the "work of my father, the Sakyan" (*pitu sakkassa kammante*), which has been explained by most commentators as a "plowing festival." The fact that on this occasion Siddhartha, enjoying the cool shade of a rose apple tree, attained to the first stage of meditation is mentioned in the discourse. The commentators have placed this incident at a very early stage in Siddhartha's life, probably in the hope of emphasizing the miraculous or wondrous powers of the *bodhisattva*. Assuming that this is a veridical memory, yet not attributing to Siddhartha a capacity such as reaching the first stage of meditation, which he probably mastered just before his enlightenment, we have attempted to make use of this incident as a starting point in our story.

The second important reference in this chapter is to the predictions of Suddhodana's spiritual adviser, Asita Kaladevala. These predictions certainly played an important role in the life of Siddhartha and seem to have some historical basis, especially as they occur in one of the earliest portions of the canon, namely, the *Nalaka-sutta* of the *Sutta-nipata* (vv. 679-698).

CHAPTER TWO

The teachings of the Upanishads, especially those of the *Brhadaran-yaka* and *Chandogya,* probably served as part of the background in which Siddhartha himself received his education. Of the teachers mentioned in these two Upanishads, Uddalaka and Yajnavalkya are prominent. Uddalaka's teachings are different from Yajnavalkya's both regarding style and temper. Uddalaka is a "systematic" philosopher, while Yajnavalkya is a mystic. In the story we have tried to maintain this distinction. Uddalaka's "systematic philosophy" is traced back to his association with Gandhara, one of the western kingdoms of India, hence having contact with the Greco-Roman civilizations. In addition to the information available in the *Chandogya Upanishad* where Uddalaka himself seemed to have been aware of the Gandharas (see VI.14.1-2), the *Uddalaka Jataka* of the Buddhists refers to his education in Takkasila, the capital of Gandhara (*Jataka* 4.298).

Uddalaka's teachings, as presented in the *Chandogya Upanishad,* probably served as a foundation for the Sankhya school of thought. The influence of Sankhya doctrines on Buddhism has been emphasized by modern scholars. Even if elements of Sankhya are not traceable in early Buddhism, Buddha certainly was aware of these teachings. For these reasons, we have made Kapila, a name associated with Sankhya, the source for Siddhartha's knowledge of the teachings of both Uddalaka and Sankhya. Since Siddhartha, as tradition rightly believed, did not go out of Kapilavatthu until the time of his renunciation, it was felt necessary that the story is presented in such a way that at least his friends had direct contact with other parts of India and through whom he was able to learn about the various schools of thought prior to his enlightenment. Therefore, following the tradition recorded in the *Jatakas,* we have decided to send Kapila to Takkasila.

CHAPTER THREE

The creation of the world by Brahma, the existence of a permanent and immutable reality or substance in man and his environment, the divine ordination of the fourfold caste system and a social ethic based upon that caste system—these were all part and parcel of the teachings of the so-called Hinduism. As pointed out in K. N. Jayatilleke's *Early Buddhist Theory of Knowledge* (London: Allen & Unwin, 1963) and our own *Causality: The Central Philosophy of Buddhism* (Honolulu: The University Press of Hawaii, 1975), these doctrines were well known to Siddhartha. He was probably trained in this Brahmanical tradition, and rather early in his life developed a critical attitude towards these. Chapter Three is an attempt to depict two of the pre-Buddhist traditions: the social philosophy embodied in Narayana's *Purusha-sukta (Rg-veda* x.90) and the doctrine of self presented by Yajnavalkya in the *Brhadaranyaka Upanishad.* References to these doctrines in the Buddhist texts are many and varied. See *Brahmajala-suttanta (Digha-nikaya* 1.18 ff.), *Agganna-suttanta* (ibid. 3.80 ff.), *Kaccayanagotta-sutta (Samyutta-nikaya* 2.17 ff.), etc.

CHAPTER FOUR

Though the Buddha rejected the transcendentalist metaphysics of the Upanishads, he was not a materialist. He was very critical of the moral philosophy propounded by materialists like Ajita Kesakambali and Pakudha Kaccayana, as is evident from discourses such as *Samannaphala (Digha-nikaya* 1.47 ff.). Chapter Four is intended to show his strong opposition to such morality.

Social events such as music festivals and sports competitions are mentioned in texts such as *Brahmajala-suttanta (Digha-nikaya* 1.6) and also in the *Jatakas.* As a prominent young man in the Sakyan kingdom, Siddhartha probably played an important role at these social gatherings.

CHAPTER FIVE

The incident with which this chapter begins is based upon a similar story occurring in *Therigatha* where a female disciple of the Buddha confronts a brahman who had been practicing the ritual of "purification by water" (see *Therigatha* vv.236-251).

Siddhartha's reflections on existence, presented at the end of the chapter, are an attempt to symbolize the ideas of the discourse on *Anusota (Anguttara-nikaya* 2.7 ff.).

CHAPTER SIX

There is very little information about Siddhartha's wife in the early sources. Following the widely prevalent view (see E.J. Thomas, *The Life of Buddha,* London: Routledge & Kegan Paul, 1960, p. 50), Siddhartha's wife is here called Yasodhara. Her two companions are characters that occur in the *Therigatha:* Rohini (vv.271-290) and Anopama (vv.151-156).

CHAPTER SEVEN

No substantial references can be quoted to support the contents of this chapter.

CHAPTER EIGHT

The story about the three palaces which Siddhartha occupied during the three seasons and his being entertained by female minstrels is mentioned in several places in the early discourses (see *Anguttara-nikaya* 1.145; *Majjhima nikaya* 1.504).

CHAPTER NINE

The purpose of Chapter Nine is to gradually move Siddhartha in the direction of the ascetic tradition, especially the contemplative life of the yogin, which was to eventually mold his philosophy of life.

CHAPTER TEN

The objections to Siddhartha's renunciation of home life came more from his parents than from his wife. In the two earliest sources that describe his renunciation there is no mention of his wife and son. Instead, one of them specifically refers to the "lamentation of his parents" when he left the household life (see *Majjhima-nikaya* 1.163). Our portrayal of Yasodhara's character is dominated by this fact.

CHAPTER ELEVEN

Commenting on Siddhartha's wife and son, E. J. Thomas says: "That Buddha should have had a wife is not only natural but according to Indian ideas inevitable. To marry is one of the duties of a person living in the world. The chroniclers did not need to start from the historic fact that Buddha had a wife and son. This may be true, and may rest on unwritten tradition, but it is certain that the early tradition has preserved no information about them." (*The Life of Buddha,* pp. 59-60). In the absence of such information, we have gone back to the later traditional stories about Yasodhara and Rahula.

232

CHAPTER TWELVE

The death of Siddhartha's mother soon after his birth and Maha-pajapati Gotami's playing the role of mother to him, even to the extent of breast-feeding him, is mentioned in *Dakkhinavibhanga-sutta (Majjhima-nikaya* 3.253).

Traditional stories refer to Siddhartha's seeing the four omens: a sick man, an old man, a dead body and an ascetic, as the reason for his renunciation. This may have been true. The exaggeration in the traditional stories is that Siddhartha saw these omens only on the day before his renunciation, and this we have avoided in our story.

The story about the mad woman is adapted from that of Kisagotami *(Therigatha* vv.213-223).

CHAPTER THIRTEEN

There are no references in the early texts to the incidents related in this chapter. Our story is based upon the incidents related in the later traditional accounts. The idea that Siddhartha may have left home in a horse-drawn carriage seems to be implied in the *Maha-padana-suttanta (Digha-nikaya* 2.29) where it is stated that a previous Buddha named Vipashyin did so.

CHAPTER FOURTEEN

This chapter contains one of the most important historical events in Siddhartha's life and is recorded in one of the earliest texts: the *Ariyapariyesana-sutta (Majjhima-nikaya* 1.160-175), as well as in the *Mahasaccaka-sutta* (ibid., 1.240 ff.) and it pertains to Siddhartha's training under the famous contemplatives, Alara Kalama and Uddaka Ramaputta.

The second part of the chapter, which refers to the practice of self-mortification, is based on the description available in the *Mahasaccaka-sutta* mentioned above.

CHAPTER FIFTEEN

The story about Siddhartha's meeting with King Bimbisara is related in the *Pabbajja-sutta (Sutta-nipata* vv. 405-425). Siddhartha's reflections as he sat under the bodhi-tree are taken from the *Ariyapariyesana-sutta.* The story of Sujata is taken from the traditional accounts. His struggle against temptations is recounted in the *Padhana-sutta* (*Sutta-nipata* vv. 425-449), and the present account is a combination of what is found in the *Padhana-sutta* as well as in the traditional stories.

In presenting Siddhartha's enlightenment, we have followed two important texts: the *Ariyapariyesana-sutta* and the *Tevijja-Vacchagotta-sutta* (*Majjhima-nikaya* 1.481-483). The *Ariyapariyesana* clearly indicates that the Buddha's freedom was due, not to the attainment of the pacification of mind following the higher dhyanas, but to the development of insight (panna). Although this insight is identified with the knowledge of the cessation of defilements (*asavakkaya-nana*), it is facilitated by two other higher knowledges (*abhinna*). There are several different forms of higher knowledge. What we have adopted is the threefold higher knowledge which the Buddha himself recognized as being important and which is referred to in the *Tevijja-Vacchagotta-sutta*.

CHAPTER SIXTEEN

Reflections of the Buddha, immediately after his attainment of enlightenment and freedom pertain to the four noble truths and the causal formula consisting of the twelve factors. These are discussed in a large number of discourses and it would be needless to list them all here.

The events leading up to the preaching of the first sermon at Baranasi, popularly known as the "Turning of the Wheel of Dharma" (*Dharmacakkappavattana*) are related in the *Ariyapariyesana-sutta*. The sermon itself is included in the *Samyutta-nikaya* (5.420 ff.). This is followed by the preaching of the famous discourse on nonsubstantiality (*anatta*) included in *Samyutta-nikaya* (3.66 ff.).

CHAPTER SEVENTEEN

The conversion of Kolita and Upatissa by Assaji is taken from the traditional life stories of the Buddha. But the enlightenment of these two famous disciples, who came to be known as Moggallana and Sariputta respectively, was placed in the context of a discourse delivered by the Buddha to a person named Dighanakha (*Dighanakha-sutta, Majjhima-nikaya* 1.497-501). The reason for this is that the *Dighanakha-sutta* seems to be the most appropriate form of instruction for two people like Kolita and Upatissa who were disciples of the famous skeptic, Sanjaya.

Samyutta-nikaya (4.388) contains a discourse where Sariputta is said to have entertained doubts regarding the saint after death. If so, obviously he had not attained enlightenment at that time. Hence it was considered appropriate to bring together material from the discourses dealing with the ten unexplained questions and the variety of reasons given by the Buddha for not explaining them. Texts utilized are *Culla-Malunkya-sutta* (*Majjhima-nikaya* 1.426 ff.), *Aggi-Vacchagotta-sutta* (ibid. 1.483 ff.) and *Samyutta-nikaya* (4.391 ff.). The reference to the four types of questions mentioned here—namely, (1) those that are categorically answered, (2) those that are answered after an analysis of the questions, (3) those that are answered after counter-questioning, and (4) those that are to be left without answers—occurs in *Anguttara-nikaya* (2.46).

CHAPTER EIGHTEEN

The story of Kassapa, the matted-hair ascetic, is emphasized in the traditional life histories of the Buddha. Our portrayal of his character is based upon his own reminiscences as recorded in the *Theragatha* (vv.375-380). The discourse delivered to Kassapa and his disciples, according to tradition, is the one popularly known as *Adittapariyaya* and is included in the *Samyutta-nikaya* (4.19-20).

Buddha's admonitions to King Bimbisara on social and political philosophy are taken from *Cakkavattisihanada-suttanta* (*Digha-nikaya* 3.58-79) and *Agganna-suttanta* (ibid. 3.80-98).

CHAPTER NINETEEN

Reference to Kaludayi is at *Theragatha* (vv. 527-536). The sermon delivered to the Sakyans led by the Buddha's father, Suddhodana, is based upon the *Alagaddupama-sutta* (*Majjhima-nikaya* 1.130-142).

Two quatrains occur in the *Theragatha* (vv. 157-158) attributed to Nanda. Traditional stories seem to preserve the contents of these two quatrains in portraying the character of Nanda. In the present story, the authors have followed the same description *sans* the mythologies of the traditional story.

CHAPTER TWENTY

Incidents related in the first part of the chapter are taken from traditional accounts. Mahanama's question and the Buddha's answer to it are taken from a discourse at *Anguttara-nikaya* (4.220). Reference to Gotami's offer of a robe for the Buddha occurs at *Dakkhinavibhanga-sutta* (*Majjhima-nikaya* 3.253-257) and the Buddha's admonition to Gotami is taken from the last section of that discourse. *Anguttara-nikaya* (5.328) refers to the Buddha getting ready to leave Kapilavatthu.

CHAPTER TWENTY-ONE

The chapter begins with an incident related in the *Vinaya-pitaka* (2.182-183). The parable of the partridge, monkey and elephant is also taken from the same source (2.161-162). The Buddha's warning that one should not ignore someone because he is young and insignificant is contained in a discourse occurring at *Samyutta-nikaya* (3.1).

Discussion between the Buddha and Janussoni is based on the Chinese version of the *Sabba-sutta* (*Samyutta-nikaya* 4.15). The Pali version does not refer to Janussoni as the interlocutor in this particular discourse, although he appears in another discussion on a similar theme (see *Samyutta-nikaya* 2.76). Buddha's discourse to Kaccayana is an elaboration of the famous *Kaccayanagotta-sutta* (*Samyutta nikaya* 2.16-17), quoted by almost all the major Buddhist philosophical traditions (see my article, "The Notion of the Middle Path in Early [sic] Buddhism," in *The Eastern Buddhist,* New Series, vol. xii. 30-48). The final discussion regarding the two kinds of knowledge is taken from *Samyutta-nikaya* (2.56-59).

CHAPTER TWENTY-TWO

Anathapindika's visit to the Buddha is related in *Samyutta-nikaya* (1.210-212). Buddha's discourse to Anathapindika is based upon *Anguttara-nikaya* (2.69-70). The story about the construction of the monastery, which Anathapindika offered to the Buddha and his disciples is related at *Vinaya-pitaka* (2.154-159).

The story of the man bereaved over the death of his son, as well as the conversation between King Pasenadi and Queen Mallika is found in *Piyajatika-sutta* (*Majjhima-nikaya* 2.106-112).

CHAPTER TWENTY-THREE

Pajapati Gotami's request to the Buddha to allow women to join the order is recorded in *Vinaya-pitaka* (2.253) and *Anguttara-nikaya*

(4.274-279). Buddha's explanation of the attitudes of man and woman toward each other is contained in two discourses included in the *Anguttara-nikaya* (1.1-2).

The ceremony connected with the opening of the Convocation Hall in Kapilavatthu as well as the Buddha being taken ill during the proceedings are related in the *Sekha-sutta* (*Majjhima-nikaya* 1.353-359). Ananda's discourse to Mahanama is in *Anguttara-nikaya* (1.219-220). Nanda's inappropriate behavior in going out for alms in pressed and ironed robes, etc. is recorded in *Samyutta-nikaya* (2.281).

CHAPTER TWENTY-FOUR

Buddha's arrival in Vesali and his confrontation with the Jaina disciple, Saccaka, is taken from *Cula saccaka-sutta* (*Majjhima-nikaya* 1.227-237). Discussion with Vacchagotta on omniscience is from *Tevijja-vacchagotta-sutta* (ibid. 1.481-483). Admission of women into the order is discussed in *Anguttara-nikaya* (4.274-279). Description of Ambapali's personality is based on *Therigatha* (vv.252-270).

CHAPTER TWENTY-FIVE

This chapter dealing with the Jain doctrine of karma is based primarily on the *Upali-sutta* (*Majjhima-nikaya* 1.371-387).

CHAPTER TWENTY-SIX

The admonition to Rahula is from *Ambalatthika-rahulovada-sutta* (*Majjhima-nikaya* 1.414-420). The traditionally popular story about the Buddha's half-brother, Nanda, is adapted from *Udana* (pp.21-24). Devadatta's relationship with Ajatasatthu is mentioned at *Samyutta-nikaya* (2.242) and Ajatasatthu's plotting against the Buddha is related at *Anguttara-nikaya* (4.160 ff.).

CHAPTER TWENTY-SEVEN

Angulimala-sutta (*Majjhima-nikaya* 2.97-105) contains the rather poignant story about Angulimala and his conversion.

CHAPTER TWENTY-EIGHT

This chapter is based upon the information available in *Therigatha:* Sela (vv. 57-59); Soma (vv.60-62); Vimala (vv.72-76); Nanduttara (vv.87-91); Sona (vv.102-106) and Mutta (vv.11). The story of Subha is related in detail in the same text (vv.366-399). The character of Uppalavanna is based upon vv.224-235.

CHAPTER TWENTY-NINE

The characters in the first part of this chapter are fictitious and were fabricated in order to illustrate the contents of the discourse on "dominances" in *Anguttara-nikaya* (1.149-150). This was done with a view to contrasting the Buddha's pragmatic teachings on moral philosophy with those of the absolutistic traditions, especially those of *Bhagavadgita,* etc. The discourse to Prince Abhaya occurs in *Majjhima-nikaya* (1.392-396).

CHAPTER THIRTY

This chapter focuses on the *Kalama-sutta* (*Anguttara-nikaya* 1.188-193). The reference to the two ways of developing right understanding occurs in *Majjhima nikaya* (1.294). The ideas expressed in the last part of the chapter are taken from the *Canki-sutta* (ibid. 2.164-177). Although the interlocutor in this discourse is a brahman by name Canki, for the sake of the continuity of the chapter we have retained the Kalamas as the interlocutors.

CHAPTER THIRTY-ONE

The first part of this chapter utilizes the incident referred to at the beginning of the famous *Mahaparinibbana-suttanta* (*Digha-nikaya* 2.72-168). The second part dealing with the five propositions of Devadatta is based upon *Vinaya-pitaka* (2.196-200).

CHAPTERS THIRTY-TWO to THIRTY-FIVE

These are based upon *Mahaparinibbana-suttanta* (*Digha-nikaya* 2.94-156).